SAMPSON TECHNICAL INSTITUTE   NORTH CAROLINA

POLITICS AND PEOPLE
The Ordeal of Self-Government in America

POLITICS AND PEOPLE

The Ordeal of Self-Government in America

ADVISORY EDITOR
Leon Stein

EDITORIAL BOARD
James MacGregor Burns
William E. Leuchtenburg

THE
SPEAKERS OF THE HOUSE

BY

HUBERT BRUCE FULLER

ARNO PRESS
A New York Times Company
New York — 1974

Reprint Edition 1974 by Arno Press Inc.

Reprinted from a copy in The University
  of Illinois Library

POLITICS AND PEOPLE: The Ordeal
of Self-Government in America
ISBN for complete set: 0-405-05850-0
See last pages of this volume for titles.

Manufactured in the United States of America

Library of Congress Cataloging in Publication Data

Fuller, Hubert Bruce, 1880-1957.
    The Speakers of the House.

    (Politics and people: the ordeal of self-government
in America)
    Reprint of the 1909 ed. published by Little, Brown,
Boston.
    1. United States. Congress. House--Speaker.
I. Title. II. Series.
JK1411.F9 1974   328.73'07'2   73-19147
ISBN 0-405-05871-3

THE SPEAKERS OF THE HOUSE

Henry Clay

From the Painting by Edward Dalton Marchant,
Department of State, Washington

THE

SPEAKERS OF THE HOUSE

BY

HUBERT BRUCE FULLER, A.M., LL.M.
Author of "The Purchase of Florida"

BOSTON
LITTLE, BROWN, AND COMPANY
1909

Copyright, 1909,
BY LITTLE, BROWN, AND COMPANY.

All rights reserved

Published September, 1909

THE UNIVERSITY PRESS, CAMBRIDGE, U.S.A.

PREFACE

In 1789, when the first Congress convened under Washington, the Speaker of the House of Representatives was merely a moderator, who presided over the sessions of that body with calm deliberation and impartial favor. The prestige of his position lay rather in its honor than in its power.

In 1909, after an interval of a hundred and twenty years, the Speaker of the House of Representatives is quite the most potent factor in American legislative life. There is some room for saying that he is even more powerful than the President of the United States. To-day the Speaker is the absolute arbiter of our national legislation. He can dictate what laws shall be enacted and what bills shall be defeated.

An attempt has been made in this volume to give a brief, dispassionate story of this development of power by the presiding officers of the lower House of Congress. Effort has been made to avoid the dry and technical mysteries of parliamentary law. The book is not intended as a text book on that intricate subject. In the effort to popularize the work all annotations and references have been omitted of purpose.

The author has sought to lend to the story a personal element by giving pen pictures of some of the greatest characters of American congressional history, and by describing some of the most interesting scenes enacted upon our legislative stage. The volume also contains many hitherto unpublished anecdotes and reminiscences of our national leaders which tend to reveal their personal and mental attributes.

An introductory chapter has been incorporated wherein is traced very briefly the origin and development of this office in England and colonial America. It was felt that this chapter might prove of evolutionary interest.

It is a privilege to acknowledge a debt of literary gratitude. Here the author wishes to express his grateful appreciation of the valuable and kindly advice and suggestions always graciously accorded him by the Hon. Theodore E. Burton, Senator from Ohio; the Hon. John B. Henderson, one time Senator from Missouri; Mr. T. Fletcher Dennis and the Hon. Asher C. Hinds of Washington, D. C.; Paul Leland Haworth and W. S. Couch of Cleveland, Ohio; and also to various members of the United States Senate and House of Representatives, who, by correspondence and in personal conferences, have contributed many of the anecdotes and personal stories in these pages.

HUBERT BRUCE FULLER.

CLEVELAND, OHIO, May 10, 1909.

CONTENTS

INTRODUCTORY CHAPTER

	PAGE
THE BRITISH AND COLONIAL PROTOTYPE	1

CHAPTER I

MUHLENBERG THE FIRST AND HENRY CLAY THE GREATEST OF AMERICAN SPEAKERS 22

CHAPTER II

REACTION AND CONTEST 59

CHAPTER III

TURMOIL AND CONTESTED ELECTIONS 82

CHAPTER IV

THE MEDIOCRITY OF THE CHAIR 120

CHAPTER V

GROW AND COLFAX DOMINATED BY THADDEUS STEVENS 149

CHAPTER VI

JAMES G. BLAINE 169

CHAPTER VII

Kerr, Randall, Keifer, and Carlisle 193

CHAPTER VIII

"Czar" Reed — The "Revolution" 214

CHAPTER IX

Joseph G. Cannon — The Present Speaker . . . 250

CHAPTER X

Résumé. The English and the American Speakers of To-day 273

Appendix 293

Index 297

THE
SPEAKERS OF THE HOUSE

INTRODUCTORY CHAPTER

THE BRITISH AND COLONIAL PROTOTYPE

IN the year 1377, the last of the reign of Edward III., the Rolls of Parliament make the first mention of a Speaker of the House of Commons in the person of Thomas de Hungerford. Peter de la Mare filled the office without acquiring the title in the Good Parliament of 1376.

The House of Parliament from its earliest inception, however, must, like all legislative and deliberative bodies, have had its master of ceremonies, its moderator, its regulator of proceedings. Yet in the paucity of records we have convincing proof of the insignificance of the office and the mediocrity of its tenants during the formative period of English constitutional history.

In 1378, Sir Peter de la Mare, for whose release the death of Edward III. had opened the prison gates, became in fact and in title Speaker of the House of Commons. During his incumbency the power of that body developed in proportion to the demands of a rapacious monarch and the House asserted with warmth and vigor its right to participate in the affairs of State. The enormous expense incident to the prosecution of the French Wars — an undesirable legacy which Richard II. had inherited with the royal title — and the customary contempt for economy always incident to a regency, impelled frequent appeals for parliamentary grants. The House of Commons, with the true human instinct of acquiring power, bartered cash for privilege and some royal concession was ever the condition precedent to parliamentary acquiescence. That the presiding officer by his strength of character and his insistence of purpose influenced the other members cannot be doubted, for the leader invariably furnishes at once the index and the guide to the general body.

The title itself suggests the clue to the official character of the early Speakers — they were the mouthpiece, the voice, of the House in all its communications to the King and the nation. Yet not for several generations did the House of Commons acquire the independence to give effect to this pleasing fiction. Even to-day the English Sovereign retains the theoretical right to veto the choice of the House of Commons for Speaker. Since 1869, however, this power has been but a tinsel ornament. But the existence of the right carries conviction that the office was, in its early stages, purely political, and its incumbent entirely subservient to regal influence. The peculiar duties devolving upon him made it a matter of supreme importance to the Sovereign that the Speaker should be in sympathy with all royal policies. It was the office of the Speaker to compose all speeches to the King and to frame all petitions and memorials to the Crown. It was in his power to inject a large element of his own personality into the proceedings. He translated according to prejudice or whim the resolutions of the House; if several matters were under consideration, he put such questions to a vote as suited his purpose. He framed the questions for decision not so much from the language of the original motion as from the general trend of the ensuing debate. Upon the reading of a bill it was his duty to declare its substance to the House and this, too, with a possible veneer of prejudice and corruption. He might in the first instance control the activity of the House and in the second translate that activity into such terms as conformed most nearly to selfish ambition and royal desire.

The cardinal principle of the Tudor period was the complete subjection of a servile Parliament. The necessary prelude to this ideal parliamentary attitude was a Speaker zealous in the interests of the Crown. If the machinery of oppression run smoothly and all the component parts of the engine of injustice give off neither noise of friction nor spark of protest, the oppressed seem never conscious of their wrongs. Lest there be any slipping of cogs, lest the House of Commons, by some untoward prejudice, might name a Speaker hostile to the Crown and thus necessitate the friction of a veto, the Tudors conceived the idea of nominating the Speaker before Parliament convened. Thus the ceremony of regal control was carried through with the same acquiescence that distinguishes a highway robbery, when the victim, bound and gagged, consents to being plundered. There is no voice of opposition because the opposition has no voice at its immediate disposal. Discreet men generally remain subservient to the forces which create them; the Tudor Speakers naturally made obeisance to royal dictate. The "Defender of the liberties of the House" then rapidly misapplied his power. Such bills as bore the stamp of royal approval he was charged with forcing through the House, no matter how wry a face it might provoke. There was a certain financial harmony about the bills; extravagant royal appetites were to be satisfied, court favorites pensioned, and royal mistresses pampered. The House must not be permitted to demand popular reform as a return for its grants and so the Speaker rapidly became the factotum of an unscrupulous master.

The House of Commons rapidly developed a mental attitude of sullen resignation alternating with obsequious obedience. Still there were occasional flames from the fire that smouldered. In 1523 Cardinal Wolsey, in a fit of indiscretion, visited the House of Commons to urge an appropriation of £800,000. Many, resenting his purpose, wished to deny admission to one who came thus to intimidate, but more moderate counsels prevailed and the royal emissary was admitted, at the request of the Speaker, Sir Thomas Moore, "with all his pomp, with his maces, his pillars, pole-axes, cross, hat, and the great seal." Wolsey's eloquent plea gained no response; the independent members maintained determined opposition. Again, the Cardinal sought to persuade them to obedience by the art of oratory; again to be greeted with hostile silence. In a show of rage the courtier demanded some answer, but no member ventured a reply until the Speaker, falling on his knees reverently sought to excuse the silence of the House "abashed at the sight of so noble a personage who was able to amaze the wisest and most learned men in the realm." Moore then declared, as politely as sentences might be framed, that the Cardinal's visit was not in harmony with the ancient and revered liberties of the House who were wedded

The British and Colonial Prototype

to the custom of debating only among themselves. Wolsey withdrew, enraged at this failure of his mission. After fifteen days of debate, a subsidy much less desirable than that demanded, both in amount, and in the terms of payment, was carried, largely through the influence of defenders of the Crown, who held the balance of power.

One of the most slavishly subservient of the Tudor Speakers was Hare, who presided over the House in 1540. Sent to the Tower for opposing the prerogative of the King, he acquired both freedom and office at the price of apostasy and, as is usual with renegades, became most zealous in the new cause.

In the reign of Queen Mary, the Speakers were selected with a view to the restoration of the Roman Catholic religion. Under Elizabeth the majority party in the House of Commons were infected with the views of Puritanism. The bolder spirits organized an element hostile to the continued royal despotism, and succeeded in repeatedly defeating the Crown party. Two matters furnished the bone of contention, namely, the further reformation of the established church and the succession to the Throne. A royal personage is quite as prone as a layman to resent interference in strictly private affairs, particularly if they be affairs of the heart. The opposition party at first sought to persuade the Queen to take a consort, that an heir might be provided. Her answers varied from the coquettishly evasive to the furiously defiant. Her amours with Sir Walter Raleigh and the Earl of Essex seemed to her preferable to the trials and restrictions of a lawful alliance. As the prospect of marriage gradually vanished, fearful lest the claim of Mary Queen of Scots should be preferred to that of Suffolk, Parliament insisted upon a proclamation of settlement.

In 1566 this question engendered probably the most serious conflict between the Crown and the Commons that had arisen since the reign of Henry IV. The Lords joined the House of Commons in the struggle. Bold and determined language was bandied about the floor of Parliament, and some peers, members of the Council of the Queen, insisted that Elizabeth should be compelled to marry or else Parliament should declare a successor despite her protests. Firmness and diplomacy were the weapons with which the Queen met this attack. The peers who had opposed her were humbled by her refusal to receive them, and the Commons were persuaded to temper their action by offering a request for a royal spouse. To this action she replied in courteous and unmeaning phrases. The Commons again opened the flood-gates of oratory upon the question of succession. The Queen, indignant at their perversity, through the Speaker, directed them, in strong terms, to cease their discussions. One member, Paul Wentworth, of unusual temerity, raised the question whether this inhibition of the Queen was not a serious interference with the liberties and privileges of the House. An earnest debate ensued and Elizabeth discreetly revoked her former command, "which revocation" according to the "Journal" was taken by the House "most joyfully with hearty prayer and thanks for the same."

Under the Tudors, the Speaker, nominally the servant, was really the master of the House of Commons, ruling that body by the dictates of the throne. Still we trace a nascent independence. With Henry VIII. only once,

The British and Colonial Prototype

namely in 1532, did the Commons decline to give sanction to a bill recommended by the Crown. Under Edward VI. and Mary, weaker characters, several bills sent down from the House of Lords were rejected by the Commons. They held out strictly for the provision in the Act of Treason under Edward VI. that the offense should be proved by the testimony of two witnesses thereto, in open court.

These disquieting signs of legislative independence were met by the organization of rotten boroughs and by the naked and unblushing interference of the Crown in subsequent elections. Edward VI. either constituted or revived twenty-two boroughs, of which fully half were places of no importance, some indeed scarcely possessing name or location. Mary devised an additional fourteen while Elizabeth thus added sixty-two members to the parliamentary enrolment. Royal interference with elections was open and shameless. The sheriffs were notified to instruct the various freemen as to the candidates for whom their ballots should be cast. The freemen being wholly complaisant, men belonging either to the court or occupying positions of trust or ornament about the King, were elected as Knights from different shires.

Similarly the Parliament summoned in 1554, to register the return of England to allegiance to the Apostolic See, was wholly subservient to the slightest whim of Queen Mary. In this instance the voters were commanded to choose as their representatives "such as being eligible by order of the laws, were of a wise, grave, and Catholic sort."

In the gradual evolution from abject subserviency we find that during the reigns of the Stuarts the position of

Speaker served as an admirable barometer, indicating the varying phases of the contest between King and Parliament. With the temporary ascendency of the Crown, the Speaker was servile, cringing, obedient; as Parliament gained control we note him confident, proud, independent.

When the first Parliament of James I. met (March 19, 1603), a struggle with the Crown seemed imminent. In reply to the address from the Throne, the Speaker, Sir Edward Phelips, reminded the King in precise terms of the limited nature of the royal powers. Under Elizabeth the House of Commons was less belligerent because of the dangers which threatened both the Reformed Church and the national independence, combined with a conviction of the unselfish patriotism of the Queen. They were not inspired to obedience by any personal esteem for the Stuarts, nor was the national existence imperiled.

The Parliament of 1628 marked the crisis of the struggle for legislative liberty. Late in February, Charles I. had directed the House to adjourn until March 2d, expecting thus to protect his favorites from the attack then being made upon them. All efforts for a compromise failing during this recess, the House, immediately upon convening, March 2d, was informed by the Speaker, Sir John Finch, that the King again ordered them to adjourn, this time until March 10th. While the Lords had from time immemorial granted the right of the King to order an adjournment of their House, this action had never been acquiesced in by the Commons. Though issue had never been joined, the House of Commons, while acceding to the desires of the King, had always been scrupulously careful to make their adjournment their own formal act. This was, of

The British and Colonial Prototype

course, but sophistry masquerading as logic. The question of adjournment, put to a vote by the Speaker, was rejected by a resounding chorus of "noes." Sir John Eliot, foreseeing an enforced adjournment and immediate dissolution of Parliament by the King, had drawn up a formal protest on the questions of religion and taxation which, if passed by the House before adjournment, would be spread through the Kingdom as both an appeal and a challenge against the arbitrary conduct of the Throne. Eliot rose in his place to address the House. He was interrupted by the Speaker, who declared that he had received the royal injunction to quit the Chair if anyone sought to address the House. The Speaker, attempting to rise, was violently thrust back into his seat by Holles and Valentine as he sought to announce the adjournment. The whole House raised its voice in uproar and the Privy Councilors rushed to the assistance of the Chair. The Speaker, breaking away from the struggling group, was again seized and hurled into his seat. "God's wounds" exclaimed Denzil Holles, "you shall sit until it pleases the House to rise." Upon the order of the House the door was locked by Sir Miles Hobart, who placed the key in his pocket. Eliot then explained his resolutions and requested that they be formally put to vote. The Speaker and Clerk, both subservient to the Crown, refused to put the question and a fiery debate ensued between the contesting factions. Eliot, giving up hope of forcing the resolutions through the House, had thrown them into the fire. At length, as the King's Guards were seen approaching the House to break down the doors, Holles, who had rewritten the resolutions from memory, read them to the members. They passed by acclamation and the House thereupon voted its own dissolution, and saved its chamber from the dangerous precedent of being invaded by an armed body of soldiers.

The next Parliament was convened in 1640. Even the lapse of twelve years had not effaced from the minds of an indignant nation and a jealous Parliament the memory of the injustice and oppression with which Charles I. had forced that other Parliament to its unwilling dissolution. At an early session of this new Parliament official cognizance was taken of the struggles between the Speaker, subservient to the King, and the independent body of the House. The Speaker, Sir John Finch, having refused to put a question to the House, was declared guilty of a breach of privilege. Thus notice was served upon Crown and nation that the Speaker of the new House of Commons should be free from all external influences or authority.

In 1640 Charles I. attempted to overawe his enemies by throwing into prison several members of the House of Commons which he had dissolved after a futile session of three weeks. Others in the ensuing year he removed from the opposition by the more effective stratagem of winning men by places.

In 1642 the Attorney-General delivered a royal message to the House of Lords impeaching of high treason Lord Kimbolton and five members of the Commons. The King demanded that the persons accused be arrested by the House and the charges immediately considered. The House of Commons refused to be thus despoiled of its primary rights and the King determined to supplement impeachment by an act even more tyrannical — in short to go to the House in person at the head of an armed

The British and Colonial Prototype 11

body and forcibly remove the leaders of the opposition. The following morning (January 4, 1642) the accused members were in their regular places; the House of Lords firmly refused to obey the royal order. King Charles, at the head of five hundred armed men, set out for Parliament, combining in one moment the extremes of tyranny and folly. The five members, forewarned, withdrew to a convenient place of hiding, by the expressed desire of the House. At the entrance to Westminster Hall the royal retainers broke ranks and ranged themselves on either side along the entire length of the Hall. Charles, passing between the two ranks thus aligned, ascended the stairs leading directly to the House of Commons. As the King passed into the lobby, just outside the House, many officers of the Army of the North and a princely crew of desperate ruffians pressed in after him. Commanding all others, on pain of death, to remain without, Charles, accompanied only by his nephew, the Elector Palatine, entered the chamber of the House of Commons. But so closely did the desperadoes follow upon his heels that the door between the chamber and the lobby was not allowed to close behind him. Standing, thus, at the very portals, and plainly visible to all, glared these hirelings of the King. Many of them had thrown off their cloaks and a large majority were armed with pistols and swords, pistols cocked and swords drawn.

Upon the entrance of the King, the members, according to tradition, rose and uncovered, Charles likewise removing his hat. The King, not observing Pym, approached the chair of the Speaker, saying, "Mr. Speaker, I must for a time make bold with your chair." Mounting the dais the King addressed the House upon the purpose of his visit and demanded the surrender of the five members whom he had accused. Receiving no response to his inquiries he turned to the Speaker, William Lenthall, and asked whether the accused were present. Lenthall, falling upon his knees before the King, replied, "May it please your Majesty, I have neither eyes to see nor tongue to speak in this place but as the House is pleased to direct me, whose servant I am here." The King continued the search in his own behalf, until, chagrined and humiliated, he was forced to admit his defeat. In rage he withdrew from the House and passed through the reformed line of his guards who in turn gave vent to angry cries of disappointment that they had not been permitted to invade and pillage the sanctum of English liberties. In the lobby they had impatiently awaited the signal which would have been the prelude to a terrible realization. For it had been the intention of Charles to remove by force the five members, had their peaceable delivery been denied.

The spirit of this historic Parliament is an earnest of what that answer would have been. In the general struggle which must necessarily have ensued, the whole body of the House would have been set upon without discrimination or distinction. Even during the days of turmoil incident to the Revolution of 1643 the Commons followed the cherished custom of submitting their choice of Speaker to the confirmation of another authority. The King not being able to give the sanction of his approval, the House in 1647 adopted the novel rule of presenting its Speaker to the House of Lords, who expressed their approval as a matter of mere formality. However, frequently during

The British and Colonial Prototype

the Revolution a Speaker was chosen upon the sole responsibility of the House.

After the Restoration, the King endeavored, whenever possible, to place in the Chair a Speaker favorable to his interests. Sir Edward Seymour although distinctly subservient was one of the ablest Speakers in the history of the English House. He was so intimately acquainted with each member and his views upon all questions, that by merely glancing over the House he could accurately predict the outcome of any measure proposed. In case any bill came up in which the King was interested, if the court party were not in the majority Seymour would resort to a novel method of filibustering, that of deliberately misreading or mistating the question, that time might be given the party whips to round up a sufficient majority. When enough of these had been summoned, so that the bill might safely be put to a vote, the question would be fairly stated.

In 1677 this doubtful method of framing the questions aroused a storm of angry protest. The Speaker had usurped what was considered the privilege of the members. It had been customary for the Speaker to frame the motion from the substance of the debate. It was openly charged and but faintly denied that the Speaker sought to supply the House with sentiments and that the proceedings of the Commons were often deliberately misrepresented and their effect upon the nation wholly neutralized. The practice of thus commenting on the motion before the House was so notoriously abused as to be no longer tolerated. Often several offices were held by the Speaker at the same time. For example Sir Edward Seymour was

Treasurer of the Navy while presiding over the deliberations of the House. This confederation of offices was bitterly denounced in 1673 and the custom was strangled by its own unpopularity.

In 1679 the Crown, for the last time, refused from political motives to confirm the election of the Speaker chosen by the members. Sir Edward Seymour, despite his seeming bias for the court, had become immensely popular and was elected in preference to the nominee favored by the Crown. Charles II. refused to confirm the election when, in accordance with custom, Seymour was presented to him upon the ensuing day. The royal attitude was severely condemned as an interference with the undoubted rights of the House. The Commons insisted that it rested with them alone to name their governing officer and that his presentation to the King was but a mere deference to an ancestral tradition, wherein the King played his innocuous part of confirming the election without hesitation or objection. The contest between a protesting House and a defiant King continued for a week, when at length the Commons bowed to the royal will, although their knees were stiff and their concession ill-humored. Yet ultimate victory was with the House for no English sovereign thereafter ventured to question the right of the House to name its own Speaker or to intimate that the royal confirmation was other than a pleasing formality.

Among the added liberties brought to England by the Revolution of 1689 was the recognition of the complete independence of the Speaker of the House from all external influence. Still the growth of the office was slow and its

The British and Colonial Prototype 15

evolution gradual. In the eighteenth century we observe this transitory stage. Pitt, in the discussion of the Stamp Act, declared with vehemence that "Even the Chair looks too often to Saint James's." Although not indifferent to the influence and glamour of the Crown, still the Speaker had graduated from the subserviency of the Tudor régime. Indeed it was not until the beginning of the nineteenth century that the English Speaker became in fact, as well as in theory, the moderator of the House of Commons, neither servant to the Crown nor dominant over the House.

From the office of the English Speaker as it existed in the sixteenth and seventeenth centuries, rather than in the eighteenth century, we trace the lineage of the American Speakership. The first Puritan colonists brought over, as not the least valued of their possessions, the English constitutional system including of course their theory of the Speakership. But as some animal, removed from its natural habitat to another clime, is influenced by the new conditions and develops differing traits, so the Speakership was modified by the different character of the people, by novel institutions, by new influences.

Following closely English precedence, the colonial legislative assemblies adopted generally the custom of electing their Speakers subject to the confirmation of the colonial Governor, who was regarded as the personal representative of the King. This right of veto, in the colonies as in England, contained the germ of many a dissension. It was claimed as a prerogative of the Crown. The insistence of the various legislative assemblies that their choice should be final frequently met with success, but the royal Governor, when the issue was actually joined, more often carried the point.

Following further the English example, the colonial Speaker was not vested with any particular political functions and the parliamentary duties of the office remained of secondary importance. To control debate, preserve order, and enforce rules, after the manner of the Speaker of the Commons, comprised his tripartite duty. He did not name committees; this important asset of the Speakership in our day then devolved upon the House; however, in many instances, the committees were nominated by the Speaker and revised or confirmed by the members.

The Speaker of the colonial assembly was generally an active politician, the head of his party, and it was rather these attributes than any pre-eminent ability as a presiding officer or any intimate knowledge of parliamentary procedure which determined his election. The attitude of the House toward the Crown and the royal Governor was invariably registered in the selection of the Speaker. Thus the Speaker elected developed into a political leader. He guided the assembly in its work and naturally impressed the stamp of his personality upon much of the legislation. As the statesman of the colony, he was often named as a delegate to frame treaties, attend conferences, and visit conventions. Contrary to the English tradition, it was not felt that a representative upon assuming the Chair should be compelled to sacrifice his privileges as a member, and a district be thus deprived of all influence. In many of the colonial assemblies, the Speaker not only voted upon all questions before the House, but even put motions from the Chair; in others he served on committees of the

The British and Colonial Prototype

House with the same freedom as the other members. Thus the office became largely political, not so much through the nature of its duties as because of the political influence of its incumbents. As if to emphasize the increasing political importance of the office, the House under the leadership of the Speaker would often adopt spirited resolutions defying or censuring the Governor. The growing prestige of the Speaker is easily understood when we reflect that he was the highest elective officer of the people and consequently regarded as *per se* the legitimate popular leader. A power was thus built up which might cope with the Governor and his Council. Men of prominence seem to have been as human in those days as now and the privileges and influence of the office were often misused.

The colonial Speaker was subject to removal or expulsion whenever he failed to command a majority of the House or refused to obey their fiat. Thus the colonial official in both practice and theory occupied a ground midway between the Speaker of the House of Commons of England and the Speaker of the House of Representatives of the United States.

In the days of our national beginnings the presiding officers or Presidents of the Continental Congresses were selected because of their personal influence and power. At first the principle of rotation in office, by States, was sedulously adhered to. But this chain of rotation was broken in 1784 by the election of Richard Henry Lee of Virginia, the first President, Peyton Randolph having also been a delegate from that State. With the custom once ignored, a return to it, in the absence of able contestants from the States not already honored, was not to be expected. Indeed New Hampshire, Rhode Island, and North Carolina were conspicuous in that none of their delegates were called upon to preside over the deliberations of the Revolutionary and pre-constitutional assemblies.

In the absence of any journals of the proceedings it is difficult to enumerate the duties and powers of the presiding officers of the Continental Congress. We may safely conclude that they were neither onerous nor distinguished. Mutual jealousies argued against conferring unequal power upon any colony, by bestowing any unwonted authority upon the presiding officer. Further, all important business was invariably transacted in the Committee of the Whole. Congress may truly be said to have governed itself rather than to have delegated that power to its Speaker. The President does not appear to have named any committees. Congress itself appointed the Chairman *pro tempore*, but he was authorized only to exercise the function of keeping order. As the ballots were taken by States we see another influence at work to neutralize the power of the office. Yet we must not deny the prestige of the Speaker as the official and executive head of the Government. He was the highest functionary of the revolted colonies. He was endowed with executive and diplomatic powers. He served in the capacity of Secretary of War, and Secretary of State, received the diplomatic representatives of foreign powers, conducted the official correspondence with the various colonies and became in short a quasi-President. The official communications of Congress were naturally signed by the presiding officer of

The British and Colonial Prototype

that body and many of these letters he framed at their suggestion. Appeals to the various States to meet their quotas of troops and expenses were invariably signed by the Speaker or President in his official capacity. Not infrequently the Speakers were guilty of an arbitrary exercise of power by refusing to recognize members who desired to speak in opposition to the views of the Chair or by failing to record in the Journal hostile motions which had been duly made and seconded.

John Hancock often employed the office as a personal asset, a cudgel to force upon the House his individual sentiments. He felt his influence as one of the leaders of the Continental Congress to be unquestionably greater than his prestige as a presiding officer. Not recognizing the natural obligation of gratitude, Hancock, after his election to the Chair, opposed the members to whom he owed his own election. Refusing to consider himself the servant of the assembly over which he presided he deliberately set about to bend that body to his will. He opposed those who, with a majority behind them, declared for decisive action against England, and by all the arts of which he was master obstructed the presentation and passage of the Declaration of Independence.

The Speakers of the Continental Congress apparently compared themselves with the English Prime Minister, and considered that the loss of a majority necessitated their resignation. In 1778 a bitter newspaper attack was made upon Congress and Richard Henry Lee. The President of Congress, Henry Laurens, proposed from the Chair that this article be read to the House that it might thereby be made the basis of certain resolutions. Congress refusing to take up the matter, Laurens, in a rage intemperately resigned his office, insisting that its further retention was not consistent with his honor. Irritated at this churlish display of temper the House adjourned. The ensuing day a new President was chosen although the friends of Laurens endeavored to secure his re-election.

Although not a powerful officer in the modern acceptance of the term, the President of the Congresses of the Confederation seems to have combined the functions of a moderator with the power of a political leader — the careful poise of the English and the strong keen prejudice of the American office. Of the fourteen Presidents of the Continental Congress between 1774 and 1789, probably only Randolph, Hancock, and Laurens are popularly remembered in that connection. Jay, St. Clair, Mifflin, and Lee built their fame upon other services. Hanson, Griffin, and Boudinot are mere names except to the close student of American history.

In the Constitutional Convention of 1787 the presiding officer, General Washington, was chosen by ballot. He was given certain extraordinary powers, as the right to determine all questions of order without submitting them to debate or appeal; two reasons conspired to this — their confidence in the wisdom and integrity of Washington, and the necessity of holding within bounds members who might in their disappointment resort to political skirmishing. The committees were selected by the ballot of the Convention. Only once did the presiding officer of the Convention offer an expression of personal conviction from the Chair.

The British and Colonial Prototype

What the artisans of our Constitution intended should be the character of the office of Speaker of Congress it is impossible to determine. There was, to all appearances, no debate in the Convention upon the subject. The whole question is disposed of in the single constitutional clause: "The House of Representatives shall choose their Speaker and other Officers ——." They must then have intended such an officer as the one with whom they were familiar. He should not be the executive head of the nation after the manner of the presiding officers of the Continental Congress for they had provided a President to assume those duties. He should not be the moderator as the Speaker of the House of Commons of England, as they knew him only through their political studies, and not by contact with such an administration of the office. The Speaker with whom they had served combined these qualities; he was at once moderator and political leader. Into the Speakership then had been kneaded the leaven of partisan politics.

CHAPTER I

MUHLENBERG THE FIRST AND HENRY CLAY THE GREATEST OF AMERICAN SPEAKERS

THERE are many delightful little traditions of our Revolutionary War — illustrating the piety of the struggle and the religious fervor with which men mingled for a moment their tears in the lamentation of the family, only to brush the mist from their eyes and march off to battle with flintlock and powder-horn.

One of these relates how a minister of the Church of England, in Pennsylvania, appeared before the congregation at the Sabbath service, clothed in the vestments of the church, preached on the perils of the colonies, and, at the climax of oratorical passion, tore off his garments to reveal the blue and buff regimentals of a Continental soldier — crying out as some celestial trumpeter, "There is a time for all things — a time to preach, and a time to fight: and now is the time to fight." Then, leading the patriotic members of his parish out on the village green, he laid aside the gospel and prayer book to instruct them in the manual of arms, and the art of killing.

This parson was Peter Muhlenberg, one of three brothers, all born in Pennsylvania and sent abroad to acquire in the universities of Germany an education such as this country could not provide. Frederick Muhlenberg likewise embraced the ministry and was ordained in the Lutheran Church. Less theatrical than that of Peter

The Greatest of American Speakers 23

Muhlenberg was his transition from religious to public life. We first meet him as a member of the Continental Congress. Later he became President of the Council of Censors, presided over the Pennsylvania Convention, and was a member of the first Federal Congress. Possessed of marked parliamentary genius, the fame of his talents had defied the artificial boundaries of political divisions.

Men, not issues, seemed at first to dominate. In the first Congress which convened at New York City in 1789, there was no distinct cleavage of political parties. Sectional jealousies which had come so near to strangling the nation at its birth still exercised a potent influence in politics, and an equitable geographical allotment of offices — the earliest concession to the theory of geographical politics which has robbed the nation of the services of many brilliant statesmen — was agreed to by common consent. The South claimed the honor of the Presidency in the commanding figure of General Washington. From the North came the austere Puritan, John Adams, to preside over the deliberations of the Senate and establish the precedents of an office of innocuous inactivity, important only in that its occupant was heir apparent to the Presidency. To the middle States some sop of patronage must be thrown. Pennsylvania, with Philadelphia the citadel of American liberty, stood forth as the symbol of the unrepresented section.

Frederick A. Muhlenberg, now a portly, prosperous man of affairs, was elected Speaker of the first House of Representatives. Signers of the Declaration of Independence, generals of the armies of the Revolution, and future Presidents combined to constitute that one of the most interesting bodies of men ever gathered in a political assemblage.

Elbridge Gerry, Roger Sherman, George Clymer had subscribed to the document of 1776; Fisher Ames, the brilliant genius, polished writer, profound lawyer, eloquent orator and political hypochondriac; Jonathan Trumbull, Jr., son of the sturdy patriot "Brother Jonathan" Trumbull of Connecticut; Theodore Sedgwick of Massachusetts, Speaker of a later Congress; the benevolent Elias Boudinot of New Jersey; the distinguished soldier and uncertain politician, Sumter of South Carolina; the eccentric James Jackson of Georgia; Scott of Western Pennsylvania, a typical backwoodsman of native prowess and picturesque attire; the talented and experienced Madison, intimate of Washington and ward of destiny; all these answered the roll call. The government of this Washington era was not by the people, but by a distinguished social and political aristocracy. In the Senate honorable mediocrity was apparent. The casual observer asks what of the brilliant Hamilton, the aristocratic Jay, the distinguished Pinckneys — why are they not in the seats of the mighty in the temple which they have built so well?

Muhlenberg was neither a great man nor an inspiring leader. As a presiding officer, or moderator, he possessed a certain adaptability to novel conditions. The House of Representatives, at this initial stage of development, gave little opportunity for the aggrandizement of the Speaker's office. There were no parties — all rather were friendly rivals in their zeal to proclaim loyalty to the administration of Washington. All vied with one another in the sincerity of their devotion at the font of patriotic endeavor. To question the wishes of the President was sacrilege, to oppose them would have been political suicide.

During the first session the House of Representatives tried the experiment of choosing its committees by ballot. But in January, 1790, they voted to give this right to the Speaker. This was the first factor in the evolutionary development of the power of the Speaker. His duty at first was simply that of any presiding officer — to apply the rules of the House so as to ensure the opportunity for unhampered debate and secure the freest expression of the legislative desire. Even after the House had conferred upon the Speaker the power of committee appointments, so long as the number of committees was small and the committee positions were in slight demand, this was an administrative rather than a political power fitting into the general theory of moderatorship.

In the second Congress, Jonathan Trumbull was substituted for Muhlenberg as the Speaker. Trumbull was an earnest Federalist whose orthodoxy was unquestioned, while Muhlenberg had wavered in his allegiance to certain administration measures. Still sectional prejudice and the plea for rotation in office — the American theory that every man fitted for office must have his turn — were probably more decisive factors in this displacement of the Pennsylvania Representative. Trumbull was formerly Speaker of the Connecticut Assembly, and later Governor of the State. Under his régime the germ of political differentiation attacked the House and from the undefined mass of political concepts arose two distinct national parties.

The year 1793 marks the birth of distinct political alignment under the Constitution; the Federalists and the anti-Federalists, or Republicans. In the third Congress the anti-Federalists elected Muhlenberg again as Speaker by a small majority over Theodore Sedgwick of Massachusetts, whom the Federalists supported.

In the fourth Congress, that of 1795 to 1797, the Republican party, formerly classed as the anti-Federalists, grown strong in numbers and dignified by a name suggesting a positive career of militant principles rather than a carping attitude of negation, controlled the House of Representatives by a bare majority.

Yet by the fortunate union of their own ranks, combined with lack of cohesion among their opponents, the Federalists were able to elect Jonathan Dayton, of New Jersey, Speaker. This furnishes the only case in our legislative history where a portion of the majority joined with the minority in electing their candidate. Dayton in his earlier career had staunchly advocated the sequestration of British debts, and it was felt that he might be counted on to oppose a British treaty. To this political influence was added the moral element of Dayton's personal popularity. In the ensuing Congress Dayton again received the nomination and election, although Smith of South Carolina was the acknowledged leader of the Federalists in the House. Smith's rabid anglomania had alienated the support of many of the Federalist leaders — so that while retained as knight of the floor he was compelled to give way in the greater honor to the more fortunate Dayton. Dayton's influence was of vast importance, not alone to the Federalist party, but also to the nation.

He succeeded, by the aid of Hamilton, in tempering the bellicose attitude of the House and in moderating the legislative reply of 1797 by the avowal of sincere gratitude at the prospect of renewed negotiations with France, and in polishing a paper which was punctuated with daggers of war.

With an orthodox and trustworthy majority, the Federalists elected Theodore Sedgwick of Massachusetts Speaker in 1799, over Nathaniel Macon of North Carolina. The vote of forty-four to thirty-eight reveals at once the size of the House and the division of the two parties.

Sedgwick felt the sting of partisan rancor. A man of marked ability, undoubted integrity, and unsullied honor, on the altar of partisanship he sacrificed both personal popularity and hope of political preferment. One of the accredited leaders of the Federalists, he invited criticism by his radicalism. He had been one of the chief plotters in the intrigue to make Aaron Burr President, and had cast the deciding vote which passed the Bankrupt and the Sedition Acts. In 1801 Sedgwick was approached by the editor of a Republican paper with the request that he be extended the customary courtesy of a seat on the floor to facilitate reporting the debates for his sheet, the *National Intelligencer*. This periodical had earned the enmity of the Speaker who despised anything that was not a missionary of Federalism. After reprimanding and expelling the applicant from the floor of the House, Sedgwick ordered him summarily ejected from the gallery whence he had retreated. The editor appealed to the House for admission and was again rebuked by Sedgwick's casting vote.

Sedgwick intensified the dissatisfaction over what was considered a deliberate affront to the opposition, and a slur upon the dignity of the House, by arguing from the Chair in support of his position.

The virulence of party feeling in the House was manifested at its dissolution when the Republicans firmly declined to join in the customary vote of thanks to the retiring Speaker. The bitterness of this sting and disappointment at the failure of his career were clearly portrayed by Sedgwick in his valedictory to the House when he renounced forever public life and turned as some soldier weak and disheartened from the wounds and privations of war to the tender ministrations of home and kindred.

In 1801 Nathaniel Macon of North Carolina was elected Speaker. A man of some mental independence and of unquestioned honor he possessed in profusion the homely, frugal traits that won the new administration so warm a place in the popular heart. Frequently he cast off the shackles of political subserviency and asserted his independence of party suzerainty. In after years he was reverently termed the "Father of the House" so constantly was he re-elected to preside over its deliberations.

The first Southerner to be chosen Speaker, his election was the offspring of that alliance between the Southern gentry and the New York Democrats which had elevated Jefferson to the Presidency and had earlier brought the Capitol to the Potomac. The administration controlled by a safe majority both the Senate and the House of Representatives. A reaction from aristocratic, paternal, "silk-stocking" Federalism had brought to Washington

The Greatest of American Speakers 29

scores of able men clad in simple homespun, permeated with the ideas of democratic equality, men who followed the plow and gloried in their rusticity.

For the first time in our national history we had an Executive who dominated, who fused the legislative with the executive will, who held Congress to the tasks he imposed. Thus the majorities of both Houses were thoroughly tractable and did yeoman's service in framing into legislation the principles to which Jefferson was pledged. This Washington had not done, for he would not; and Adams had not for he could not. The one would not countenance the prostitution of Congress to partisan purposes, the other would have broken in the effort.

This Congress was subservient to the administration as probably no succeeding Congress has ever been. Yet it seemed a willing obeisance to the external authority — and not the cringing subserviency of fear, the trembling before the rod. The presence in the Cabinet of two of the most adroit and skillful congressional leaders of the earlier day may have been an influence but probably not a controlling one. Certainly no questionable methods were enlisted: nor was public patronage then, as at present, held out as a crumb of reward or a cudgel of revenge. A master mind dominated the government — not crudely as brute force compels, but smoothly as the diplomat persuades — and a single principle permeated all of its departments. Jefferson found in Macon as Speaker of the House an able ally and forceful friend. Probably the ablest of the early Speakers, Macon was essentially a party man and his record reveals a mild tinge of partisanship. Henry Adams has drawn a neat pen picture of him — "a typical homespun planter, honest and simple, erring more often in his grammar and spelling than in his moral principles, but knowing little of the world beyond the borders of Carolina. No man in history has left a better name than Macon, but the name was all he left." An ardent lover of horses Macon entered the births and pedigree of his blooded stock on the fly-leaf of the family Bible.

Macon was the first Speaker to assert his constitutional right to vote despite a regulation in the rules of the House to the contrary. Also he was the first Speaker who led his party from the Chair: although he did not take the floor — as did the later Speakers — he exercised a powerful influence, through his lieutenants, in controlling and directing legislation. Naturally opposition slowly but clearly developed. In 1805 sectional jealousy and local pride united in the clamor for a change. Northern Democrats, weary of Southern domination, and keenly disappointed with the Southern appropriation of offices, suggested the name of Joseph B. Varnum of Massachusetts and only after a sharp struggle was Macon re-elected. Macon's apparent subjection to the turbulent John Randolph of Roanoke fanned the spark of dissatisfaction into the flame of discontent and in 1807 the revolt culminated in the election of Varnum by a majority of one vote. He was re-elected in 1809, though the Southern Democrats still remained loyal to the honored Macon.

The period from 1789 to 1811 in the Speakership may be characterized as the epoch of commanding mediocrity. The first three Speakers, Muhlenberg, Trumbull, and Dayton, were men of ordinary ability. The House of

The Greatest of American Speakers

Representatives at that time did not revel in the carnival of intellect which appeared in the following years, and did not in the first two decades attract the brilliant men of the nation. These Speakers were representative, they were the leaders of their party in Congress and the best to be secured from the material that offered. Sedgwick, embittered by the strife which he had engendered, contributed nothing to the history of the office. Macon and Varnum approached in some measure our theory of party leaders, though Varnum did not incur the charge of subserviency to executive influence.

The Speaker was still only a moderator, a presiding officer as compared with his successors of our generation. He had not named committees for the framing of legislation, he had not denied recognition or bestowed it to advance partisan ambition; he had not counted a quorum when those present declined to vote. He had not smothered filibustering with the bed clothes of cloture — he was the servant of the House, not its ruler.

This was still the heroic age of the Republic. The Revolutionary heroes were still in the land, lingering a little as if to give their benediction to the nation whose infancy they had baptized, and the American people were still under the hypnotic influence of the Revolution. The leaders were yet those who had helped to achieve our independence. So great was the veneration with which they were regarded that even those who had performed the most menial offices were considered, like the equerries and chamberlains of sovereign princes, entitled to a high rank. In that blinding glare of patriotism many a man, mediocre or even without ordinary ability, played a rôle in the public favor. The brazen age of commerce had not opened, but in the intervening thirty years a new country had grown up west of the Appalachian mountains — a country of strong, virile, hardy men, proud of their native ruggedness, setting physical prowess above mental keenness, applauding the coonskin and deriding the beaver — men who felt small affection and little respect for the dilettante East, or for elegant manners and effeminate courage. The Westerners had long chafed under the continued domination of the country along the seaboard. The East they felt supplied the aristocrats, the officeholding class of the nation, although they themselves were the bone and sinew, the iron and steel of the country. As this feeling crystallized they insisted upon official recognition.

A new generation too had grown to man's estate since the Revolution; ambitious, their blood thrilling with the enthusiasm of youth, they had become the local leaders. In the Congress which convened in special session at Washington, November 4, 1811, a host of new faces were seen; a new atmosphere pervaded the halls of the Capitol. Dignified age — aristocratic, patriotic, self-esteemed, service proud — the legacy of the Revolution — was no longer in the ascendency. Seventy new members appeared, to assume the unfamiliar duties of legislative life. They were another type — younger men plumed and knighted for the combat — the glory of their lives yet in the future, not pointing the finger of pride ever to the past.

First of all, Henry Clay in his thirty-fourth year; John C. Calhoun not quite thirty, Langdon Cheves of South Carolina thirty-five, Felix Grundy of Tennessee of the same age

The Greatest of American Speakers 33

as Clay, William Lowndes, David R. Williams, Peter Buell Porter of New York, and Richard M. Johnson of Kentucky, all leaders and under forty. None of these remembered the battles of Lexington and Bunker Hill; Yorktown was a dim and uncertain memory; they had not entered public life until we had become a nation. Even honored Federalism was now reduced to mere protest and driven to guerilla warfare.

These younger statesmen had only contempt for the ponderous, heavy-eyed ideals of the past. They were statesmen of conquest, not pleaders of self-preservation. Bold, defiant, aggressive, they were disciples of militant patriotism. They flaunted the cry of treason and cowardice in the face of conservatism. They cheered the heroes of war and toasted the gods of battle. They demanded war with England, they boasted of conquering Canada, they scanned the horizon for other fields, they suggested the occupation of Mobile and Key West and the acquisition of Florida; they even squinted longingly at Mexico and South America. National bankruptcy was a matter of supreme indifference; an unsuccessful issue of the struggle which was a bogey concept not to be considered.

With the issue joined the House proceeded to the election of its Speaker. On the first ballot the strength of the war movement was apparent. Henry Clay, the leader of the war Republicans, received seventy-five votes to thirty-eight cast for William Bibb of Georgia, the peace candidate, and three scattering for Nathaniel Macon, now returned to party allegiance.

"Who is Clay?" demanded the country, confusing him with a member from Virginia of the same surname.

The uncertain answer was that he was a new member of some talent and considerable oratorical ability who appeared to preside without prejudice. The reply was unsatisfactory and the country demanded to know more of this unsung prophet of the West — this youth who had been chosen Speaker on the day of his first entrance into the House. His election seemed remarkable, for the House was filled with members of recognized ability who had grown old in the country's service; still more striking was the fact that the new Speaker was from the unknown wilderness beyond the mountains — from one of the only two states that touched the great Mississippi; and there were only fifteen members from beyond the Alleghanies. But this was merely the prelude to the most wonderful, the most picturesque career of success and disappointment, of ambition and failure, in the annals of American history.

Clay had entered the Senate when not quite thirty and died while still a member at the age of seventy-six. He was introduced to that body during the Presidency of Jefferson and delivered his valedictory under the administration of Fillmore. Other Senators have served longer terms than Clay but none at times so widely separated. Other men in American history have excelled him in intellect — Hamilton did, so did Marshall and Story — but he combined those incomparable qualities which made him at once the adored party leader, the brilliant statesman, and the matchless orator.

To-day it is difficult to perceive the real Clay in the web of eulogy and reproach that a century has woven about him. Like Washington and Lincoln he is fast becoming a mythical personage, yet through an intervening century he stands out clearly the typical American — not a demigod like Washington, not an enigma like Lincoln. He was sent to the United States Senate by Kentucky to serve an unexpired term when still lacking three months of the constitutional age. Tiring soon of the dignity and quiet demeanor of the Senate, he turned to the aggressive turbulence of the House and was elected to a seat from the Lexington district. From the day he took the oath of office until 1852 Henry Clay was a compelling figure in American politics.

Probably never did a physical structure so naturally respond to its own emotions and passions; nor did a voice so perfectly harmonize with what it felt and uttered. This perfect union of voice and person was probably the secret of the masterful eloquence which shivered the dynasty of Jackson in the person of his successor. Wonderful as he was, Clay can hardly be ranked as one of the half dozen great orators of the world. He spoke rather to the hearer than to the reader — more to the present than to posterity.

Clay was pre-eminent in the delivery of a philippic wherein he could combine an attack upon a measure with an assault upon personal conduct, marshaling under his banner the forces of impassioned eloquence, bitter invective, and taunting sarcasm. Contests always attracted him. From an early habit of taking a share in animated discussion he derived that readiness of resource, and that knowledge of the temper and understanding of an audience which were far more valuable to him than Calhoun's careful reasoning, clear narrative, fair statement, and sharp retort. Clay seemed to lack the power of analysis — to prefer the plausible to the solid.

A man of adaptable personality, he was as much at home among European monarchs as with his constituents at a Kentucky barbecue. The Kentuckians remembered with pride his boyhood of dire poverty, his widowed mother and the fatherless family, his struggles for an education, his wonderful success. The "Mill Boy of the Slashes" appealed to the populace, it suggested the basic theory of democracy — the poor boy grown famous. His life was a pulsating lesson on the blessing of penury — an epic of democracy. He was one of the children of poverty who have built the world's greatness.

Clay was schooled in the vicissitudes and hardships that are potent factors in character building, and that furnish such splendid material, withal, for biographers and historians. He would have perished without human companionship, which was not alone his life and entertainment but the fount of his information. Whomsoever he touched, he drained — he read men instead of books. Without affectation, he allowed no pride of position, no conceit, no vanity to tarnish the beautiful homeliness of his character. A free liver, he would sit at cards far into the night, studying his political associates while the puritan Adams, alone in his study, indulged his literary taste. He drank to excess — but that must be judged by the standards of his time. This passion later became a source of pitiful reproach to himself, and of apology to his friends. In his last years, chastened by the vicissitudes of fortune, he became a most devout Christian.

While still in his twenties, Clay had rendered brilliant service in the Kentucky legislature, and as presiding officer had given some hint of those incomparable parlia-

The Greatest of American Speakers 37

mentary talents which later won for him an enduring fame in the broader arena of national activity. At the opening of the twelfth Congress he seemed the embodiment of the young and spirited West which had forced an entrance into the council chamber of the nation. His very life typified those influences. What more fitting than that he should be leader?

There were certain elements in Congress that had long provoked both fear and hatred. Of these was Josiah Quincy, the talented Representative from Boston, who had translated to the National Congress some of the harsh and uncompromising fervor of the New England town-meeting, where opposing factions held opposite sides of the hall, and in the bitterness of their quarrels recognized neither the dictates of courtesy nor the precepts of parliamentary law. Quincy had long been distinguished for his savage personal attacks when parliamentary decorum had been contemptuously ignored. And with him John Randolph of Roanoke; a talent for turbulence — the incarnation of erratic genius — what better summary of the most picturesque yet fascinating character of American civil life? His friends called him "A Chatham in eloquence, a Cato in incorruptibility," while his enemies declared him a nuisance and a scourge. He used to shake his long forefinger, the "javelin of rhetoric," in the face of the indignant House and manifest a vindictive pleasure in outraging the opinions of his fellow members. Priding himself upon his descent from Pocahontas, he showed much of the native virility of her race. An aristocrat by birth, a patrician by education, no man in Congress dared incur his enmity, for no opponent went free from his scathing denunciation and withering sarcasm. He ridiculed the dogmas of parliamentary law and showed his contempt for all forms of discipline by ignoring them. He was guilty of the most violent outrages upon decency and propriety. He seemed to recognize only the dictates of his own volatile caprice. His mind apparently had slipped its moorings and was like a rudderless ship in a heavy sea. The House for twelve years had been forced to tolerate his insolence and his unrefined bullying. Macon, as Speaker, had indulged him from motives of personal and political friendship, and Varnum from a less worthy motive — the dread of his keen and malicious sarcasm against which even the dignity of office had been insufficient protection. The Congressmen who had been pierced by the sharp shafts of his personal attacks demanded that his profligate career be arrested, that he be compelled to show some regard for the dignity of the assembly.

Clay was thought to be a man of such parliamentary ability, of so much dignity, that he would surely resent — and that effectively — any disrespect offered him either in his personal or official character. Through him the House wished to protect itself from the vipers in its midst. His relations with the mercurial Randolph were now friendly, now hostile, but ever dignified; the picturesque climax was reached as they faced each other on Virginia soil some years later with duelling pistols leveled, awaiting the count. From that day the bitterness of personal antipathy disappeared and one of the last visits of the "Baron of Roanoke," when the hectic flush and the brilliance of his eyes alone disguised the ravages of decay, was for the purpose of hearing in the familiar halls the well-known voice of his ancient adversary. During his career in the House, Randolph had been the uncompromising opponent of every measure proposed or supported by Clay — the War of 1812, the tariff, the early recognition of Greece and the independence of South America, the Missouri Compromise, and the election of John Quincy Adams to the Presidency.

Clay was the youngest man ever elected Speaker of the House of Representatives, and one of two to be so honored during the first term of service, William Pennington of New Jersey acquiring that honor during his first term in 1860, after a long and acrimonious contest. The election of Clay was a positive tribute, that of Pennington a negative compliment. Clay was chosen because of his acknowledged ability, his recognized talent, because the measures which he advocated were popular with his fellow members — in short, because he was known. Pennington was elected because his views were not matters of common information, because he had no enemies, nor for that matter friends — in short, because he was not known.

Clay's election was a protest against the old order of things — the prelude to the new. The battle cry was "War with England" — the slogan, replace listless inactivity with dynamic patriotism. Clay was the first Speaker to realize the possibility of his position and his assumption of the Chair marks an important epoch in the growth of the office. He became the first great party Speaker, using the enormous power and prestige of his position to carry out partisan policies. There are six or seven committees of the House, which, if properly organized and framed to do the bidding of the Speaker, will give to that official absolute and unquestioned control. To the keen intellect of Clay, this was at once apparent. He immediately took steps to so construct the committees that he might command their deliberations. War had been the desideratum, patriotic defiance to insolent Britain; therefore Clay organized the committees for war. That on Foreign Relations, of most immediate importance, was put in control of Porter, Calhoun, and Grundy. David R. Williams was named as Chairman of the Committee on Military Affairs, Langdon Cheves was given control of the Naval Committee, while Ezekiel Bacon and Cheves ruled the Committee on Ways and Means.

With intense fervor Clay set about the task that confronted him. Madison was weak and had been elected President largely because he stood in the line of Virginian succession. He had neither the knowledge nor the spirit of war. His advisers took counsel of their timidity. The vitriolic Josiah Quincy was the leader of the Federalists who decried war. Being the party of the opposition they felt that they must consistently oppose, although they laid themselves liable to the accusation of being traitors, than which nothing could have been more dangerous from a political standpoint. Quincy took up the cudgels and had something to say about young politicians with pin feathers not yet grown. Others have made the same mistake with like grievous results in underestimating the powers of youth and insisting that years are essential to leadership.

The plea of the venerable Quincy seemed to ridicule patriotism. No subject was so well suited to Clay's native talents; he touched the keys of inspiration and the nation echoed one strain; the boundless resources of the country, the glamour of successful war, the magic of enlarged domain, the prestige of victory. This stamped Clay, not the traditional moderator of the House, but rather party leader who could control the House. In becoming Speaker he did not sacrifice his rights as a member. Indeed there was scarcely a question of importance that he did not debate in Committee of the Whole. To govern or rule the House from the Chair, and to persuade it from the floor were clearly his purpose. In the stirring times of his first term in the Chair, with all the bitterness of party feeling, there was scarcely a day when he did not give voice to his sentiments. He never failed to cast his vote on any measure before Congress, refusing to deprive his State of her full representation.

While often arbitrary in his decisions he seldom aroused personal antagonism. He employed the tact of Talleyrand rather than the violence of Napoleon. He never gave reasons for his decisions on matters of parliamentary law. Impetuous, swift in decision, unflinching, of an imperative will, he seemed to have an instinctive consciousness not only of his own strength, but of his special capacity for leadership. Therefore he would himself take the lead — as if unconsciously — whatever the occasion, and as naturally and gracefully as if it were his unquestioned right. He never failed to overrule the eccentric Randolph when it could be done by any strength of justice, Randolph invariably appealing from the decision and the House, without exception (though often by a strict party vote), sustaining the Chair. Clay was frequently guilty of manipulating the rules in an endeavor to throw an advantage to his party — after the manner of those earnest characters who, determined upon realizing an end, care less for the means than the results.

He never hesitated to deprive Randolph of an opportunity to address the House if that could be accomplished without scandal or open rupture. A notable instance of this was in connection with the debate on the declaration of war, May 29, 1812. Randolph gained the floor; Clay ruled that he could not speak unless he submitted a motion to the House. Having complied with this requirement, he again essayed to argue the question and was informed from the Chair that the question could not be debated until the House consented to hear. A majority rallied to the support of the Speaker, refusing to consider the question, and Randolph was forced to desist. Thus we detect somewhat of the method of Clay's domination, the saving influence of his personal popularity, that inspired the House to endorse his action. During the entire period of his Speakership not one of his decisions was overruled.

Upon Clay fell the burden of advancing and at the same time defending the war which he had inspired. For only reverses need excuse and palliation; victories, whether they be of accident or design, of intention or blunder, need only heralding. The House repeatedly went into Committee of the Whole that Clay might address it, that his magnetic eloquence might draw doubtful members into line. On one occasion, Randolph, ever quick to grasp the point of a situation, queried: "After you have raised these twenty-five thousand men, shall we form a committee of public safety to carry on the war, or shall we depute the power to the Speaker, shall we declare that the Executive not being capable of discerning the public in-

The Greatest of American Speakers 43

terest, or not having spirit to pursue it, we have appointed a committee to take the President and Cabinet into custody?"

The war was almost a failure, indeed the posthumous battle of New Orleans alone cast the balance in favor of the United States. Clay was sent abroad to seek by diplomacy the conquests which had not been secured by arms, to garner whatever harvest there might be. With him went John Quincy Adams, James A. Bayard, Jonathan Russell, and Albert Gallatin, and their gleanings were scarce worth the effort. To Clay's political ambitions the war was destined to become a Nemesis. As it had built him up so it was later to tear him down. From the field of New Orleans there sprang a hero, who was three times to wave him back from the entrancing goal of his career.

Clay was re-elected Speaker in 1813, but resigned January 19, 1814, to take up at Ghent the diplomatic battle of his country. In his stead was chosen Langdon Cheves of South Carolina, one of that brilliant coterie of younger leaders who then controlled the country's destinies. This was the first time that a Speaker had resigned, under the Constitution. Only twice later did it occur — again in 1820, when Clay voluntarily retired from public life, and in 1834, when Andrew Stevenson of Virginia gave up the position to enter the diplomatic service. Nothing could have been better calculated to bring out in bold relief the ability and force of Clay's rule than this transition. The Congress of 1814, like some vast ship without compass or rudder, floundered hopelessly and won the unenviable distinction of personified incompetency, while that of 1815, when Clay was again in power, was long known as the most efficient and industrious that had ever met.

Upon his return to the United States after the treaty of Ghent, where he had so successfully defended the prestige of his country and won a peace hardly supported by the issue of battles, Clay was at once re-elected to Congress. He was chosen Speaker immediately upon the convening of the House of Representatives, and again took up the reins of authority which he had so successfully handled during his previous service.

The fourteenth Congress had been elected as a Congress of reform: the dissatisfied electorate demanded national bank legislation, a protective tariff, and a score of other matters of only secondary importance. Congress, although in session three months, had made no apparent progress in their legislative duties. Only seven bills had gone to the White House. The people could not understand why two hundred and eighteen men, presumably chosen for their conspicuous ability, should consume six months or more, each year, over business which with reasonable diligence might be concluded in one half that time. In the congressional salaries was thought to lie both the reason and the remedy. A Salary Act was framed by this "Reform Congress." It was entirely proper. The salary of Congressmen had been fixed by the salary law passed by the first Congress in 1789. Although many of the members of that first Congress were men of marked ability, proficient in various lines of activity, they passed a salary law fixing their compensation at what seemed to them a generous figure, though to us it appears niggardly. Six dollars a day for each day on which they were in attendance upon the sessions of Congress, and a reasonable mileage — this they deemed suitable pay for Senators and members of the House. The Speaker, from the dignity and the added duties of his office, was allowed a per diem of twelve dollars. Members who spent six months at New York or Washington, as the case might be, away from their business and their homes, incurring the additional expense of a changed residence, were paid, mileage included, only nine hundred dollars.

Shortly before adjournment, in the summer of 1816, a bill was introduced by Richard M. Johnson of Kentucky, providing an annual salary of $1500 for members of each House and double that amount for the Speaker. The arsenal of debate was immediately raided for weapons and the members rushed to the contest.

Randolph made a characteristic speech in support of the motion. "The present manner of payment," he insisted, "is disgraceful. Is it wonderful that we are considered by the people at large as no better than day laborers when we are willing to come here and work for something less than a dollar an hour, which is something more than you pay a man for sawing wood? There should, too, be another change made. A member should be paid whether he attends or not. Is it to be presumed that because he is out of his seat he is idle? Is the only diligent member the one who comes each day, writes and franks so many letters, reads so many newspapers, stitches together as many documents as he chances to find on his table and adjourns when the clock strikes four?" The bill was passed with its unsavory retroactive clause, although Randolph declared that he would as soon be caught with his hand in some other gentleman's pocket as to draw any of the back pay. It was further rushed through with suspicious haste. In the House it was introduced one day, read and considered the next, and passed the third. In the Senate, postponement, commitment, and amendment were all defeated. The harvest was ready for the sickle and the sickle was poised for the stroke.

It was natural that the people should feel that their Representatives had voted money to themselves, but that the whole nation should gasp in the convulsive spasms of political hysteria, was not expected. Every man who had voted for the bill was attacked with the venom of personal hatred. "Pirates," "looters of the treasury," "thieves," "traitors to the people," — such were the epithets bandied about the country. Grand juries of Vermont and Georgia returned presentments against the members who had voted for the nefarious bill and demanded the election of a Congress pledged to its repeal; the people seemed all at once infected with the germ of madness. The popular outburst was an interesting and valuable historical contribution to the psychology of political caprice.

Even Henry Clay, "our Harry," always nominated and elected by acclaim, was forced to conduct a spirited contest for re-election and was rescued from the cataclysm only through his personal popularity. Others were less fortunate. Georgia returned but one of its former delegation to Washington; South Carolina three out of nine; Maryland four out of nine; Pennsylvania thirteen out of twenty-three; Connecticut but two out of seven. The entire delegations from Ohio, Delaware, and Vermont were relegated to private life. Nine members disgusted with the popular clamor resigned before the opening of the second session of this ill-fated Congress and were superseded by men rancorous in their hostility to the compensation law. Both the popular rage and the punishment thus summarily inflicted were unreasonable and, like most exhibitions of popular anger, unfortunate. The fourteenth Congress thus ruthlessly destroyed had been, by far, the most efficient of any as yet convened under the Constitution.

In December of 1824 it became the duty of Henry Clay officially to extend the greetings of the United States to General Lafayette then visiting this country after an absence of forty years. No task could have been better suited to Clay's temperament — warm, ardent, patriotic, imaginative. The return of Lafayette to the scenes of his early fame was quite the most inspiring and picturesque feature of the first half century of our history.

As the guest of the nation he visited Washington, and Clay, as Speaker, when he was received in the hall of the House of Representatives, rose to greet him. It was a solemn and inspiring scene. With delicate instinct united with his inimitable grace of oratory he touched upon the poetic side of Lafayette's visit. It was generally felt that Clay had honored not alone Lafayette but Congress itself with the beautiful pathos of his speech and the subtle grace of his demeanor on this occasion.

In the intervening period since his return to Congress in 1815 Clay had been offered, by the prevalent harmony of political and industrial conditions, an opportunity to exploit his great program of internal improvements, the protective tariff and a national bank. They were but a chapter in the volume of his brilliant conception of the American nation.

He was always the leader in debate, and the organ of his party. His leadership was not alone the result of his position as presiding officer but depended upon his marvelous activity as a Representative. He had never contemplated resigning his right to vote or neglecting the opportunity to exercise the persuasive talents of his oratory when he assumed the Chair. He established the valued tradition that a party in elevating its leader to the Speakership does not thereby lose his services on the floor. Clay even pursued this policy to greater extremes. As far as possible matters of importance were discussed in Committee of the Whole that he might be given the opportunity to express his views. Indeed the House often went into Committee solely for this purpose. On one occasion he reproved the House by innuendo for failing to extend him this usual courtesy. As the dominant figure in national life and the leader of a great party he felt that he should be awarded every opportunity to defend himself and to persuade others.

Although other Speakers, notably Carlisle and Reed, have sought to combine these functions, none ever quite so thoroughly blended the duties of the Chair with the privilege of the floor.

Again, Clay's domination of the House arose not alone from the parliamentary power of his office; he frequently took advantage of his position to guide, if not indeed influence, the members of his party. To him fell the duty of framing the questions from the turmoil of debate. Clay's mind quickly conceived the advantage thus afforded.

The Greatest of American Speakers

At times he would even descend to sharp practice, especially when necessary to foil the thrusts of the troublesome Randolph. March 3, 1820, the turbulent genius from Roanoke moved that the vote of the previous day on the bill embodying the Missouri Compromise be reconsidered. Clay ruled the motion out of order until the regular business of the morning had been considered. Shortly Randolph moved that the House again retain in its possession the Compromise bill until such time as his original motion would be in order. Clay refused to consider this motion and at last when Randolph was recognized to restate his original motion he was coolly but politely informed that the proceedings of the House on the bill had already been communicated to the Senate by the Clerk and therefore the motion to reconsider could not be entertained.

Winthrop of Massachusetts furnished us probably the most accurate and impartial criticism of Clay's parliamentary ability. "He was no painstaking student of parliamentary law, but more frequently found the rules of his governance in his own instinctive sense of what was practicable and proper than in 'Hartsell's Precedents' or 'Jefferson's Manual.'" While the House was ever harmonious under the magic of his dominion it was more the harmony of mastery than the concord of freedom.

But Clay's empire was not the House alone. He was easily the presiding genius of the federal government during Madison's administration. The shibboleth by which Clay had been first elected Speaker was "War with Great Britain." To him must go the credit for that struggle. He forced the Senate and the President into acquiescence. Madison was not a man of commanding will — rather he was timorous; while not hostile to war he reflected mentally this physical indifference and was glad to cast the burden of framing and pursuing the foreign policy upon broader and more willing shoulders. Such shoulders were those of the rugged Speaker of Congress — whose blood seemed to tingle, whose every fibre seemed to vibrate, with the militant patriotism and blind enthusiasm of adolescence.

When a different type of man succeeded to the Executive Chair, Clay, who had enjoyed the taste of power, sought to retain control. Monroe declined to receive Clay in the capacity of political mentor — he was determined to be President in fact as well as in name. When Clay could not rule he must oppose and from the hostile camp he trained the batteries of debate and oratory upon the Executive. Mustering his cohorts from the different States, Clay gained for the House the glory of the victory while himself appropriating the spoils of the contest. Internal improvements, protective tariff, recognition of the South American governments, the Missouri Compromise — all of these measures, children of his acknowledged paternity, were carried to a successful maturity despite the frequent opposition of an unwilling Executive.

Clay had indeed created the office of Speaker and like a mother who has nursed a child through youth and sickness and finds therein the image of her own soul, he was loath to give it up. Realizing its power, and feeling in it the pride of creation, he declined various executive appointments. In 1825 when he finally bade farewell to the position it was because he stood in the magic presence of that still greater ambition — the Presidency. The Speaker-

The Greatest of American Speakers 51

ship, however pleasant its duties and however honorable its influence, was not in the line of succession to the White House.

In 1820, Clay, hampered by the stress of his private fortunes, voluntarily retired from public life. However loose his morals or free his manners Clay was withal a man of inflexible integrity. He held himself aloof from even the appearance of corruption although in severe pecuniary difficulties during the larger part of his congressional career.

John W. Taylor of New York — on the platform of loose construction, protective tariff, internal improvements, and opposition to slavery extension — was elected to the Chair. Friendly to President Monroe and loyal to John Quincy Adams, his election was an index of the strength of the latter in Congress. Taylor, while an able man, was dwarfed into insignificance by the fame and ability of his predecessor. His conduct of the office, however, met with general commendation.

The political intrigues inspired by the approaching Presidential struggle exerted a powerful influence upon the conduct of the seventeenth Congress which convened December 3d, 1821. Immediately an animated and exhilarating contest over the Speakership was launched. Three competitors were presented to contest for the honor with John W. Taylor who, though he had proved acceptable to the last Congress, was far from attractive either in manners or personality. McLane, the venerable Rodney of Delaware, and Samuel Smith of Maryland, were the original entries. On the following day Philip P. Barbour of Virginia gradually fused the opposition until on the twelfth ballot he was elected by a modest majority. Taylor's supporters never once wavered during the balloting and even then his strength gradually increased from vote to vote, but the combined power of the Cabinet and the dissensions of the Middle State Republicans proved too great a handicap.

The success of Barbour could easily be translated into a victory for Crawford; and Calhoun, embittered against Taylor by an attack upon the War department during the late Congress, had made this consummation possible — though he soon rued his vengeful course. The New York "Bucktails" voted against Taylor because he had supported Clinton for the Presidency in 1812, and had since been regarded as a Clintonian. Taylor denied the charge but could only plead neutrality — which in politics always alienates the support of both victor and vanquished. Taylor's attitude on the Missouri question had also displeased a powerful faction.

Barbour, an active partisan of Crawford, was hostile to the Missouri slavery restriction and to the proposed tariff bills. His election was generally heralded as a complete triumph for the South. The narrow partisanship of Barbour's administration was quickly apparent from the roster of the House Committees. Smith and McLane were favored with desirable assignments but both Taylor and Rodney were singled out for humiliation and embarrassment. Jonathan Russell, bitterly opposed to Adams, then Secretary of State, was placed at the head of the Committee on Foreign Relations. Taylor's supporters, including Adams, burned with the bitterness of vexation and chagrin. Rodney tasted the apples of Sodom.

The Greatest of American Speakers 53

His family, long famous for its devoted attachment to high federal, state, and colonial office, felt a stain upon its escutcheon which was barely removed by his speedy election to the Senate. Early in the session the waves of dissension broke upon the legislative ship and the Crawford faction at the pilot wheel was forced to carry her through a stormy course. Within the first ten days all the turmoil of the preceding Congress had been forgotten in the unseemly discord of its successor. The commanding genius and steady hand of the talented Clay were sadly wanting.

There being no issue of immediate importance, Congress took the course of all deliberative bodies under similar circumstances and resolved itself into an arena of oratory and debate. Business became increasingly distasteful and was soon neglected in the prevailing passion for speech. Orators of considerable talent, some half dozen of them, then as now, pre-empted the floor; other stars of less magnitude would then consume from three to six hours in utterly commonplace speeches to which nobody listened — the whole affair invented for a pleasing deception of guileless constituents.

In 1823 Clay returned to the House stronger in popularity than ever before and in better sympathy with the administration. Of the two men who had occupied the presiding Chair since his retirement, Taylor declined to offer himself as a candidate, while Barbour's rashness was rebuked on the first ballot by a poll of forty-two votes to one hundred and thirty-nine for Clay.

The legislature of Kentucky in 1822 had nominated Clay for the Presidency. It was then as a presidential candidate that he became Speaker. From that time for the remainder of his life there were two Henry Clays, Clay the statesman, and Clay the candidate for the Presidency. These two rôles ever met, often in conflict and each at length fatal to the other. Clay was five times a candidate for national leadership, twice rejected by his party and three times by the people. It is plain then that he was far better loved than trusted. The people seemed to appreciate his failings, his lack of fixity of purpose, his inconsistency, his latitudinarianism of thought and life. Personally popular, his opportunism was unpopular.

During this Congress Clay displayed his wonderful tact and inspiring honesty. A cowardly attack was made upon William H. Crawford of Georgia, then Secretary of the Treasury, and a prominent candidate for the Presidency. Charges were filed in Congress by Ninian Edwards, late Senator from Illinois but now Minister to Mexico and then en route to his post, accusing Crawford of illegalities and misconduct. This conspiracy, because of the signatures to the accompanying documents, is known as the "A. B. Plot." Apparently its author believed that the charges would not be investigated at this session of Congress and, remaining unanswered, would be an effective club against Crawford in the presidential canvass.

Crawford's friends rallied at once to his defense and Floyd of Virginia upon the reading of the charges moved the appointment of an investigating committee clothed with power to send for persons and papers, administer oaths, take testimony, and report to the House, and with leave to sit after adjournment if necessary and publish their report. In the appointment of the committee Clay

The Greatest of American Speakers 55

admirably acquitted himself of a delicate and embarrassing task — for the Speaker was himself a candidate for the Presidency, and every member of the House a friend and ally of some candidate, including the accused. The committee consisted of Floyd of Virginia, Livingston of Louisiana, Webster of Massachusetts, Randolph of Virginia, J. W. Taylor of New York, Duncan McArthur of Ohio, and Owen of Alabama. The committee conducted a thorough investigation, completely exonerating the aged and paralytic Crawford.

The severest struggle of this Congress centered about Clay's tariff measure. Christening his policy "The American System," as opposed to what he called "The Foreign System," he delivered one of the most masterful speeches of his life, pitted against the renowned Webster. It was the clever, graceful, pleasing thrust of rapier against the heavy, sweeping, more awkward blow of the broadsword; the keener weapon scored the points. The debate added another chapter to the volume of Clay's popularity. He was not only popular, he was great. Clay was immediately heralded as the people's candidate. There were no issues, therefore it became a campaign of personalities with the shafts of debate aimed at the candidates. Such a campaign is the prolific breeder of slander and infamy, of vituperation and billingsgate. There was no popular choice, the militant Jackson led with ninety-nine electoral votes, the austere puritan John Quincy Adams received eighty-four, the infirm Crawford had forty-one, and Clay, the most brilliant of all, thirty-seven.

Under the amended Constitution the House of Representatives was called upon to name one of the highest three. Clay was bitterly disappointed that he had not been one of the eligible trio, and to the bitterness of this humiliation was added the sharp sting of apparent corruption. It was rumored that he had been cheated out of five votes in Louisiana by a contemptible trick in the legislature. These votes would have placed him ahead of Crawford.

But Clay was now the Warwick of American politics. From President-seeker he became President-maker. Such was his power and prestige in the House, that his will would determine the choice of that body. The aspirants for his favor courted him in every conceivable manner. Even the unforgiving Jackson, oblivious for the moment of the Seminole question, sought to curry favor. But Clay needed no particular mental effort to determine his course. Crawford, now a confirmed and helpless invalid, could not be considered. Nor did he feel that the defeat of an ill-advised English expedition at New Orleans constituted the requisite training for the discharge of executive duties. Suspecting this course on the part of Clay the Jackson supporters endeavored to browbeat him into submission by the cry of "bargain and corruption " — "the union of the puritan and blackleg," Randolph called it — that he had agreed to support Adams in return for being named as Secretary of State. This cry, manifestly false, rose up through Clay's political life like some restless ghost of a palsied past, and was stilled only in the silence of death.

Although Clay, as Speaker, dominated the House at all times, yet his dominion was felt to be fair and beneficent. Through the bitter personalities of the Seminole debate, the keen strife of the Missouri question, the rancor and dissension of the tariff and internal-improvement legisla-lation, he guided the House with calm and judicial deliberation.

He is to-day universally accorded the first place among the noted Speakers of the House. Six times elected to the position, his choice never met with formidable or even serious opposition. Frequently he was almost unanimously chosen in direct contrast to the strife and turmoil of elections when he was not a candidate. The resolutions of thanks, customarily voted at the end of each Congress, were extended to him unanimously with only one exception, and that too, when many felt obliged to consent, although they were his personal enemies. He was reelected oftener and served longer than any other Speaker in our national history. Elected six times he presided four full terms and portions of two others.

Yet despite the imperious nature of his sway and the political coloring of his rulings, three principles were established during his service; the increase of the Speaker's parliamentary power, the retention of his personal influence, the establishment of his position as legislative leader. Clay was certainly the boldest of the Speakers — never did he consider the idea of effacing himself. No other Speaker has ever so harmoniously combined the functions of a moderator, a member, and a leader. Few Speakers have known so well how to measure their power that they might achieve the greatest results, and yet not transgress that unwritten standard of fairness which exists in every legislative body — how to observe the subtle yet essential distinction between "political" and "partisan" dominion. His success was also due in part to that singular charm of personality so pronounced that the impartial observer unconsciously became the admiring partisan.

He combined a rare mastery of parliamentary law, with a quickness of decision in its application, a never failing presence of mind and power of command in moments of confusion and excitement, and a charming dignity of bearing — all unequalled in the history of our National Legislature. He was never assailed with the cries of tyrant, Czar, or despot — which have been so often heard against Speakers less autocratic.

His conduct in the Chair was largely that of a party leader determined to force through a sometimes unwilling assembly the measures which he advocated. His friends applauded while his enemies found nothing to denounce. He added more to the power of the Speakership than has any subsequent Speaker. His fervid temperament, commanding intellect, strong will, daring courage, and pleasing personality combined to gain for him the complete supremacy of his own party and the ready control of the House. His warm heart and buoyancy of temperament won him a multitude of admirers; his impulsive nature raised up enemies; but if he was not the master of the art of self-restraint and self-government he never cherished a feeling of resentment. At his death he left not a single enemy. After the briars of bitterness and the jungles of past struggles, triumphs, and disasters, he bequeathed only peace and a cherished name. Other Americans have been intellectually greater; others have been greater benefactors to their nation, but few men have ever been loved as the people of this country loved Henry Clay.

CHAPTER II

REACTION AND CONTEST

HISTORY teaches us that after heroic periods of national grandeur the State sinks back into an era of mental and physical lassitude; tired of the strain and effort of action, it embraces the repose of inertia. Great men are succeeded in office by mediocre types and gain added prestige by the comparison — as does a mountain, rising stern and clear from surrounding plains. So Clay is the one commanding figure in the office of Speaker prior to the Civil War. Other able men were elected to that position both before and after him, but they added naught to the power of the office, they left no personal impress.

After Clay had quit Congress in 1825, to accept the portfolio of State under President Adams, John W. Taylor of New York was elected by a small majority (99 to 94) to the office which he had held five years previously. His term was without particular incident — it was the darkness that brightened the candle of Clay's glory.

It was a very different Congress which assembled in Washington on the 3d of December, 1827. Encouraged by the recent elections, the Jackson followers had swooped down upon the Capitol eager for power. Their victory, while not overwhelming, had been decisive. With all but six members of the House in their seats upon the opening day, but a single ballot was necessary to settle the question of control.

Andrew Stevenson of Virginia, a well disposed man of pleasing personality and easy habits, was elected Speaker by one hundred and four (104) votes out of two hundred and five (205). John W. Taylor polled ninety-four, Philip R. Barbour four, and scattering, three. Stevenson immediately organized the House along strictly partisan lines. The committees named by him, after many conferences and much scheming, were dominated by the Jackson party in the ratio of four to three. Randolph, the caloric McDuffie, Cambreling, Ingham, and Barbour were given posts of power and prestige. Everett was named chairman of the Committee on Foreign Relations — this not so much to mollify the administration as to humiliate Sergeant, who in line with unwritten law was entitled to that honor. Taylor who had been the administration candidate for Speaker was visited with the injustice of successful foes.

Under a change of rules and procedure the Senate chose its own committees. These too were inimical to the President, fully as hostile as those named by Calhoun when the power of appointment rested in him. For the first time in our history, both Houses of Congress were organized in opposition to the administration.

The President's message fell on deaf ears, the executive recommendations were ignored — particularly in the second or long session of this Congress. The entire six months were devoted to the cause of partisan politics. Efforts were continually made to discredit the administration of Adams, to regard even the most patriotic suggestion with the leer of suspicion — they stopped at nothing which might help elect Jackson to the Presidency.

Reaction and Contest

Investigations, inquiries, examinations into the conduct of the administration were daily voted by the lower House. Public accounts were audited, were reviewed and scrutinized as if some embezzlement were to be discovered in high office. Resolutions of inquiry, constantly voted, were framed so as to insinuate, if not openly charge, that wrongdoing was rampant in official circles. Suggestions were daily made upon the floor as to the best methods of retrenchment in this puritan administration. Laws were passed for the punishment of defaulters, and then constantly amended, as if to insinuate that the treasury was being looted by its guardians.

The Congress which was elected with Jackson was overwhelmingly Democratic in its organization. Stevenson who had earned the gratitude of the new President by his services in the last Congress was re-elected Speaker to become now even more strongly partisan. Jackson's personality dominated the whole government — the legislative as well as the executive; the judicial alone seemed free and untrammeled.

Throughout the entire session of Congress he followed its proceedings with the care and solicitude of a parent. The picturesque Major Lewis, now in the government service, or Jackson's nephew Donelson, now his private secretary, were charged with the task of bringing to the Presidential ear the news of each day's session. Not a single speech, no motion of importance, not a resolution nor a vote, but was promptly reported at the White House. Jackson's devotion to his friends, his unwavering enmity towards his enemies were widely heralded. The rewards of party loyalty and the penalties of insurrection were the subject of stirring communications. His administration was a stirring tribute to the "cohesive power of public plunder." He did not lead Congress by the art of persuasion; nor did he sit idly by until its pleasure was manifested. He offered them rather the mailed fist of discipline; patronage was the reward of submission; anger, flashing and terrible, was the return for revolt.

If Congress at times ignored his commands he straightway had recourse to the executive veto to throw contemptuous defiance in the face of the hostile majorities. He would frequently anticipate the attitude of Congress and complete some performance before they could checkmate him by adverse legislation. He was ably supported by that select and picturesque coterie of personal advisers known as the "Kitchen Cabinet," and by the editorial staff of his official organ.

The twenty-second Congress was brilliant in its membership. In the House of Representatives a power over all was John Quincy Adams from Massachusetts. Respected as ex-President, he won his greatest renown as a member of the House. The volatile Rufus Choate, the renowned Edward Everett, and John Davis constituted a worthy trio from the Bay State; the caustic Tristam Burgess was there from Rhode Island, and Churchill C. Cambreling and Gulian C. Verplanck from New York; Virginia was represented by William S. Archer, John Y. Mason, and the able though subservient Andrew Stevenson; South Carolina had sent George McDuffie, and Georgia James M. Wayne; James K. Polk and John Bell — both destined to be elected Speakers and one to become President — answered to the call of Tennessee; John Adair and former Senator Richard Johnson were from Clay's State; Thomas Corwin of Ohio for the first time took the oath as member of an assembly wherein he was destined to win fame as the keenest wit and one of the greatest orators of our national life — and then, as if embittered by disappointment, to die with the pathetic admonition that did one seek to achieve distinction and win enduring fame, he must renounce all forms of pleasantry. Thus it has been asserted that a sense of drollery is a bar to success — that the world's greatest men had no appreciation of humor. Tom Corwin said to Don Piatt, referring to his disposition to joke with a crowd: "Don't do it, my boy; you should ever remember that the crowd always looks up to the ringmaster and down on the clown. It resents that which amuses. The clown is the more clever fellow of the two but he is the despised. If you will succeed in life you must be solemn, solemn as an ass. All the great monuments of earth have been built over solemn asses." Many a statesman has owed his success in life to the length of his legs and the solemnity of his countenance.

Stevenson was again elected Speaker, this time, however, by a bare majority, so powerful was the strength of the anti-administration forces in the House. Stevenson had slight respect for the rules and precedents of the assembly, violating them constantly, whenever it suited his purpose, to promote purely partisan interests. So sharply had his official acts been tainted with partisanship that in 1832 General Root moved that the committee to investigate the National Bank should be chosen by the House itself by ballot. Upon this motion the vote stood 100 to 100. Stevenson then cast the deciding vote against the resolution, thus virtually electing himself to appoint a committee at the dictate of a higher influence.

On the second of December, 1833, the twenty-third Congress convened with two hundred and twenty-nine of the two hundred and forty members answering the roll-call. In the rear of the regular rows of cushioned seats sat the privileged members who occupied a slightly raised balcony among the marble columns. John Quincy Adams was still by common consent declared the most illustrious. Three of these members were destined to become Presidents of the United States. James K. Polk from Tennessee was now the floor leader of the administration forces — a man of no marked brilliancy yet entitled to this honor as the reward for tireless and methodical industry. Franklin Pierce of New Hampshire, a Democrat and a tyro in national politics, won the esteem of the entire House by his delicately chiseled features and his charming manners. Millard Fillmore, a member of the opposition from New York, like Polk, possessed the genius of industry, unburnished by any particular power of intellect.

In this twenty-third Congress, Everett and Choate were again present from Massachusetts and Burgess from Rhode Island. There was Horace Binney, lawyer by profession and statesman by way of diversion, from Pennsylvania; the long-honored Stevenson and the brilliant consumptive Wise from Virginia; from Alabama among others Dixon H. Lewis, huge of girth, whose chair was fashioned expressly for him; the keen and ingenious Corwin from Ohio was again returned to lighten the dull hours of official routine; in the Kentucky delegation were the renowned and familiar Richard M. Johnson, and

Reaction and Contest 65

Tom Marshall, who, combining brilliancy with pitiful dissipation, furnished another illustrious witness to the theory that great intellects are generally reared at the sacrifice of private morals; from Tennessee came John Bell and Cave Johnson, both able Representatives, and the picturesque Davy Crockett, bear hunter and author, uncouth pioneer and nascent statesman, whose very presence lent a touch of nature to the somber surroundings. For then it was the general custom for the members to sit with covered heads after the manner of the English House of Commons.

On the first day of the session Andrew Stevenson of Virginia was re-elected Speaker by a large majority on the first ballot. Walter S. Franklin was elected Clerk to succeed the faithful Matthew St. Clair Clarke who was displaced. Stevenson continued to administer his office for the benefit of the White House. The committees appointed to investigate various executive measures were so constituted as to insure reports favorable to the President. The removal of the public deposits was successfully engineered in large part through the subserviency of the Speaker. It is of course impossible to state, with any degree of accuracy, how far Stevenson's official conduct was the result of his own volition and how far he was coerced by the power of Jackson. Yet this subserviency to the Executive, or, if you will, this harmony with executive desire, was not to go unrewarded. As early as April of 1833, Stevenson had received an inkling from the Secretary of State that he would be appointed ambassador to the Court of St. James. Apparently that he might be inspired by the promise of preferment or restrained by the fear of punishment, the nomination was delayed until May, 1834, some six months after Congress had first convened. Ever ready to assist his political associates, and now particularly desirous of aiding the administration, he rode rough-shod over the prescribed limits of his office with mirthful contempt for both parliamentary law and official precedent. No Speaker of Congress, not even Macon, has ever been so brazenly responsive to executive dictation.

So flagrant was this subserviency that he was rebuked by his own constituents who, differing with him on the question of the public deposits, demanded that he either amend his conduct or resign. In a letter of May 9, 1834, he declared his willingness to adopt either alternative. He finally resigned the Speakership on the 30th of June, 1834, but so strong were the animosities which he had aroused that the usual vote of thanks were not tendered him until a month after his withdrawal from the House.

In length of service Stevenson ranks next to Clay; four successive elections had been bestowed upon him; and with Clay he shares alone the peculiar distinction of having resigned from the Speakership. Yet his reward, like that of most political adherents, was subjected to the whims of a fickle jury. The triple alliance in the Senate, where a bitter war was being waged against Jackson, determined for the present at any rate the fate of the recent nominees to office. The Senate showed its animus by rejecting the name of Stevenson. He failed of confirmation, however, by a bare majority, for he counted many personal friends among his political opponents. In an impressive speech he had resigned his congressional honors while his nomination was still pending. Jackson with the dogged tenacity of purpose which was his chief characteristic, left the ambassadorship to Great Britian vacant for two years, when Stevenson's name was again presented under a more auspicious constellation and this time confirmed.

Stevenson's career gave little prospect of the election of a partisan successor. The two candidates for the unexpired term were from Jackson's own State, — John Bell who, in 1860, became the candidate of one of the smaller parties for the Presidency, and James K. Polk, who later became the chief Executive. On the tenth ballot the more moderate Bell was elected over the strictly partisan Polk, who was looked upon as the personal representative of Jackson on the floor of the House.

If the opinion of John Quincy Adams may be taken, Bell was an able Speaker and, when left to his individual discretion, was impartial though inclined at times to heed the voice of the administration. Bell was openly accused of subserviency to Jackson, but party sheets always paint their pictures in sensational colors.

With the opening of the twenty-fourth Congress in December, 1835, the tempestuous waves of slavery discussion were breaking on all sides. With sky darkening and clouds lowering all minds were turned at once to the approaching storm. Sectionalism became the dominating force in national politics. All legislation was tainted with its flavor, all discussion bore its impress, all debate heralded its influence. On every side the parading of local, as above national, feeling and interests was apparent.

The administration forces, clearly in the ascendency,

elected James K. Polk of Tennessee Speaker on the first ballot, by a vote of 132 against 84 for Bell, the Speaker of the last Congress. Bell was feeling the penalty of insubordination — he dared to support the claims of Judge White for the Presidency. The task before Polk was a difficult one — no Speaker had ever been called upon to preside in a House torn by such bitterness of feeling and so severely lashed by party passion. Polk, however, was a success from the parliamentary standpoint, but like Stevenson he was primarily a party man and aroused much bitterness among the minority.

During this Congress it was that the political seas were lashed to fury by the slavery memorials and petitions. On the 26th of May, 1836, the first gag-resolution, offered by Henry L. Pinckney of South Carolina, was adopted. This day became a milestone in the history of the nation. John Quincy Adams — now a man of almost threescore and ten, of forty-two years in the service of his country — denouncing this as a violation of the Constitution, unsheathed his sword and engaged the enemy. The South, as though mad with its zeal for slavery, rushed blindly forth to combat, with sword broken and with the warnings of devoted friends falling on unwilling ears.

In the next session of this Congress the Speaker ruled that the order of May 26, 1836, for rejecting slavery petitions expired with that session. On the 18th of January, 1837, on the motion of Hawes a similar gag-measure was passed by a majority of over two thirds. Adams refused to be either cajoled or clubbed into the "surrender of his constitutional privileges." He could die, he would never surrender. When the presentation of petitions was the order of the day he invariably offered a number of memorials relating to the abolition of slavery in the District of Columbia. Under the tactics of Adams the House was a perfect sea of turmoil and the vessel carried no oil of diplomacy to sooth the troubled waters.

February 6th the storm burst in renewed fury. Having first presented a petition for the abolition of slavery in the District of Columbia Adams caught up from his desk a bundle of papers which he said came from twenty-two slaves and appealed to the Speaker for a decision as he was uncertain whether such papers were embraced by the gag-rule.

Bewildered silence prevailed for a moment. Then the very elements seemed to rage. Members, their faces livid with rage and tense with fury, rushed quickly in from the lobbies. On all sides were heard cries of "Expel him! expel him!" His age and the dignity of his preceding office alone preserved him from personal assault. One motion to punish the intrepid statesman was followed quickly by another, all vying with each other in severity and all dictated by the fever of passion. Even the mildest demanded that at least he be censured before the bar of the House by the Speaker.

Lewis of Alabama accused the ex-President of inciting a slave insurrection. Thompson of South Carolina, in tones keen-edged with passion, warned of the existence of grand juries, declared his belief that if the petition were presented the House would all have the pleasure of seeing Adams "within the walls of a penitentiary." Adams was defeated if one estimate defeat as a question of numbers.

But his defeat was a great victory — for no defeat of a right principle can ever be permanent.

The tragic features of the contest suddenly yielded to a comic denouément. Adams appealed to the Speaker to declare whether he had not merely asked for a decision upon a preliminary question of form, instead of having presented or offered to present the petition itself, which he declared was in fact hostile to abolition rather than to its favor. The more hot-headed members cursed inwardly at having been forced to play the fool's rôle.

Thompson declared that Adams should be censured. There was much discussion as to just how such a censure should be cloaked. Dromgoole of Virginia insisted that it should be administered "for giving color to an idea" that slaves were entitled to the right of petition. Adams turned on his assailants and lashed them with the flail of denunciation, and into every laceration he poured the acid of sarcasm and the salt of ridicule. His opponents routed fell back in a confused retreat and the resolutions of disapproval were defeated even after the words of censure had been erased. Over such turmoil and bitterness Polk presided with fair and impartial hand.

The twenty-fifth Congress was organized on the 4th of September, 1837, with the re-election of Polk as Speaker on the first ballot by a majority of eight votes over John Bell, his Whig opponent. Again in this session the contest between slavery and its opponents carried the House through many exciting days. The Pinckney resolutions of the twenty-fourth Congress were again adopted under a suspension of the rules and the previous question by a vote of 122 to 74; Adams again registered a prophetic

Reaction and Contest 71

protest. Eighteen months of gag-rules had multiplied the anti-slavery petitions tenfold, and in 1838 they numbered 300,000 signatures, yet the South, blinded by the myopia of passion, read not the lurid writing across the heavens.

Long after midnight of Sunday, March 3d, 1839, the Speaker's gavel announced the close of the storm-swept Congress. After long hours of excited debate the usual resolution of thanks, admittedly an empty courtesy, was tendered to Polk by a vote of 94 to 57, Bell, Wise, and Sergeant S. Prentiss leading the opposition. The vote, however, did not register accurately the purely national sentiment toward the Speaker. Polk was an aspirant for the gubernatorial chair of Tennessee and a portion of the opposition was inspired by the politicians of his own State, in an effort to rebuke this ambition. Polk was admittedly an able moderator and a Speaker of considerable talent, yet on one illustrious occasion he had been tricked and outwitted — when Slade in 1837, at the time of the "secession" of the Southern members, was able to deliver an abolition speech. Securing the floor through the temporary abstraction of the Speaker, despite repeated calls to order, furious blows of the gavel, and Polk's demand that he take his seat, Slade persisted in his remarks until some of the members had forced through a motion to adjourn.

But Polk, like Stevenson and like Mason, was charged with subordinating his official powers to the dictates of the Executive. It was not that Polk or Stevenson had been partisan in their rule of the House — for Clay had been thus — but they had assisted in bending the body of the Legislature to the will of the Executive. Congress has always been keenly jealous of its own prerogatives and has bitterly resented any encroachment by the Executive upon the realm of its independence.

Polk after a service of fourteen consecutive years in the House left the impression of an able man, of clean person and high morals, an indefatigable worker, a clever parliamentarian and able presiding officer, but withal an intensely narrow and partisan politician. It required a skillful parliamentarian and a firm moderator to restrain Adams from dominating and defying even the Speaker himself. The House, not Polk, was the author of the gag-rules. It was his honest duty to enforce their dictates — to him belongs none of the opprobrium for that inexpedient legislation. After the resolutions of 1836, 1837, and 1838, Polk was compelled to forbid the reading of slavery petitions or to permit motions for their reference or debates upon their merits. The sharp controversy over the question of the independent treasury contributed something to the hostility toward Polk's conduct of the office. After his retirement from the House he was elected Governor of Tennessee for a term of two years, but defeated for a re-election. Still clinging faithfully to the remaining prestige of Jacksonian Democracy, he was carried into the White House when the people turned from the glare of dazzling talent to the softer lights of conspicuous mediocrity. Polk however failed to carry Tennessee. It was the only instance in our history that the successful candidate for the Presidency did not secure the electoral vote of his own State.

The first of the four memorable and prolonged contests for the election of a Speaker was that which inaugurated the twenty-sixth Congress which convened on the second

Reaction and Contest

day of December, 1839. At that time the so-called general ticket system, by which members were elected by entire States rather than by congressional districts, prevailed in several of the States, notably in New Jersey. In those States this meant the unit rule and before the development of political independence resulted in solid congressional delegations.

The New Jersey delegation thus chosen consisted of six Whigs. Only one of them, J. M. Randolph, had received an unquestioned majority. However, all six of the Whigs were declared elected and were supplied with the usual credentials. The New Jersey Democrats promptly and loudly protested, disputing the validity of the seal and the certificates which had been presented to the entire delegation with the single exception of Randolph. They insisted that the Democratic candidates had been honestly elected and cited the official returns to prove their contention. The Whigs maintained that the election returns had been tampered with.

The panic of 1837, attributed, whether justly or unjustly, to the party in power, had aroused keen dissatisfaction with the Democratic administration, and had inspired surprising Whig successes in the congressional elections of 1838. The strength of the House, on the face of the election returns, was so evenly divided between the two parties that the State of New Jersey with its delegation of six held the balance of power. Eliminating the five members whose seats were contested, the alignment was 119 Democrats to 118 Whigs. The complexion of the New Jersey delegation thus became a question of national importance. It was evident that if the names of the five

Whigs were included in the first roll-call the Whigs would elect the Speaker and organize the committees in opposition to the administration. Conversely, if their names were omitted the Democrats would, by the small though effective majority of one, be able to control the organization of the House.

Upon the opening of Congress it is the first duty of the Clerk of the preceding House to call the names of those persons who have brought with them the legal certificates of their election. This roll-call having been completed — the requisite number being present, the House proceeds to the election of its Speaker.

The Clerk of the previous House was Hugh A. Garland of Virginia, who had held that position for a year, completing an unexpired term. Garland was a Democrat, a candidate for re-election, and naturally had his own interests to subserve. If the Democrats prevailed his re-election was assured, but if the Whigs organized the House his decapitation was certain. It was Garland's duty to make up the roll of the House and preside until a Speaker was elected.

Beginning with Maine as was then the custom, he called the various New England States and New York, and then came to New Jersey. Having called the name of Randolph, Garland paused and announced that the elections for the five other seats were contested; that as he did not feel warranted in presuming to settle the issue, he would pass over the other names and proceed with the roll-call until the House should be organized, when the question might be officially determined. He insisted that until the House was duly organized he could put no question to a vote.

By that sudden and subconscious impulse that often moves a large number of men to adopt spontaneously the same course and arrive at the same decision, the members of the House of Representatives quit the hall after Garland had declined to put a motion for adjournment. Opportunity was thus given the members of both sides for reflection and the party leaders for evolving a definite plan of campaign.

On the next day the situation was equally critical. The self-serving Garland, concealing unworthy motives behind the pleasing mask of modesty, had arbitrarily disfranchised a State which was entitled to vote in the constitution of the House — either by one set of delegates or the other — and had then effectually fortified his position by obstructing all business in an effort to compel that body to bow to his purpose.

Much to Garland's apparent surprise, an animated debate sprang up instantly upon the first announcement of his position. The third of December he sought an opportunity to read to the House an exposition of his reasons for obeying "the stern call of duty." The day was consumed in foolish discussion as to whether he should be permitted to make such an address to the House. Again the members adjourned despite his determined efforts. On the third day, another attempt was made, but the New Jersey question was an impassable moat beyond which stood the glittering castle of the Speakership. Garland, however, relaxed slightly from his position of the preceding sessions and put the motion to adjourn.

Still a member of the House, whither he had been returned with honored regularity, was the staunch and dauntless ex-President. A silent listener and a patient witness to all the confusion and turmoil of the struggle he declined the entreaties of members of both parties to throw himself into the breach and, by the force and example of his own personality, rescue the House from its own shame. The debate grew more spirited, more venomous, was diplomatic in name rather than in verbiage, but still there was no indication of progress. At length on the fourth day, Adams, taking the initiative, arose in his seat and addressed the Clerk. Immediately a hush fell over the House — it was the silence of reverence and anxious expectancy. Addressing his "fellow citizens, members-elect of the twenty-sixth Congress" he explained the reluctance with which he had entered the dispute: he begged them to believe that it was a painful sense of duty alone which inspired him to his present course. He reviewed the conduct of the Clerk and reminded them that that official, in the performance of his apparent duty, had refused to complete the roll-call in the manner prescribed by usage, and had also persistently refused to put any question to the House. He declared that unless some alternative were found the columns of the Capitol itself were not fixed more firmly or more immovably than was the House. "But I say," he continued, with the glowing eloquence of his peroration, "that we have solemn duties, too, and the first duty is to organize. It is in the power of this House to set the Clerk aside; thank God, it is not in its power to obey despotic dictates! If we cannot organize in any other way, — if this Clerk will not consent to our discharging the trusts confined to us by our constituents, — then let us imitate the example of the Virginia House of

Burgesses when the colonial Governor ordered it to disperse, and like men —"

The pent-up emotions of four days of raging strife, of bitter animosity and troubled mentality broke forth in an eloquent testimonial of applause. Having thus suggested the solution of the dilemma Adams now offered a resolution ordering the Clerk to call the names of those members from New Jersey who had produced the credentials from the Governor of that State. He made the further suggestion that any member so disposed might offer an amendment to the resolution and thus bring the matter to an immediate issue. In reply to the spontaneous question which broke from many lips as to how or by whom the question should be put, Adams replied in stentorian tones, clear and distinct as a trumpet call to victory above the doubting tumult, "I intend to put the question myself." This single sentence seemed to fuse all the discordant notes into a soothing harmony. An impotent effort on the part of Garland to explain and justify his position was drowned out by the swelling chorus "Organize without him." The House with loud acclaim demanded that Adams take the Chair and a motion to that effect was unanimously carried. Adams was conducted to the Chair amid enthusiastic applause; the Clerk was forced to submit to the situation and, though asperity still lingered, business proceeded with decorum. Adams continued to preside until the organization of the House had been completed. Never in Congress had law and right been prostituted more openly and more shamelessly to the dictates of party expediency.

The only lawful title to participate in the organization

of the House was the legal certificate of election and this was held by the five Whigs. Not only did the Clerk of the House have no right practically to decide the question between the two contending delegations as Garland essayed to do, but officially he should not have recognized even the existence of a contest over the seats. Similarly the members-elect of the new House had nothing except the certificate of election upon which to base their action, and certainly no other rights than those emanating from such a certificate. True to the axiom that consistency is the crown jewel of no political party, it is interesting to note that the party which prated most of the "States' Rights" was guilty of this ruthless contempt for the rights and privileges of the State of New Jersey. Party passion had won a signal victory over political conscience.

The House decided after some discussion to suspend the question of seating the New Jersey delegates until a Speaker had been chosen. But the purpose of this decision was defeated. A number of Democratic malcontents, suspected of close connection with Calhoun, withdrew from their party allegiance and on the eleventh ballot joined with the Whigs in electing Robert M. T. Hunter of Virginia Speaker by a vote of 119 out of 232.

By a bare majority the other officers of the House were chosen, Garland being again named Clerk through the exclusion of the New Jersey Whigs. In the meantime — for now twenty days had elapsed since the House first convened — the Senate had adjourned from day to day. At length the joint announcement was made to the President that Congress was ready for business. On the day before Christmas, during a heavy blizzard which hindered

Reaction and Contest 79

its transmission to the press of the country, the President's message was sent to Congress after it had stood in type in the office of the Globe for three weeks.

The New Jersey question was promptly referred to a committee for investigation and report. Let us here insert a leaf, under date of March 14, 1840, from Adams's diary, that treasure house of American history: — "Neither the report of the committee, nor their journal, nor one particle of the testimony, has yet been printed. Not a word of the testimony against the illegal returns rejected by the governor and council of New Jersey was even considered by the committee. They gave the parties time to take their testimony till the second week in April. Six weeks before that time, the House passed a resolution instructing them to report forthwith which set of the candidates had a majority of the lawful votes of the people of New Jersey: and they report forthwith that the non-commissioned claimants have a majority of the lawful votes: with an argument proving that whether the majority was of lawful votes or not depends entirely upon evidence yet to come, and for the procurement of which the committee had given the parties time till the second week in April. In this state of things evidence is received by the House proving the illegality of the South Amboy election: in the face of which, under the screw of the previous question, the House passed a resolution directing the Speaker to swear in the non-commissioned members as having the majority of the lawful votes without waiting for further evidence, and without ever having heard the parties. Jenifer has probed this state of proceedings till the majority of the committee writhed in agony."

Scarcely had Congress entered upon the course of its duties before it again decreed its own muzzling. It sought not so much to emulate as to surpass the example of its predecessor. It adopted as one of the standing rules of the House a resolution decreeing that henceforth petitions touching upon abolition should not be received at all.

Hunter, elected to the Speakership, because of his advertised "independence" — generally synonymous with entire absence of political conviction — gave moderate satisfaction in the discharge of his duties, although he seemed entirely lacking in decision. Adams denominated him "a good-hearted, weak-headed young man."

The general tone of his character — or possibly lack of it — may be inferred from a letter which he wrote to certain of his constituents in 1840 in which he declared his determination not to support either Van Buren or General Harrison for the Presidency and therefore, because of his inability to properly advance or represent the wishes of his constituents on either the one side or the other, he announced his intention of quitting public life at the conclusion of his present term, or his entire willingness to resign immediately did his constituents so desire.

Hunter declined to lend his position to the furtherance of political interests, therefore his influence was simply that of a moderator, although he did much to develop the parliamentary prestige of the Speakership. His conception of this office is clearly portrayed in his valedictory remarks: — "It is something if I can hope I have made it easier for those who succeed me to act on some better principle than that of giving the whole power of the House to one of the parties without regard to the rights or feelings of others. Clothe this station with the authority of justice and how much may it not do to elevate the views of the parties from themselves to their country! But arm it with the mere power of numbers and administer it with an exclusive eye to the interests of a part and it may become an engine of as much fraud and oppression as can be practiced in a country as free as ours."

CHAPTER III

TURMOIL AND CONTESTED ELECTIONS

NOWHERE do we see more eloquently portrayed the bitter antagonisms, the jealous hatred, and the livid rage of the ante-bellum days than in the history of the popular branch of the National Legislature. The battle of slavery was twice fought; once it was a political struggle and it lasted with varying fortunes, of victory, compromise, and final defeat, for forty years; the other was the battle of blood, where lives took the place of ballots, and it too ended in defeat — though the course it ran was shorter and the final issue more certain. So keen was this feeling between the slave and the free, the South and the North, and so evenly balanced their forces in the House of Representatives that it became impossible to elect as Speaker any member who expressed or entertained decided views and had thus incurred the enmity of either section. It may be set down as an almost invariable rule that the man without enemies is the man without decided conviction, strong character, or ardent ambition. Otherwise he must have inspired opposition and aroused enemies among those whom he has opposed or has outdistanced in the race for the honors of life — enemies who while they respect him for his genius stand ever ready to encompass his ruin. Thus, perforce, weak men were Speakers of the House during this era and this became the age of unadorned mediocrity.

Turmoil and Contested Elections 83

When the twenty-seventh Congress assembled in extra session, May 31st, 1841, the Whigs were dominant in both branches. John White of Kentucky, a personal friend and protégé of Henry Clay, was immediately chosen Speaker of the House by a *viva voce* vote, and the former Clerk, Matthew St. Clair Clarke, was elected to succeed the bold and daring Garland of uncertain fame. The Whigs had flourished, like the green bay tree, since the preceding Congress; they now had a majority of nearly fifty in the lower House, and controlled the Senate by a margin of seven votes.

Clay as the leader of the Whig party attempted to rule the administration and was both surprised and indignant at the prompt insubordination of Tyler. Their friendship finally split upon the rock of national banking.

At the extra session John Quincy Adams, growing more bold and defiant in the passing years, still the champion of petition, moved to rescind the rule against anti-slavery petitions; his motion prevailed after a spirited debate only to be shortly reconsidered and voted down by an alliance of southern Whigs with the Democracy. A similar effort in the long session met a like fate, even the northern Whigs shying at the fangs of the slavocracy.

White had made Adams chairman of the Committee on Foreign Relations as a tribute to his conspicuous merit; obeying still the dictate of conscience he remained the sturdy friend of all petitioners and clearly demonstrated his consistency when the issue was raised. Further efforts to chastise and discipline the ex-President failed as signally as in former years.

Emulating the example of the venerable Adams, a young

Whig, Joshua R. Giddings from Ohio, massive and muscular in physique, bold and fearless in intellect, presented on the 2d of March, 1842, a petition from Austinburg, Ohio, praying for the dissolution of the Union. No such words as "censure," "infamy," "disgrace," "perjury," and "treason" were bandied about the House as on the occasion a few short weeks before, but, with no particular discussion, by a vote of 116 to 24 the House refused to receive the petition intimating at the same time that further contumacy might inspire radical punishment. Not to be thus easily muzzled, Giddings presented a series of petitions and resolutions based upon the "Creole" case, bitterly denouncing the coasting trade in slaves.

There exists in man a certain intuition which leads him to pay instinctive reverence to silver locks. Similarly there is an intuitive hostility in age to anything which savors of youth. This intuition had been an armor of defense to Adams, but it became a sword of attack against Giddings. He had at times been rudely jostled by some of the younger members from the South, and had barely avoided a physical encounter when one of them attempted to push him from the aisle.

After Giddings had withdrawn the latter petitions, a resolution of censure was moved. The resolution was carried by a large vote and Giddings forthwith withdrew from the hall, prepared a letter of resignation and departed for Ohio. At a special election held a few weeks later he was returned by an increased majority. After the death of Adams, Giddings continued the fight, standing at his post for twenty years, his white locks, like the plume of

Turmoil and Contested Elections 85

Henry of Navarre, showing where the battle of freedom raged most fiercely.

White, owing his election to the favor of Henry Clay, recognized the debt of gratitude and liquidated the obligation. Determined, though futile, objection was raised to the customary vote of thanks on the ground that White had been guilty of notorious partiality both in the appointment of his committees and the tenor of his parliamentary decisions.

The twenty-eighth Congress met on the fourth day of December, 1843, with a Whig majority in the Senate, while the House was controlled by the Democrats by the overwhelming majority of two to one. John W. Jones of Virginia, a rather clever politician but a mediocre Speaker, was elected to the Chair. The election of Jones constituted a dangerous precedent. He had been returned to Congress by the doubtful majority of thirty-three and his seat was contested by his opponent, John W. Botts. From the closeness of the popular vote on a heavy poll and the certainty that there are always many illegal votes cast in exciting political contests there was at least a possibility that Botts was entitled to the seat. Clearly the decision of a committee chosen by Jones, and composed in the majority of his friends and supporters, could not carry the moral force of an impartial verdict. Supposing the right of the issue to have been with Botts or that the result was extremely doubtful, could such a committee be expected to consider the evidence rationally and apply the law with absolute impartiality — to analyze the immense amount of testimony presented with the single aim of securing exact justice? However, in this particular instance scandal was obviated by the unanimous agreement that Jones was lawfully entitled to the seat. It is axiomatic, certainly, that no man can properly be the presiding officer of a legislative assembly at the same time that his right to sit in that body is honestly contested, and when he is liable at any moment to be adjudged not even a member and his seat declared the rightful property of another.

Matthew St. Clair Clarke was relegated to private life to make room for an unknown partisan who expressed his gratitude and fitness by promptly becoming a defaulter. Blair and Rives were elected public printers as a mark of contempt for the avowed wishes of the President. In this Congress appeared for the first time several men who were destined in the course of years to play important roles in the great national drama. Among them were Howell Cobb, a Democrat from Georgia, and Alexander H. Stephens, small in physique but a giant in intellect, a Whig from the same State; Robert C. Schenck, an able debater and consistent Whig from Ohio; and, destined to become most famous of all, Stephen A. Douglas of Illinois. Schouler gives an excellent portrait of this wonderful commoner who had risen from the privations of poverty to an acknowledged position of authority. "Douglas had a small and compact frame, whence issued a surprisingly stentorian voice, and his type of eloquence at once startled the House by its novelty. As he warmed up in speech, his grave face became convulsed, his gesticulation frantic, and, while roaring and lashing about with energy, he would strip off his cravat and unbutton his waistcoat to save himself from choking, until his whole air and aspect, as he stood at the desk, was that of a half-

Turmoil and Contested Elections 87

naked pugilist hurling defiance at the presiding officer. But all this gave at once to his person that picturesqueness which goes half-way towards making one a figure in public life; and, like Disraeli among the English aristocracy, Douglas rose by making himself indispensable to the slave-holding class who needed just such a commoner for a foil and northern ally."

In the second session of this Congress the dominant party, grateful for the efficient aid of the abolitionists in the late campaign, extended to them marked courtesies. John Quincy Adams, even before the reading of the President's message, received as a reward for his valiant services the repeal of the "gag-rule." This rule had been repealed during the first session but was then reconsidered and retained by a small majority. Wise, the fiery leader in the contests against the petitioners, was no longer in Congress and Adams's motion was carried without debate.

The twenty-ninth Congress assembled on the first of December, 1845, with the administration party dominant in both wings and both Houses on the *qui vive* for the latest news on the Oregon question and the status of our relations with Mexico. Polk's campaign cry of "54° 40' or fight" had touched a martial chord in the popular heart. A general air of expectancy pervaded the Capitol. Webster and Calhoun were in their accustomed places after brief absences. Reverdy Johnson of Maryland and familiar Tom Corwin, keen and humorous as ever, both consistent Whigs, were there to delight and instruct. For the first time appeared Robert Toombs, the "fire-eater" from Georgia, he who promised to call the roll of his "niggers" on Bunker Hill and was never "reconstructed";

Lewis Cass, a prominent figure in his own State, now for the first time a member of the National Legislature; and Simon Cameron, of Pennsylvania, a practical politician with a contempt for reformers and "them damned literary fellows" who cried out against the shameful corruption which has so long held the Keystone State in her corroding grasp. The northern abolitionists felt that now the fate of the Union hung in the balance. So depressed was Horace Greeley with the gloomy outlook for national existence that in 1845 he republished in his almanac the Declaration of Independence, the Federal Constitution, and Washington's Farewell Address.

In the House John W. Davis of Indiana, a pro-slavery Republican, was immediately elected Speaker, while the remaining offices were filled at a later date.

No bit of legislation can portray more accurately the manner in which it was possible to gag the House, and force through partisan measures, than the act which declared war against Mexico on the 13th of May, 1846. The President was expected to submit to Congress a message reviewing our relations with the Central American Republic and therein suggesting the declaration of war. The program to be pursued was mapped out days in advance — the administration leaders were bound to drive the swaying chariot of war madly through the House and ride down all opposition since the merits of the cause were so meager as certainly to collapse in the face of even superficial criticism. Theirs was to be the victory of votes, not of logic, of whips and spurs, not of words and arguments.

After the Clerk had read the President's message to the

Turmoil and Contested Elections 89

House, Winthrop of Massachusetts moved the reading of the accompanying official correspondence. This motion was promptly voted down; the House at once resolved itself into a Committee of the Whole and proceeded to debate the question of peace and war, with no further authorities than the mere unsupported statements of an inflammatory and specious message. The Committee on Military Affairs had already prepared the bill for adoption and the Committee of the Whole proceeded to its immediate consideration. The bill was forthwith reported to the House, the previous question effectively closing all debate at every step of this remarkable procedure. With the opposition thus muzzled, and the weaker members silenced by the taunts of cowardice and treason or inspired by the cries of "the nation, right or wrong," and "save the flag from dishonor," a bill was passed by a vote of 174 to 114 authorizing the President to call fifty thousand (50,000) volunteers to arms and appropriating ten million dollars for the war. This the preface to the Mexican war; thus was the wolf rather than the eagle suggested as the national emblem; thus they pushed through Congress the legislative approval of so bold a piece of national brigandage that threescore years have not served to drive the blush of shame from the cheek of Americans when they contemplate the despoilment of Mexico and the seizure of her richest provinces.

Three men of very ordinary ability had now enjoyed the Speakership. The prestige of the office had materially deteriorated during their incumbency. In the thirtieth Congress the mists of mediocrity were dispelled by the warm sun of ability, and in the election of Robert C.

Winthrop of Massachusetts the House selected of all its members the one best qualified by ability, temperament, and character to preside over its deliberations. Although political considerations played some part, yet the chief reason for Winthrop's election was his admitted fitness for the position. He united with the vigor and strength of youth the discretion of age. From the organization of the first Congress a majority of the Speakers at the time of their first election had been under forty-five years of age — many of them under forty. In recent years Congress has bestowed this honor upon older members apparently as a crowning reward for long terms of honorable service. Henry Clay when first elected was but thirty-four, James K. Polk thirty-nine, John Bell thirty-seven, Howell Cobb thirty-three, and Robert M. T. Hunter, the youngest man ever elected Speaker, was but thirty. Winthrop at the date of his election was thirty-eight. In his youth a law student in the office of Daniel Webster, at twenty-five he was elected a member of the General Assembly of Massachusetts, and soon promoted to the Speakership of the lower House. In that position he soon acquired a national reputation as a presiding officer; his decisions were quoted as precedents on the floors of Congress, and were generally incorporated in authoritative treatises on parliamentary law.

Elected to Congress at the age of thirty he was now serving his fifth term in the House. While without particular skill as a debater he was a graceful and pleasing orator. His early career promised the highest political honors but the promise failed of fulfillment. He served for a short time in the Senate, succeeding Daniel Webster

Turmoil and Contested Elections 91

when that statesman entered the cabinet of President Fillmore. His attitude on the slavery question was not sufficiently radical to satisfy the demands of his constituents and in 1851 he was defeated by George S. Boutwell for the governorship and forced to give way to Charles Sumner in the United States Senate. At the age of forty-two he had already read his political obituary.

Winthrop's conservative attitude on the slavery question with his Whig proclivities made him an acceptable candidate to both northern and southern members of the controlling party. The election was close; not until the third ballot was Winthrop elected and then only by a majority of one vote. This election portrayed the transition from old traditions and marked the appearance of the Free Soilers who two years later became a deciding factor in the organization of the House.

Samuel F. Vinton of Ohio, a member of the House since 1823, and the defeated Whig candidate for the Speakership in the twenty-ninth Congress, might have had the honor had he been willing to accept. Declaring himself too feeble from his advanced age to assume the onerous duties of the office he had voluntarily pledged his support to Winthrop and thus insured his election. However, such radical abolitionists as Giddings and Palfrey declined to vote for Winthrop because of his conservatism.

The thirtieth Congress marks another of those national epochs when familiar faces disappear; when, as though inspired by a single purpose, whole delegations of time-honored Representatives are retired in favor of novitiates. They appear to constitute well-defined periods of national unrest, of acute dissatisfaction with existing conditions.

These political periods seem to resolve themselves into cycles corresponding somewhat closely to one-half the average length of human existence involving six or eight political eruptions in each century.

Of the two hundred and twenty-eight members of the House of Representatives which convened in December, 1847, fewer than one hundred had served in the twenty-ninth Congress—the proportion of new members was quite as great as at any other time in our national history. One of the most striking of these new members, and destined to become the most famous, was a member from Illinois — Abraham Lincoln. We know the impression this wonderful character made upon those with whom he was associated that first winter of his national career — for no other American has been so largely the study of historians and biographers. Awkward, gaunt, clumsy, ill dressed, painfully embarrassed at social functions, yet possessing the easy manners and the simplicity and integrity of rural character, he inspired the confidence and esteem of his fellow members. In a sense he was popular with his colleagues, who accepted him as a type of the sturdy, unpolished West; they were entertained by his peculiar humor and his stories of the farm and frontier. Without fear he grappled in debate with the most famous statesmen of the House, but the impression he made upon his audience was not altogether favorable. His type of speech harmonized better with the hustings, where the crude and uncultured take more kindly to homely illustrations and spicy stories. Native keenness and a pleasing sense of humor — for these things he was probably remembered by his associates.

Turmoil and Contested Elections 93

Nature delights in contrasts. She loves to play tricks upon the imagination, to startle us with her whims and impress us with her versatility. On the 6th of December, 1847, there entered the Senate chamber a well-groomed member of medium height, of close, compact frame, and the easy grace and courtly bearing of the southern gentry. His erect carriage pronounced him a soldier, indeed a West Pointer; the visitors pointed him out with pride and whispered of his daring bravery in the Mexican war, of his relationship to Zachary Taylor. Jefferson Davis was this patrician who first entered the United States Senate on the same day that Lincoln took the oath of office at the other end of the Capitol. The one a disciple of States' rights and the defender of slavery — the other a soldier of Unionism and later the emancipator of millions. Andrew Johnson of Tennessee — risen from the cobbler's bench, and destined to assume the mantle of leadership fallen from stricken shoulders — was re-elected member of the House of Representatives.

Winthrop made a dignified moderator, always courteous, ever studious to fulfill the demands of his office and yet arousing an occasional sneer of envy by his boast of pride in birth and name. No man has ever left the Speaker's chair with a more enduring reputation for dignity. He adopted the ideals of Hunter, though he frequently failed in their application. He fulfilled the promise which his service as Speaker of the Massachusetts Assembly had given. The unquestioned master of parliamentary law, many of his decisions were either incorporated in the standing rules of the House or became well recognized precedents of its parliamentary practice. He possessed the sternness of will and promptness of decision necessary to dominate the House during the days of storm and confusion when Giddings and the other abolitionists joined issue with the war dogs of slavery. Toombs and Stephens and the other southern leaders never hesitated to accept the challenge of battle, and in the heat of conflict which raged during the thirtieth Congress rare presence of mind and unquestioned self-confidence were needed in the Speaker's chair to preserve the dignity and order requisite to the maintenance of national honor.

Yet Winthrop by his charm of manner, his unfailing courtesy, and modest dignity commanded the respect and friendship of the entire House. While he recognized the political possibilities of his office and sought to fuse with it the attributes of a political leader, he was, first and foremost, a moderator; as such he recognized neither the lines of party allegiance nor the ties of personal friendship. And yet his lofty conception of the office was rebuked by the very members who ought indeed to have led the applause. The "whole-loaf-or-none" attitude of most reformers has frequently invited their own humiliation and the ridicule of impartial spectators. The anti-slavery Whigs, particularly the radical Giddings, and the discountenanced Palfrey, could not be appeased with anything short of unfairness toward the southerners.

The cleavage of parties on the slavery question and the turbulence of political conceptions was clearly reflected in the uncertain character of the thirty-first Congress, which assembled on the 3d of December, 1849. Although the Whigs were numerically stronger than the Democrats they were less devout in their reverence for

Turmoil and Contested Elections

party decrees. The southern Whigs were insolent and defiant, and the northern Whigs were not inclined to yield even for the sake of organizing the House. Thirteen members, ostensibly Whigs but aligned under the banner of the Free Soil party — a name which sacrificed meaning to euphony — held the balance of power. These were the radicals and, quickly recognizing their power, they intended to dominate. One hundred and twelve Democrats, one hundred and five Whigs, and thirteen Free Soilers were the party alignment. Winthrop was again the Whig nominee but eight of the Free Soilers, inspired by Giddings, declined to support him because he had ignored the anti-slavery sentiment in framing his committees in the thirtieth Congress and would not pledge himself to give that recognition in the event of his re-election. They demanded — and their ultimatum was not a severe one — that the Committee on the District of Columbia, the Judiciary Committee, and the Committee on the Territories be so constituted as to report honestly on all petitions and memorials favorable to the abolitionists. Winthrop declined the bargain. Naturally there was no prospect of their supporting the southern candidate, Howell Cobb of Georgia, whom even some Democrats had already bolted.

Another band of non-conformists under Toombs and Stephens, violent in their opposition to the Wilmot proviso, fought to dislodge the Whigs from their position on that measure at the risk of disrupting not alone the party but even the Union. They foresaw the ultimate union of Whigs and the Free Soilers resulting in an anti-slavery party.

On the first ballot Cobb led by seven votes, the followers of Giddings and the adherent of Toombs scattering their support over a wide field of candidates. From day to day the House remained unorganized as the balloting proceeded, no one attaining the requisite majority. The members became daily more exasperated, while the people grew impatient under a situation so unprecedented and so full of dire possibilities.

On the thirty-sixth ballot Winthrop declined to permit the further use of his name. The Democrats, convinced of the impossibility of electing Cobb, by a coalition with the Free Soilers placed in the field William J. Brown of Indiana. On the fortieth ballot, cast December 12th, Brown lacked but two votes of election. At this juncture Stanly, a southern Whig from North Carolina, moved to invite the Democrats to appoint a committee of three members for a conference with a similar delegation of Whigs with the hope of breaking the deadlock. Suspecting this to be the countersign for a retreat of the Whigs, and fearing some trickery, a sharp debate ensued. The suspicions of the southern Whigs had been excited by the votes which Brown received from the ardent Free Soilers. Brown was sharply catechised as to the rumor that he had bargained off his committees to these extremists. At first he replied with an equivocal shake of the head but when forced to an answer admitted that some desultory negotiations had been attempted. Nor was this the climax. A letter addressed to Wilmot was produced wherein Brown had agreed, in return for their support, to appoint the disputed committees at the dictation of the Free Soilers. The southern members cried out against this Judas in their midst, and proclaimed him another Benedict Arnold without his courage. So great was the excitement on one

Turmoil and Contested Elections

side and the chagrin on the other at the exposure of this almost successful alliance that the House adjourned without attempting another ballot. The choice of a Speaker seemed now to present a more doubtful issue than ever.

The prelude to the balloting of the next day was a fiery encounter between Meade of Virginia and Duer of New York in which the epithets of "liar" and "traitor," and such sinister terms as "disunion" and "secession" were freely bandied about. Toombs and Stephens brazenly preached the gospel of rebellion. Colcock of South Carolina, carried beyond the depths of his intellect by the swift tide of party passion, announced that he would introduce a formal motion for the dissolution of the Union immediately after the abolition of slavery in the District of Columbia should be resolved upon, or the Wilmot proviso enacted.

The warnings sounded by these disciples of slavery were not lost upon the northern members and although they created no wild panic yet they did much toward securing the final organization of the House by serving notice that there was a limit to southern endurance. We have the word of Stephens that such financial considerations as unpaid board bills and importuning creditors helped much to bring the battle-mad members to a saner state of mind. Except on credit no money was available until the organization of the House, and the money lenders of Washington did a brisk business.

Still the balloting continued, punctuated and adorned by passionate oratory, sinister threats, and amusing declarations of undying party loyalty. The days had grown into weeks and no choice seemed possible. Confusion indescribable and disorder which Horace Mann — who had succeeded the lamented John Quincy Adams — characterized as "infernal," prevailed with the duration of each day's session. The Sergeant-at-arms with his mace alone prevented actual personal violence. Between ballots frenzied oratory held sway. The members spouted flame and they acted flame. They were not merely incandescent, they were a roaring fire, they reddened the sky with their glow; they filled the air with burning brands.

On the twenty-second day of December a motion, agreed to by the committees of both parties, and passed by a vote of 113 to 106, provided for an amendment to the rules of the House. If on the next three ballots no choice should be made the candidate who, on the ensuing ballot, received the highest number of votes was to be declared the duly elected Speaker. In short the plurality was substituted for the majority vote. Sixty-two ballots had been cast without a choice. On the sixty-third ballot, taken the following day in accordance with this motion, Cobb was elected by 102 votes, to 100 for Winthrop, with 20 scattering.

Three weeks of the session had thus been consumed in a contest frequently determined by a single ballot. The Senate meantime had adjourned from day to day — its members crowding into the Hall of Representatives, interested spectators of the gladiatorial combat.

December 24th — as in the previous contest, the day before Christmas — the President's message was transmitted to Congress. The intervening three weeks, during

Turmoil and Contested Elections 99

which it lay on Taylor's desk, had already placed the stamp of inconsistency upon several paragraphs of the document. When the clerks of the Senate and the House read the sentence which heralded the United States as "the most stable and permanent government on earth" a smile played across the faces of various members as they called to mind the tense days which brought ridicule upon so fulsome a eulogy.

Giddings in the flush of victory boasted that Winthrop was the first man ever defeated because of his devotion to the slavocracy. His decade of legislative service had failed to impress upon Giddings one great truth — that though there may be times when great moral convictions must not be compromised even so much as a hair's breadth, yet generally some slight concession of principle is preferable to complete defeat. Such a case was this. Had Giddings and his radical devotees voted for Winthrop he would have been chosen on the first ballot. Through their contumacy Cobb was elected. Horace Mann who had, with becoming wisdom, voted consistently for Winthrop "as the best man we could possibly select" declared of Cobb: — "He loves slavery; it is his politics, his political economy, and his religion." Devotion to the slave doctrines was easily his guiding star, indeed constituted his entire solar system.

Cobb at the time of his election was one of the leading statesmen of the South, of unquestioned ability and great strength of character. In the previous Congress, as the leader of his party, he had conducted the defense of Polk's administration. The organization of the committees, overwhelmingly favorable to the South and slave interests, was an index to his conduct of the office. An excellent presiding officer, he lacked, however, the dignity and impartiality of Winthrop; he lent his position in every possible way to the advancement of party and sectional interests. His ability served slightly to neutralize the partisan tone of his Speakership.

On the first day of December, 1851, the thirty-second Congress gathered in Washington for a session of frivolity and trifling approached but not equaled even by the twenty-third Congress. Despite the general tenor of inactivity and lack of purpose that pervaded this session it was one of the longest, as if to make up by quantity what it lacked of quality. The gradual decline of the Whig party was now clearly portrayed. Its attempt to straddle the question of slavery had miserably failed. In the Senate composed of sixty-two members — two seats being vacant — the Whigs counted but twenty-four, while the opposition numbered thirty-three; the remaining three were Free Soilers. In the house eighty-eight Whigs, as against one hundred and forty opposition men and five Free Soilers, were a pathetic reminder of former glory. Many of the members even ignored the party caucus which made no nomination because a nomination would have served the doubtful purpose of advertising their impotence — though a resolution was adopted to sustain the compromise settlement. The Democratic candidate for Speaker, Linn Boyd of Kentucky, was elected by a large majority. While a man of no inspiring ability he was at least blameless. He emulated in a feeble way the example of his predecessor. So well did he subserve the ends of his party that he was re-elected Speaker of the thirty-third

Turmoil and Contested Elections 101

Congress, serving from December 1, 1851, to March 3, 1855.

Popular interest in political contests can be aroused to fever pitch only when there is involved some great principle or some commanding personality. Otherwise indifference and apathy prevail despite the wildest pleadings of hopeful candidates. The issue is simply whether one set of men or another equally honest, equally efficient, or equally rapacious, shall hold the remunerative positions — and as to that the people are quite indifferent. In ordinary times political opinion is not bisected any more than opinion on other subjects. If it be an issue of personality two parties will accurately record the opposing sentiments. If some moral principle is involved the issue cannot be so clearly drawn; and we have varying keys, as it were, in the scale of public opinion. The larger parties lose their grasp and new ones spring up. This was clearly illustrated by the party alignments in the United States before the Civil War, particularly in the decade immediately preceding that struggle. There were Democrats and Whigs both with northern and southern factions, Free Soilers, Know-Nothings, Republicans, all equally tenacious of their convictions, none willing to compromise a single idea even for the advancement of their general purpose.

The issue that promised to concern the thirty-fourth Congress was the Kansas-Nebraska act. The South had resolved to acquire control of the large territory of Kansas while the North was equally determined to baptize it to the cause of freedom. This is neither the place nor the occasion to portray the disgraceful scenes enacted on the western stage prior to the war. Suffice it to say that those scenes were a worthy sonata to the grand opera of bloodshed so soon to open. In the new Congress the anti-Nebraska men numbered one hundred and seventeen, but they were of uncertain convictions. They were presumably pledged to the cause of territorial freedom. While all were from the North, seventy-five of them had been elected as Know-Nothings. There were seventy-nine Democrats, friendly to the administration, likely to support the Pierce-Douglas slavery policy. Twenty of these were northerners, thirty-seven members were Whigs, or Americans, friendly to the cause of slavery and all, except three of them, from the slave States.

The *Congressional Globe*, formerly in the habit of indicating the political allegiance of the various members by printing their names in different types, now abandoned even the attempt at classification. At the convening of the next Congress when the parties were again more solidly fused the editor returned to his former custom, using three sets of type. As soon as the House convened it proceeded to organize. The anti-Nebraska men had a safe plurality over the administration Democrats, yet a third coterie, composed of Whigs and southern Know-Nothings, hostile to all manner of agitation, held a clear balance of power — able to crown or defeat. On the first ballot five candidates appeared: — William A. Richardson, Democrat of Illinois, seventy-four votes; Lewis D. Campbell, anti-Nebraska of Ohio, fifty-three; Humphrey Marshall, Democrat and Know-Nothing of Kentucky, thirty; Nathaniel P. Banks, anti-Nebraska of Massachusetts, twenty-one; Henry Fuller, National Know-Nothing of Pennsylvania, seventeen; and twenty-nine scattering

Turmoil and Contested Elections 103

votes for candidates of various factions. The administration party appeared, outwardly at least, a compact mass, while the majority was a hybrid made up of various elements unable to agree on a single issue. The opposition was a unit only in their hostility to the slavocracy and it was a serious question whether some of them might not subordinate this issue to some question of less moment.

One hundred and thirteen votes were necessary for an election; the leading candidate was Richardson of Illinois, who as chairman of the territorial committee had led the Democrats in the Kansas-Nebraska fight. Richardson's friends rallied so faithfully to his standard and remained so loyal to his fortunes that they were soon heralded as "the immortal seventy-four." Some twenty candidates had received at least one vote each on the first ballot. On the tenth ballot, taken on the third morning of the session, there was no change in the relative position of the candidates: the five leading candidates divided one hundred and ninety-eight votes, the remaining twenty-two being scattered. On the twelfth ballot Richardson gave way to Campbell but regained the lead on the seventeenth ballot; on the twenty-first ballot Campbell fell to forty-six. On the seventh of December Campbell — to whom defeat was inevitable since he scorned to accept office as the cost of principle — withdrew from the contest.

After Campbell had drawn out of the race the anti-Nebraska members united in support of Banks, whose mental qualifications and past history marked him as easily the most acceptable to that coterie. The friends of freedom, in an effort to veil their plan of battle and so gain the support of the unsuspecting, gradually united on Banks and their diplomatic caution nearly won them the victory; on the thirty-eighth ballot cast on the 10th of December, he received 108 votes; several votaries of freedom had not yet supported Banks and his friends were unable to force him above the high-water mark; despite their most valiant efforts his following began slowly to disintegrate.

Had the Democrats united with the Know-Nothings on Fuller his election would have been assured at any time. Declining this course they invited the Know-Nothings to join them in the election of their candidate, after having adopted resolutions in their party caucus denouncing them as enemies of civil and religious liberty.

The dreary hours of balloting were constantly enlivened by charges of combinations, deals, and understandings; by suspicions of covenants; by rumors of bargains; and above all by many unjust charges and dishonorable misrepresentations that only aroused bitterness and more deeply inspired the determination to stand by previous candidates lest they later awake to find themselves tricked.

The renewed balloting and the incidental debates and discussions indicated that the majority of the members could be classified into three parties — the Republicans numbering 105, the Democrats 74, the National American party 40. It soon became apparent that further balloting along the lines already pursued was a profligate waste of time and various novel plans were suggested by which it was hoped that an organization might be speedily effected. Letcher and McMullen of Virginia even demanded that all the members resign their commissions and that new elections be held throughout the country with a view to securing a Congress more truly representative of the

Turmoil and Contested Elections 105

popular opinion. Other remedies were suggested. On the 26th of December it was first resolved that no motion to adjourn should be in order until a Speaker was chosen. But even before another ballot had been cast a recess was taken which in effect repealed the first resolution. The serio-comic pose of those members who had so unctuously announced their purpose to continue the contest to its termination exposed them to ridicule and the next day the heroic resolution was repealed.

Thus day after day new combinations were built up only to disappear under the hail of ballots, new arguments were devised to win those susceptible to persuasion, only to be pierced by the ridicule of the opposition, new charges and insinuations were bandied about to fill the air like some sudden flurry of snow then to disappear before the reappearing sun of investigation. The year 1855 was rapidly drawing to its close and the House was apparently no nearer its organization than it had been on the first day of its session.

On the eve of the new year — the 31st of December — as if to mock the dying hopes of party concord, the President's message was transmitted to Congress. The message was directed to Congress and no Congress existed since the House had not organized; after a prolonged and bitter debate the House declined to permit its reading. Their contention was correct in principle no matter how embarrassing might be its application. Again a return to fruitless balloting. January 9th (1856), the Democratic members having resolved to vote against adjournment until a Speaker had been elected, the northerners took up the gauntlet. The friends of slavery had thus sought by pressure to compel a Republican surrender. But on the morning of the 10th as the minutes slowly lengthened into hours and the hands pointed to nine, the Democrats convinced of the failure of their manœuvre voted to adjourn.

Men were too strong of conviction, too determined of purpose, to be either tricked or forced into a compromise. This artifice of the Democrats served the double purpose of fostering a stronger resolve in the minds of the opposition — and of writing a scandalous page in the history of Congress. Ruffin, the Democratic Representative from North Carolina, said: — "I was well satisfied what these night sessions would bring about. We have seen within the last twelve hours scenes that would disgrace the wood-sawyer's house on the canal or the lowest tipping shop on English Hill. — My section of country has nothing to expect from this Congress or its legislation, and it is a matter of perfect indifference with me whether it ever is organized. The government can get along without it." Thus had one long night of vile incrimination, ribald witticisms, and disgusting inebriety impressed one of its members.

The ingenuity of Congress and its friends had been sorely tried in the determined effort to accomplish the organization of the House. A novel plan was suggested reminding one of the catechisms of our Sunday-school days or of the spelling matches of the rural districts. The position of the various candidates on the main point at issue was not clearly appreciated by the majority of the members. By resolution an afternoon was set apart, that of January 12th, for a careful scrutiny of the ideas and purposes of the three principal candidates. Such an open declaration of principles, it was thought, would certainly

Turmoil and Contested Elections 107

clear the atmosphere of charges, would relieve all of the suspicion of deals and enlighten the various members. Pledges, promises, declarations thus made in the open would serve ample notice on all concerned. If the failure of past efforts was due, as some suggested, to ignorance of the sentiments entertained by the various candidates, such a course promised most for the prompt election of a Speaker.

The replies of Richardson, Fuller, and Banks to the queries propounded by an eager House, and the support accorded by their friends thereafter, clearly portrayed the general sentiment in the different sections of the country and furnished a criterion for the presidential contest.

Richardson advocated without reserve the Douglas theory of popular sovereignty. Fuller held that, the territories being the common property of all the states, neither Congress nor a territorial legislature had the power or the right to permit or prohibit slavery within their limits. Upon their application for admission into the Union the slavery question should be determined by the State constitution. Fuller, supposedly an anti-Nebraska man at the time of his election, had during the early days of the contest received his support largely from the North, but a month before the day of catechism it became evident that his views were at least acceptable to the friends of slavery, and thereafter his votes were mainly derived from the South. But for the stubborn adherence to party names Fuller would have been elected weeks before by a combination of the Democrats with the Know-Nothings — unless perchance such a union of slavery men had at once inspired an alliance of all members hostile to the slavocracy.

Banks declared that he would unreservedly favor a congressional prohibition of slavery in all the territories where such legislation was necessary to keep it out. On the Kansas-Nebraska question he strongly demanded "the substantial restoration of the prohibition as it has existed since 1820 — for which the southern States contracted and received consideration." His unflinching declaration of faith won for Banks the applause of the North and a strong following in Congress.

Still, after this moral and political examination the atmosphere was not wholly cleared. None of the candidates had been entirely frank. Richardson talked vaguely as to whether the territorial legislature had the right to prohibit slavery in Kansas. Banks was silent on the question of how far he was still a Know-Nothing, and refused to say anything on the subject of slavery in the District of Columbia. He had indiscreetly remarked in a speech delivered some years before that he would, if necessary, "let the Union slide" rather than yield to the slave owners. This was now used effectively against him. Fuller had changed his political coat; elected as an opponent of the Kansas-Nebraska Act he had now swallowed the slave theory even more completely than Richardson. He insisted that the Kansas-Nebraska bill encouraged the creation neither of free nor of slave States. He then denied without qualification the legislative power of Congress on the slave question; and finally he insisted that the power of the territorial legislature on this question was confined to protecting citizens of the territory in the constitutional right of the enjoyment of "property."

Gradually it became apparent that none of the one

Turmoil and Contested Elections 109

hundred and seven who had voted for Banks for weeks could be drawn from their allegiance. The Democrats had the choice of three possible courses of action: they might agree to an election by a plurality vote and admit their defeat; they might persist in their present conduct and thus make impossible the organization of the House; or they might renew negotiations with the Know-Nothings. They were unwilling to grasp the gaunt hand of despair; the second course they dared not undertake for it involved the certainty of swift retribution at the hands of the people at the next election. Thus the third alternative alone remained. After the manner of the coquette, they flirted, politely however, with the Know-Nothings. The Democrats were willing to surrender personalities but not principles.

They intimated that they were prepared to compromise upon another candidate, a Democrat, however. January 23d, Richardson declared that on the following day he would irrevocably withdraw from the contest. Rust of Arkansas, in a puerile effort to clear the situation, moved to summon all candidates to withdraw that the balloting might be taken up *de novo*. This motion was tabled the next day, Fuller in the meanwhile having declined further participation in the contest as a candidate.

The Democrats now united upon Orr of South Carolina, but he was no more successful than Richardson in winning the southern Americans, and soon retired from the field. On the second ballot the Know-Nothings again united on Fuller. Thus were the Democratic overtures defeated. Horace Greeley, radical abolitionist, the faithful chronicler of this period and an ardent supporter of Banks, wrote, "our plans are defeated and our hopes are frustrated from day to day by perpetual treacheries on our own side." On the morning of January 28th he wrote: "We hope to elect Banks to-day." His hopes were not realized and that afternoon he denounced as the cause of his disappointment "thirty double-dyed traitors, ten of them voting against us, and the other twenty cursing me because they cannot do likewise."

But the treachery and complaints were not confined to one party. Alexander Stephens had declared that "if men were reliable creatures" Banks could never be elected. "But my observation has taught me," he said, "that very little confidence is to be placed on what they say as to what they will do."

On the 30th of January, Clingman, without the consent of his party, moved an election by a plurality. The motion to table was lost but the resolution itself was defeated by a small majority. His purpose was to force the Know-Nothings to join the Democrats; but they firmly declined the attempted coercion.

Clingman's motion tended, with one other feature, to focus matters. A message from the President on the Kansas situation, received and read to the House on the 24th, after a stormy debate, warned Congress that the welfare of the country demanded the immediate organization of that body.

February 1st, a resolution was presented by Howell Cobb, that Aiken of South Carolina should be elected Speaker. The vote on this motion was 103 in the affirmative and 110 in the negative. Aiken, a large slave owner, and ardent follower of Calhoun, was a man of admirable qualities and undoubted personal popularity — much more agreeable to the southern Know-Nothings than Orr or Richardson. Although the resolution had been lost, still the Democrats were pleased with the prospective chance of success, and the Northerners correspondingly depressed. It was universally conceded that this motion to elect by a plurality, so often offered, would carry on the next day. It was felt that Aiken's election was certain. That same evening at the White House reception President Pierce heartily congratulated him upon his success. The anti-Nebraska men, however, resolved to stand loyally with Banks, no matter what the issue.

Immediately after the reading of the journal on the 2d of February, Smith, a Democratic member from Tennessee, offered a resolution providing that, if three further ballots should not result in a decision, then on the fourth ballot that member of the House receiving the largest number of votes should be declared Speaker. Smith counting on the support of the Know-Nothings expected the election of Aiken.

The supporters of Banks voted solidly for the motion for they had early advocated a plurality election. Twelve Democrats voted with them. The ballot was 113 yeas to 104 nays. Orr at once withdrew in favor of Aiken.

Now that an election seemed imminent, after months of turmoil, interest and excitement were at white heat. The Democrats convinced that Smith had blundered fought desperately to recall the motion after it had passed. The 132d ballot, the last on which a majority was necessary for election, brought no result. Rust immediately moved to adjourn, but the motion was defeated by a decided majority. Fuller rose to declare again that he was no longer a candidate but could hardly be heard in the feverish turbulence of partisan strife.

The House proceeded to the 133d roll-call. The Know-Nothings who had persistently voted for Fuller were implored to save the nation by uniting on Aiken. The roll-call was completed. Members mounting their chairs, clamored for recognition, or cried in clarion tones the varying fortunes of the contest. A motion to adjourn, shouted trumpetlike, was declared out of order by the presiding officer, John W. Forney, Clerk of the former House. The precedent of 1839 provided that a resolution should be adopted declaring that member who had the largest number of votes duly elected Speaker. Forney, afraid lest another vote in the delirium then spreading would defeat the question, resolved upon an heroic measure. After a consultation with the tellers representing both parties it was decided to announce the result. The Republican teller having secured the attention of the House shouted in firm clear tones: "Gentlemen, the following is the result of the 133d vote: Banks, 103; Aiken, 100; Fuller, 6; Campbell, 4; Wells, 1; therefore, according to the resolution which was adopted this day, Nathaniel P. Banks is declared Speaker of the House of Representatives for the thirty-fourth Congress." The feverish emotions of eight weeks burst forth like a volcano; the uproar was deafening. Cheers of victory mingled with howls of derision; hisses of disapproval accompanied vigorous applause; darkened visages answered countenances bright and cheery with the flush of success.

When at length some semblance of order had been se-

Turmoil and Contested Elections 113

cured, an American (Know-Nothing) declared that since the precedent of 1849 had been broken, Banks had not been duly or properly elected Speaker. This protest was promptly and decisively rebuked no less by the southerners, whose chivalry is traditional, than by the successful northerners. Clingman, Aiken, Orr, and other southern Democrats led the chorus of indignation at this effort to renounce the honorable agreement. A resolution declaring Banks the legally elected Speaker was carried by a conclusive majority. Governor Aiken rose, and, conceding the election of the member from Massachusetts, requested permission of the House to escort him to the Chair. Aiken's chivalry and nobility in defeat won him a notable ovation.

Thus ended the most sensational contest for the election of a Speaker that our national halls have ever witnessed. Two whole months of balloting, of argument, of attempted coalitions, of unconvincing debate and abortive alliances; and yet during all the nervous strain and physical torture of this contest surprising good humor had prevailed. Dignity and honor were distinguishing features of the sensational struggle. Threats of disunion were indulged in by sensational southerners, but they fell on incredulous ears — in fact were not accepted seriously. The mock heroics of one Virginian, who shouted that the restoration of the Missouri Compromise or the repeal of the Fugitive Slave Law would force the dissolution of the Union, were greeted with merriment and cries of "Oh! No!" The only act of the entire contest which reflected any discredit upon the legislators was the cowardly assault upon Horace Greeley in the streets of Washington by Rust, a member from Arkansas, who smarted under the keen editorial shafts of sarcasm aimed at a resolution which he had fathered.

Vastly more was at stake than the mere election of a Speaker. It was the travail of a great issue. It clearly demonstrated that a new alignment of parties on the slavery question was no longer to be postponed. The fusion of the slavery advocates was now assured. This would compel the coalition of the disciples of freedom. Whigs and Know-Nothings were but names without life, honored ghosts of departed bodies. They were, even in the Speakership contest, all referred to as Republicans, thus bestowing upon them a common name if not a single purpose. One thing was clearly established — the parties of the future were to be the Democratic and Republican.

The election of Banks was a victory for freedom, the first defeat of slavery in a quarter of a century. When Banks mounted the dais an important victory had been won by a party still in its swaddling clothes. For the Republicans had been organized scarcely two years. It gave added prestige to the Republican National Convention which had been summoned by the Republican State Committees of nine northern States. It seemed a significant fact — not unnoted — that the successful contestant had come from the North, from Massachusetts, and the unsuccessful one from the South, from South Carolina. The Speaker had been elected wholly by the votes of the free States and all the southern votes with but two exceptions had been cast for Aiken. For the first time in our history a Speaker had been elected without material support from both sections.

This marvelous spectacle of a national House requir-

Turmoil and Contested Elections 115

ing two months in which to organize for the transaction of business suggested serious questions to the statesmen of that and later date. It was mooted whether there ought to be some legal provision to cope with such a dangerous situation. It was felt that some alternative ought to be provided for the sake of national safety so that when passion is at fever heat and party alignment uncertain, the country should not be obliged to subsist for weeks or months, deprived of their legislature by reason of inability to agree upon a Speaker. The framers of the Constitution had apparently not contemplated such a contingency as this; had not supposed it possible that disruption would thus endanger not alone the organization, but even the very existence of the House. The Constitution had provided the method of electing the Speaker and organizing the House. It had made this the prerequisite to its legislative functions. It had not set any time within which that right should be exercised; it had left the mode of election entirely in the discretion of the House; it had not clothed any other factor of the government with the right to act in event Congress failed to organize — either by supplying a moderator, or in decreeing a dissolution and requiring a new election. Yet the alternative was serious. If the House failed to organize, legislation was impossible, and through the failure of the necessary appropriations the whole mechanism of government must be deranged unless the finances were bolstered in some way not suggested or contemplated by law. Then as now the only safeguard lay in the congressional conscience and possibly that greater force, the moral pressure of public opinion.

Men studied, too, over another question of scarcely less

import. Since the control and organization of the committees was the real point at issue would not the interests of the nation be better subserved if the appointment of the standing committees were no longer left to the single power of the Speaker? In short, deprive the Speaker of his power and thus obviate the struggle by withholding the spoils of victory. Indeed some spirits, far bolder than most, whispered of a radical change in our fundamental institutions which might permit the House of Representatives to be prorogued by the Executive and new elections ordered. This seemed beyond the realms of possibility — the fundamental spirit of our government depends upon the co-ordination and independence of the judiciary, the legislative and the executive. But that these questions should be mooted furnished evidence of the realization of danger.

Banks was the ideal type of the self-made man — the allegorical figure of American genius and the institutions of the Republic. In his youth he was a bobbin-boy in a cotton factory, and later a skilled machinist. With a natural aptitude for oratory he gained practice not as Clay had done by declaiming before the animals of the barnyard and the majesty of the forests, but by delivering addresses on the temperance question. From this he assumed the roll of an actor and was seen on the stage of Boston in the part of Claude Melnotte. He had been elected to the preceding Congress as a Democrat but had strongly opposed the Kansas-Nebraska bill. For this meteoric career he had been wonderfully blessed by nature, which had bestowed upon him an impressive bearing, a sonorous and pleasing voice and that valuable legacy —

although some whispered that he was "not as wise as he looked" — personal presence. He had been elected to the thirty-fifth Congress as a Know-Nothing but in the political struggle of 1855, emulating the varied rôles of his private career, he had deserted their ranks and presided over the Republican Convention of Massachusetts. A Democrat, at least in his sympathies, he possessed a discreet conservatism of action which stamped him as eminently qualified to occupy the position to which he had been elected. "The iron man" he was called in the years which ensued. With a natural genius for administration, coupled with personal popularity, he promised a career of eminence which, like Winthrop's, failed of later fulfillment.

The new Speaker's committee appointments were honestly and judiciously made. Maintaining that the office of Speaker was not political but simply executive and parliamentary, he gave the anti-slavery men only a bare majority in the various committees. Campbell was made chairman of the Ways and Means Committee; some of the enemies of the Kansas-Nebraska bill were given the chairmanships of the lesser committees.

In accordance with his firm conviction that the Speaker should be merely moderator, he added nothing of consequence to the political development of the office. This conviction he retained during the entire sixteen years of his subsequent congressional service. Yet he commanded to an eminent degree the respect and admiration of the House by his prompt and impartial decisions, his unfailing affability and consummate tact. Efficient and popular, he remains to-day one of the most prominent Speakers of our legislative history. He guided the House through the dangerous eddies of the Kansas struggle and retired with the tribute that, even in those days of bitter partisan strife, not one of his decisions was overruled.

In 1856 Congress passed a new salary act. Warned by the prompt vengeance of an outraged public in 1816 Congress voted no further increase of salary for nearly forty years, although two or three sporadic efforts had been made. In the meantime the salaries of the prominent Federal officials had been augumented at various times.

The cost and standard of living had materially increased and the country at large was basking in the sunlight of material prosperity. Moreover, with the enlarged territory of the Union the compensation law of 1818 had contrived to work serious inequalities, owing to the mileage clause which provided an allowance for Congressmen of eight dollars for every twenty miles up to one thousand two hundred and fifty miles, then six dollars for every twenty miles of the remaining distance from their respective homes to Washington and return. At a rough estimate the gross income for a Senator or Congressman from California was seven thousand dollars a year, while his confrère from Maryland or Virginia received but one thousand five hundred dollars. The cost of travel was high, yet it was surely not so exorbitant as to warrant the rate of forty or even thirty cents a mile.

Senator Weller of California frankly admitted, though with some embarrassment, that he was receiving five thousand four hundred dollars as mileage. Naturally the net income of Congressmen varied materially and the

Turmoil and Contested Elections 119

members from the far West were looked upon with ill-concealed envy.

In 1856 a bill was introduced in the Senate providing an annual salary of two thousand five hundred dollars for the members of both Houses of Congress and double that amount for the Speaker of the House and the President pro tem. of the Senate. No change in the mileage provision was suggested and the action was to become effective only upon the adjournment of that session of Congress that the scandal of a retroactive clause might be avoided. After an acrimonious debate and much parading of figures, the House of Representatives amended the bill making it retroactive and increasing the salary to three thousand dollars a year for the members and six thousand dollars for the Speaker and President pro tem. of the Senate. In this form it was at length carried.

The newspapers denounced the "Steal" suggested by the retroactive clause and declared the increase to be wholly unwarranted. However, the nation was absorbed by the greater issues, then so near the frightful climax of blood and arms. But for a few isolated cases there were no such visitations of condign punishment as had marked the enactment of the Salary Bill of 1816.

CHAPTER IV

THE MEDIOCRITY OF THE CHAIR

ON the 7th of December, 1857, the House of Representatives convened for the last time in the small elliptical chamber where the greatness and the follies of half a century had been revealed. This chamber is now called Statuary Hall. It was occupied by the House of Representatives from 1807 to 1814, the year of the ruin of the Capitol by the British invaders. After the restoration of the building, two or three years later, the House reconvened in this hall and here continued its sessions until 1857, when the present chamber was occupied. The House met here when Dickens made his first visit to the United States, and a portion of his American unpopularity was due to his description of the hall and the personal habits of the Congressmen. He said: — "It is a beautiful and spacious hall of semi-circular shape, supported by handsome pillars. One part of the gallery is appropriated to ladies, where they sit in front rows, and come in and go out, as at a play or concert. It is an elegant chamber to look at but a singularly bad one for all purposes of hearing. The house is handsomely carpeted but the state to which these carpets are reduced by the universal disregard of the spittoons, with which every honorable member is accommodated, and the extraordinary improvement on the pattern which has been squirted and dabbled upon in every direction, does not admit of being described. It is strange enough to see

The Mediocrity of the Chair

an honorable gentleman leaning back in his tilted chair, shaping a convenient plug with his penknife, and when he was quite ready to use it, shoot the old one with his mouth as from a popgun and clap the new one in its place. I was surprised to learn that even steady, old chewers of great experience are not always good marksmen."

It was in this chamber that many of our early Presidents were inaugurated. Here it was that the House of Representatives had elected John Quincy Adams President, when neither candidate had a majority in the electoral college. In the resultant bitterness John Randolph called Henry Clay a "blackleg" — the charge that was the prelude to a bloodless but dramatic duel. It was in this chamber that the maniac Lawrence attempted to assassinate Andrew Jackson on January 31, 1835, while the President was attending the funeral services of a deceased member of the House.

Here Congress had applauded the eloquence of Clay, Calhoun, and Webster; here it had smarted under the vituperative lash of the volatile Randolph; here the spirit of the Revolution had been embraced in the figure of Lafayette; here Adams, denounced and vilified in life, had been revered in his tragic death; here Giddings had battled like some crusader of a later day; and here three times the chapter of struggle, bitter and uncompromising, had been written in the history of its Speakership. From the pleasing panorama of an historic past this Congress turned to the unpainted canvas of the future. On the 15th of December it moved into its new abode — the new wings of the Capitol extension having been completed — grateful to find that here the laws of acoustics had been consulted and speeches were no longer a confused jargon of unintelligible sounds.

The administration had a decided majority in both branches of Congress, yet in each House was a compact minority fighting under the banner of freedom where during the last session several distinct shades of political opinion had contended without coherence or discipline. The House speedily organized in sharp contrast to the scenes of two years before, and to the strife attendant upon the opening of the thirty-sixth Congress. James L. Orr of South Carolina, a man of southern views — whom we recognize as one of that galaxy of candidates in the preceding contest — was chosen Speaker by 128 votes over Galusha A. Grow of Pennsylvania, the Republican candidate, who received 84. Orr was a man of attractive personality and of strong southern prejudice. In 1860, the year after he quit the Speaker's chair, he declared in favor of "prompt secession from the Union in the event of the election of a Black Republican to the Presidency." Determined to preserve the decorum of debate, he found his task a difficult one in the violent scenes which were of daily occurrence in the House during the bitter struggle over the Lecompton constitution. His period of service was without doubt the most difficult of any during the entire history of the Speakership.

On the 5th of December, 1859, while John Brown's remains were still without a sepulchre, and only three days after the more prominent of the Harper's Ferry executions, the thirty-sixth Congress convened in Washington. The sensations, both North and South, over the Virginia arsenal tragedy and its dénouement portrayed vividly the

The Mediocrity of the Chair 123

rapidly widening breach between the sentiments of those two sections. Party lines were now definitely marked by latitude and longitude, by metes and bounds — the divisions were purely geographical and such alignments are always fraught with the gravest danger. North of the Mason-and-Dixon line Democrats had been relegated to private life while in the South intense partisans graced the seats formerly occupied by more moderate friends of slavery. This movement was only less marked in the Senate than in the House because the personnel of that body changes much less frequently, and serves less as a barometer of public sentiment. In the upper House, Houston, picturesque, Union-loving, the hero of Mexican days, gave way to Wigfall, a man stronger of voice than of intellect, who provided entertainment for the galleries by his rabid tirades against the Union. Bragg of North Carolina, Powell of Kentucky, and Nicholson of Tennessee were other new Representatives of the militant slavocracy; while in the North, Bingham, Anthony, Grimes, and Ten Eyck had been elected by legislatures bitterly hostile to the perpetuation of slavery.

The mantle of leadership was still shared by James A. Bayard, Hunter, Toombs, Mason, Slidell, Judah P. Benjamin and Jefferson Davis representing the administration; by Douglas representing none knew just what, except probably his own presidential ambition. The Republicans still looked to Hamlin, Fessenden, Wade, Collamer, Hale, and Wilson, while Seward, with broken health partially restored, soon took his place in the Council of Elders. Thirty-eight were Democrats, two — a curious anomaly — were South "Americans," and twenty-six were Republicans.

An unusual number of new faces were to be seen wandering strangely about the other end of the Capitol. The Republican party, although in the majority, was such a loose coalition that it was unable to complete the organization of the House except by assistance from without the party. Colfax of Indiana, the eloquent Burlingame of Massachusetts, Morrill of Vermont, Grow and Covode of Pennsylvania, all were destined to political fame. Tom Corwin and Thaddeus Stevens were back again amid the unfamiliar scenes of the new legislative chamber. William Pennington, a former Governor of New Jersey, took the oath of office for the first time. Charles Francis Adams, now a national figure of heroic proportions, mingled with such novitiates as Train of his own State, Windom of Minnesota and Roscoe Conkling of New York.

Upon the minority side of the hall sat "Sunset" Cox and Pendleton of Ohio, together with Vallandigham from the same State, one of the most partisan slave advocates; the talented Lucius Lamar answered the roll-call from Mississippi; Sickles of New York, who in defense of his family honor had but recently shot the brother of that Keyes who wrote the "Star Spangled Banner," Logan and McClernand from Illinois. Among the so-called independent members were Gilmer and Vance of North Carolina, Hickman of Pennsylvania, Henry Winter Davis of Maryland, and Maynard and Etheridge of Tennessee.

The House was composed of one hundred and nine Republicans, eighty-eight administration Democrats, and twenty-seven Americans, all but four of whom were from the South. No party controlling a majority, a spirited contest for the Speakership was inevitable. The vote on

The Mediocrity of the Chair 125

the first ballot was divided among sixteen candidates and gave no prophecy of the manner in which the struggle might terminate. On this ballot the Republicans divided their votes, John Sherman of Ohio receiving 66 and Galusha A. Grow of Pennsylvania 43. Thomas S. Bocock of Virginia led with 86 votes. As soon as the ballot was announced, Grow withdrew his name from the list of contestants. After some discussion as to his right to address the House in the absence of any question before that body, Clark of Missouri offered the following resolution:

"Whereas certain members of this House, now in nomination for Speaker, did endorse and recommend the book hereinafter mentioned, Resolved, that the doctrines and sentiments of a certain book called 'The Impending Crisis of the South — How to Meet It,' purporting to have been written by one Hinton R. Helper, are insurrectionary and hostile to the domestic peace and tranquillity of the country, and that no member of this House who has endorsed and recommended it, or the compend from it, is fit to be chosen to be Speaker of this House."

The motion, met by mingled hisses and applause, shouts and jeers, from the gallery, was the traditional spark in the powder house. The book in question had been written by a poor white of North Carolina in an effort to demonstrate that slavery was ruinous to the non-slaveholding whites of the South. Written in an impassioned and hysterical style, it was, however, based upon facts largely correct. The arguments were logical and in the main incontestable though they were foolishly clothed in the garb of threat and invective. "Uncle Tom's Cabin" had furnished already its martyr; was Helper's book to do likewise? Published in 1857 its circulation was at first very limited but in 1859 with the renewed agitation it was widely read by those of Republican faith. A compendium of its contents was published in a cheap edition for gratuitous distribution. This had been endorsed by many members of Congress, Sherman and Grow among them.

While Helper showed clearly his prejudice against the negro, his arraignment of the slave institution was made in behalf of the "poor whites." He prayed for the day when the blacks would be deported from the nation and their part of the industrial order filled by whites. The abolition of slavery, he maintained, would advance the material prosperity of the South by inspiring manufacturing and commerce, thus increasing the value of land, and providing a larger market for agricultural products. The population would increase — both in the city and country — schools would be established for the proper education of the children of the poor and the general tone of southern civilization and refinement thus materially uplifted. His arguments were founded on census statistics and upon statements of men of experience in the South. They were quite unanswerable. The only difficulty which presented itself was that the poor white, to whom the book was particularly addressed, could neither read nor comprehend the work. Otherwise the doom of slavery would have indeed been written. For beyond doubt seventy per cent of the electorate in the South were non-slave-owning whites. The slaveholders continued their power largely by encouraging and compelling the ignorance of their less fortunate brethren. In this we find the explanation of

The Mediocrity of the Chair

southern wrath at Helper's contribution to American literature.

Clark's motion was immediately followed by unsuccessful motions to adjourn. Stevens declared "These things must come out, and they might as well come out now." The battle was on; the light musketry of the skirmish line was giving way to the heavy siege guns of the battle regiments; the pickets were called in and the signal for a general advance rang clear.

The Republicans sought to postpone the conflict until after the election of the Speaker, but the Democrats, quick to see their advantage and the momentary panic in the ranks of the opposition, hastened to press their point. Kilgore of Indiana sought delay and insisted that although he appeared as one of the signers of the compendium, he had no recollection of affixing his signature to any such doctrine, and furthermore he was not in sympathy with such radicalism. To this statement Clark replied with effective scorn: "I am glad that the gentleman is beginning to flee from the wrath to come." Some members arose to deny having even read the book, although their names had been published as endorsing the baneful compendium. Possibly many had committed the indiscretion, so common among men in public life, of affixing their signatures to all sorts of memorials and petitions, frequently without comprehending either the spirit or purposes of the papers which they thus endorse. A motion to adjourn finally prevailed after Clark had ironically expressed his assent "if the gentlemen wanted time to deliberate and prepare themselves in secret."

The demoralizing influences of political panic were rampant among the Republican ranks. Torn by contending emotions of conviction and expediency, swayed by calm logic and partisan prejudice, depressed and buoyed up alternately by fear and hope, the Republicans knew not whither to turn.

To desert Sherman whom they had supported on the first ballot would be a confession of error and an admission that they had been bullied by the "fire-eating" slaveholders. On the other hand, to persist in their support of this candidate would proclaim their adherence to Helper's doctrines, and for this they were not prepared. Lack of moral courage held them hesitating between the alternatives of humiliating repentance and persistence in tactless imprudence. Clark's ironical suggestion that the Republicans sought the opportunity to consult together over some method of escape from their own folly, was all the more distasteful because it revealed the truth. And yet the outcome of the conference where no one seemed able to present a bold, clear, logical plan was simply confusion worse confounded.

The following day Clark opened fire on the scattered ranks with the flash and sputter of oratorical pyrotechnics. He quoted from the ill-starred compend to prove his assertion that it was highly incendiary, and then he read the names of all who had subscribed thereto.

Millson hotly declared that "one who consciously, deliberately, and of purpose lent his name and influence to the propagation of such writings is not only not fit to be Speaker, but is not fit to live." Clark's speech, a forceful blending of mad invective and scathing denunciation, had its inspiration in an effort to win the Americans to the sup-

The Mediocrity of the Chair 129

port of the Democratic candidate; not to drive the Republicans from their position.

Gilmer, an American from North Carolina, declared that he could see no logical connection between Helper's book and the election of a Speaker. He bitterly decried the agitation and insisted that it was the duty of all patriotic citizens to oppose steadfastly any and every attempt to renew slavery agitation either in Congress or out of it. The question should be ignored, there should be a sort of "gentlemen's agreement" on the entire subject. Gilmer thus served dual notice to the nation. The Americans would not support a Republican so long as one of the subscribers to the compendium was their candidate; and they would not assist the Democrats in any effort to turn the present confusion to their partisan advantage or encourage the propagation of sectional bitterness. He offered no syllable of hope to either party, no promise of support in consideration for any declaration of principle.

The speech of Millson which followed — of which one sentence has been quoted — was typical of the southern attitude. The North should return thanks for being wrong and ask pardon for being in the right. It should come to the South on bended knee, offering the olive branch of peace and balm for wounded feelings. The South should not demand a confession of wrong from the North; the North of its own prayerful volition should bow to receive absolution.

So direct a challenge could not be ignored, and Sherman arose to the attack or more properly the defense. He read a letter anent his subscription to the compendium which indicated that the signatures were received before the publication of the volume, and were to be used only in case of its appearance as an expurgated work. At best the letter was a poor weapon of defense in such a battle as now raged. At most it showed that Sherman agreed to recommend the work in case it appealed to some third party as deserving such commendation. We confess little sympathy for the embarrassment of one so careless in the use of his name. Sherman asserted with fervor that, whether his name had been attached to this troublesome document in good faith or otherwise, he had never seen either Helper's original book or its compendium. He insisted that there was no question likely to arouse sectional strife unless it be of southern brew. His statement carried neither persuasion nor conviction. And his assertion that the Republicans would prove their ability to conduct the proceedings of the House while carefully protecting the rights of all parties, was looked upon rather as a threat than a promise.

The impression left by Sherman upon the House, and the public as well, was distinctly unfavorable. His case, weak enough in the beginning, was now no whit stronger. Leake of Virginia immediately translated Sherman's remarks into different language, and tauntingly dubbed him the "abolition candidate." Badgered still further, Sherman, in his appeal for votes, at length declared that he was "opposed to any interference whatever by the people of the free states with the relations of master and slave in the slave states." Yet even this declaration was only an unskillful parrying of the real question which stalked as an avenging Nemesis about the aisles of the House, — Did Sherman retract his signature to the Helper compendium

The Mediocrity of the Chair

or did he ratify it? The slavocrats stood eagerly awaiting his avowal or disavowal, ready to either fight or taunt.

Sherman sought to drown the question and confuse the audience in a flood of unmeaning words. He had not learned that lesson ever so difficult for politicians to acquire, that the people are not to be deceived by the vague generalities of oratory into forgetting the question upon their lips. Sherman had clearly been guilty of the common folly of lending his name to matters of which he knew absolutely nothing. As it happened, this particular folly was to ripen into a tragedy. To disavow the signature would be to repudiate such leaders as Weed and Greeley, and cause a serious rupture in the Republican party. To endorse it was to invite defeat.

No political forecaster could foretell the probable length of the impending struggle. Crimination and recrimination, charges and countercharges, threats and vituperation were hurled about the hall in extravagant profusion. Keitt of South Carolina, denouncing the Republicans for the Helper book and the John Brown raid, declared with apoplectic wrath: "The South here asks nothing but its rights. I would have no more. But as one of its representatives I would shatter this republic from turret to foundation-stone before I would take one tithe less." Thaddeus Stevens did not spurn the challenge. "I do not blame gentlemen of the South," he cried, "for the language of intimidation, for using this threat of rending God's creation from the turret to the foundation. All this is right in them, for they have tried it fifty times, and fifty times they have found weak and recreant tremblers in the

North who have been affected by it, and who have acted from those intimidations."

Crawford of Georgia joined issue with Stevens in a heated debate; the din of conflict could be heard over the Capitol. The Clerk, unable to preserve even the semblance of order, stood helpless in his place; members rushed madly down to the area in front of the Speaker's desk, and cooler heads alone prevented a physical collision. Only the pervading dignity of their situation restrained the contestants. "A few more such scenes," declared Morris of Illinois, "and we shall hear the crack of the revolver and see the gleam of the brandished blade."

The southern members flaunted their challenge in the face of the North. They declared their willingness to assume whatever censure the public at large might care to visit upon them for the delay in organizing Congress. All the weapons offered by the rules of parliamentary law, they insisted, would be requisitioned in their determination to prevent the standard bearer of the Republican party and the principles which he represented from dominating this Congress.

Iverson, in the Senate, voiced the attitude of the southern extremists. "If I had control of the public sentiment," he declared, "the very moment that you elect John Sherman, thus giving to the South the example of insult as well as injury, I would walk every one of us out of the halls of this Capitol, and consult our constituents; and I would never again enter until I was bade to do so by those who had the right to control me. Sir, I would go further than that. I would counsel my constituents instantly to

The Mediocrity of the Chair   133

dissolve all political ties with a party and a people who thus trample on our rights."

On the second day of the session another ballot had been taken. Sherman received 107 votes — nine short of the number necessary for his election. Bocock, a Democrat from Virginia, received 88, Gilmer, an American from North Carolina, 22, with 14 votes scattering.

The assembly rapidly degenerated into a society of debate with the burden of speech carried by the southerners. Balloting was ignored in the mad riot of logic and vituperation. Each speech, and there were no interims, added fuel to the blazing fires of southern wrath. The Republicans were bitterly denounced, and their leaders were verbally drawn and quartered. Seward was a particular target for the shafts of southern venom. Lamar accused him of culpable connection with the John Brown raid. Reuben Davis of Mississippi denounced him as a traitor. Threats of dissolution were uttered as though the Union were a mere house of cards to be destroyed by a breath. Mingled applause and shouts of derision re-echoed through the legislative chamber.

Nor was Seward alone in his defensive position. Greeley, John Sherman, Helper, John Brown, were similarly denounced and stigmatized. The election of Sherman to the Speakership, declared Pryor with bitterness, would be the preface to "the ultimate catastrophe, the election of William H. Seward for President."

The Republicans willingly granted the slavocrats the monoply of speechmaking. Unhampered by the chastening rules of parliamentary law, the southerners freely gave way to the blazing emotions which burned within.

The flame of passion burned more fiercely as the fuel of oratory was piled on.

And as the Democrats gathered about the fire of their own harangues, they warmed with wrath and indignation. Eloquence of every type had been displayed — harsh, fierce, tender, pathetic, passionate, pleading, hortative, monitory, appealing, warning, comforting, commanding everything in the wide gamut of expression and emotion. These fires of oratory were banked at times but only for the vain effort of engineering new and impossible combinations for the organization of the House. Appeals were frequently made to the popular indignation at the riotous waste of public time. This availed nothing, for the sentiment of the different sections of the country was clearly represented by the attitude of the members of Congress.

The Republicans seized every possible opportunity to secure a ballot, and then voted consistently for Sherman. On some days it was impossible to procure even a single ballot.

A novel change of the seating arrangement of the House intensified the bitterness of the struggle. A resolution, adopted by the previous Congress, ordered that all desks be removed from the floor of the House and that the seats should be rearranged in such a manner as would bring them into close proximity. This it was felt would dispense with the practice, even then so prevalent, of writing letters and reading papers during the sessions, and would materially assist in the effort for legislative reform. Mental as well as physical presence would thus be secured and the members would perforce participate more generally in the discussions and proceedings of the House. The size of

The Mediocrity of the Chair 135

the chamber rendered it difficult for a man of ordinary voice to be heard from the farther side and this bred inattention and listlessness.

In compliance with the resolution benches were installed so that the House was drawn into a comparatively small compass. This new arrangement did not suit the majority of the House and the resolution was rescinded and the desks and chairs ordered to be replaced, although the return to the old order was not actually accomplished until after the close of this session.

During these days of turmoil and strife the members were thus in closer contact and were more easily impelled by the prevailing passions. As a result there was much shaking of fists under noses, much hurling of threats of personal violence and much assuming of insulting and defiant attitudes.

On one occasion Kellogg and Logan, both of Illinois, reached the threshold of personal encounter in an angry debate over charges against Senator Douglas. Again a bitter personal argument between Branch of North Carolina and Grow of Pennsylvania was the prelude to a challenge to mortal combat issued by the former member, but declined in dignified manner by the latter. Both were later subjected to arrest and put under bonds to preserve the peace. The climax came when Haskin, an anti-Lecompton Democrat from New York, was in the midst of a bitter verbal assault upon a colleague. A revolver accidentally fell from the breast pocket of Haskin and struck the floor with tragic resonance. Many members believing that he had purposely drawn the weapon from his pocket to do murder in the very Halls of Congress, were livid with rage. Several Democrats rushed forward "to be in at the killing." The more reckless bravely crowded about the principals while the timorous nervously cried out for the Sergeant-at-Arms and many were rudely jostled in their efforts to withdraw speedily from the scene of impending slaughter. The wildest confusion prevailed. The kind fortune, which has been said to watch especially over the United States, and imbeciles and inebriates, alone prevented a bloody contest. "The members on both sides are mostly armed with deadly weapons," wrote Senator Grimes of Iowa, "and it is said that the friends of each are armed in the galleries." "I believe," declared Senator Hammond, "every man in both houses is armed with a revolver — some with two and a bowie-knife."

The southern members were but following the custom, then so prevalent in that section of the country, of carrying weapons. Many of the northern members felt themselves forced to adopt the custom by the threats which were hurled at them from across the chamber. While they steadfastly declined the appeal to the code duello they took the precaution of being prepared for such assaults as might be forced upon them — the recent tragic death of Broderick of California had well taught them what little show northern inexperience with the duelling pistol would stand against the skilled hand and practiced eye of a southerner. Any considerable blood-letting in Washington would be the signal for graver tragedies throughout the country — and this danger exerted a restraining influence.

After two weeks of vain balloting which revealed only the same results, an effort was made by the Democrats to

The Mediocrity of the Chair 137

switch candidates in the hope of thus wooing success. December 19th, after the announcement of the result of the eleventh ballot, Bocock withdrew from the contest. The Democrats then united in support of Millson, whose speech early in the session had revealed him as a "moderate conservative," — whatever that doubtful term might mean. This move, intended as a bait for the Americans, failed signally and after a few more ballots the Democratic votes were again scattered over the field of the southern aspirants.

The country at large, like spectators grouped at the ringside, alternately applauded and denounced the legislative strife. The advent of Christmas brought no prospect of any agreement and gave no promise that the interests of the nation would receive any attention whatever from the new Congress. As if, by innuendo at least, to remind Congress of its paramount duty to the country whose interests were suffering from the legislative neglect, President Buchanan on the twenty-seventh day of December forwarded his annual message to the two Houses. Even then he appears to have felt that he had been remiss in so long delaying its transmission for the official publication in the *Congressional Globe* bears the date of December 19.

The Senate received it at once and thus its contents were communicated to the nation at large. But the House, following the precedent adopted by the thirty-fourth Congress, after a short debate ordered that it be received by the Secretary and laid upon the table. Thus, although the members read the message in the daily journals, the House remained in official ignorance of its contents for several weeks.

The House continued in session the entire week between Christmas and New Year's Day. The war of words and ballots continued without abatement. The Democrats changed their candidates with each successive ballot in the vain hope of effecting a "winning combination." On the twenty-fifth ballot, taken January 4th, 1860, Sherman lacked but three votes of election — but then as if rivaling the fate of Sisyphus the boulder again rolled down the hill. He came no nearer the coveted prize on any subsequent ballot. Frequently the plurality rule, adopted in previous contests, was suggested but was not forced to a vote as the Republicans realized that the Southerners would defeat such an attempt by filibustering.

On the 8th of January ten members — self-constituted representatives of the administration Democrats, anti-Lecompton Democrats, and Americans — met as a conference committee to devise some concerted plan of action for the conduct of the parties represented. The conference, understood not to be binding even upon the participants, was entirely unauthorized. They reached no agreement on a candidate to be supported by them; the most they could accomplish was to frame a compromise on the original Clark motion. Even this amounted to nothing, for, from the first, the three parties had been a unit in the belief that the election of a Republican was not desirable. No logical analysis of the situation, and the result of the conference thereon, is possible.

The Republicans, by skillful parliamentary tactics, had prevented a vote upon the Clark resolution. The success of the resolution was possible only by overcoming the determined opposition of the smaller parties to the election

The Mediocrity of the Chair   139

of an administration Democrat to the Speakership. On the 12th of January, Sherman, roused to action by the taunts of Houston of Alabama, opened the debate with the statement that he would gladly give a frank exposition of his views upon every sentence of Helper's book as soon as Clark's resolution was withdrawn; he viewed the resolution as a personal insult and so long as it was pending before the House his sense of honor would seal his lips. Clark, immediately disavowing any intention of attacking him as a man, declared that the political status of the question remained unchanged, and therefore he must decline to withdraw his motion. Again he demanded a vote on his motion and indignantly spurned the substitution of any "bastard conference resolution." The action of the conference committee, intended as a secret to be sprung upon the House in proper season, had leaked out and had been published in a New York paper, although each participant indignantly denied that he had been guilty of this serious breach of confidence.

Further discussion revealed the fact that the published report was but a minor detail of the conference program. The main feature was the union of the three parties interested against the adoption of the "plurality rule," in case an election by a majority was impossible.

This hinted at a startling conspiracy against the organization of the House. For it was apparent that the conferees, despite their diligent efforts, were unable to agree on any candidate for whom the three parties would unite.

On the 19th of January, Colfax forced from their unwilling lips the admission that they had agreed in writing to exhaust every parliamentary rule to prevent a plurality election; to this document, it was later proven, fifty-seven Democrats and one southern American had attached their signatures — a number sufficient to defeat the adoption of the plurality rule. Burnett boldly declared that they would persist in their course no matter how great the majority in favor of its adoption. If this were literally true these fifty-eight members had bound themselves absolutely to prevent the organization of the thirty-sixth Congress unless they were convinced that no Republican could be elected.

This exposure of the McQueen plot — for he was its author — aroused the North to the conviction that the southerners had been guilty of a revolutionary conspiracy. Although no northern Democrats had signed the instrument, they still persisted in their allegiance throughout the ensuing ballots.

This startling exposure materially assisted in the ultimate organization of the House, for it aroused the conservative Americans of the South and the more numerous conservatives of the North to a realizing sense of danger. The Douglas Democrats were furious, for its practical result would be the destruction of all hope of reconciling the two wings of the Democracy in the next national convention.

On all three ballots cast on the 26th of January the Americans voted solidly for William N. H. Smith of North Carolina and on the following day he was announced as the candidate of that party. Mallory, in reply to a query from Crawford, asserted the opinion that all the Americans could be induced to vote for this new nominee. Smith, a Democrat from Virginia, quoting a resolution adopted

The Mediocrity of the Chair 141

by his State calling upon its Representatives to support the cause of every "sound, conservative, national man," invoked the co-operation of all faithful Democrats in the election of his namesake of the American party.

A ballot was then taken. Before the vote was proclaimed Mallory arose to declare that, all of the Americans having voted for Smith, it remained for the Democrats to insure his election. There ensued a wild scramble on the part of the members of that party to withdraw their votes already cast and bestow them upon Smith. This required considerable jockeying and vigorous persuading. Smith would have been declared elected had the vote been announced immediately after the Democrats had finally switched their votes. But the infection thus started spread beyond the confines of the Democratic party and forthwith three Republicans from Pennsylvania, and one American from New Jersey, who had voted for Smith, transferred their votes, some to Corwin and the others to Pennington. As a result Smith received 112 votes, three short of the number necessary to secure his election.

While various specious reasons were advanced by these Republicans in explanation of their early votes for Smith, it was apparent that they were bestowing their suffrage upon a non-Republican only because they were convinced of the impossibility of his election. This ballot was the preliminary to a complete change of front by the Republicans. Tom Corwin had shouted something about the last blast of Gabriel's trumpet and insisted that that direful sound alone would terminate the Republican support of Sherman. Thaddeus Stevens, the inveterate foe of slavery, had sworn that the very crack of doom would find the

Republicans marshaled still about their original candidate. But, however they might feel, the large majority of the Republican Representatives felt little sympathy for "everything-or-nothing" brand of politics. They were not persuaded that they must stand or fall with their original candidate. The thirty-ninth ballot brought them face to face with this very proposition. This ballot taken on Friday, the 27th, immediately preceded an adjournment to the following Monday, the 30th of January.

It was now felt that Sherman's race was run. He had fought a good fight, but his personal candidacy must be sacrificed to the higher interest of party success. Amid all the bitter personalities exchanged during the seven weeks of impotent balloting he had borne himself with exceptional personal dignity. He had been denounced as an abolitionist by the Southern members who cared more for taunts than for logic; he had been more vilified in the slave States than even Seward, whom they religiously traduced. He had explained fairly that his name had been attached to the Helper compendium by proxy — though that could not wipe out his own liability to censure. He had made a dispassionate speech in which he had declared his allegiance to "the Union and the Constitution, with all the compromises under which it was formed and all the obligations which it imposes." He blamed the Harper's Ferry affair for the prevalent bitterness of feeling and declared that every northern member came to Washington sincerely regretful of that incident, and animated by the most kindly feelings towards the South. Poor John Brown had been sacrificed; but then as ever the stones that pelted the martyr to death formed the altar at which men were to worship in generations long after.

Greeley insisted that the Republicans should have demanded a vote on the plurality rule and, to accomplish this end, should have even held night sessions. This, he thought, would ultimately win the election for Sherman. But it could have had no other result than to exaggerate the already intense friction between the contesting parties. The fact that Sherman, though a man of undoubted integrity, lacked personal magnetism, the invaluable asset of political aspirants, furnished some explanation of the ultimate failure of his ambition to become Speaker.

When Congress again convened on the 30th of January, and before the House proceeded to another ballot, Sherman, in harmony with the action of a party caucus, formally withdrew his name, declaring that the possibility of the election of an administration Speaker was such a grave danger that he felt it incumbent upon him to withdraw in favor of one on whom the Republicans could center enough votes to win. The candidate then brought forward was Pennington, an ex-governor of New Jersey, now serving his first term as a member of the national House. In fact his only legislative experience had been gained in a single term as a member of the lower House of the New Jersey State Legislature, and he was utterly without national reputation. In this very lack of experience lay his chief and only recommendation.

The Democrats still held to Smith, and on the three ballots taken that day Pennington received 115 and Smith 113. On the 31st of January, Smith withdrew from the contest, convinced of the futility of his efforts.

McClernand received only 91 votes while Pennington, with 116 votes, still lacked one of the necessary majority. Still the new vote which had been added to his previous ballot was of vast significance. Henry Winter Davis, a southern American from Maryland, had joined the Republicans. The ultimate success of Pennington was now assured since Briggs of New York had promised on the 30th of January to switch his vote to Pennington when that would accomplish his election.

On the first day of February, and on the forty-fourth ballot, Pennington received 117 votes, exactly the number requisite to his election.

For eight weeks the battle had raged; the rival armies, constantly prepared for surprises, attacks, counter attacks, and ambushes, had literally slept upon their arms. The contest lacked only three days of running the course of that contested election when Banks was finally raised to the Speakership. The bitterness and intensity of feeling are indicated by the fact that in this struggle only forty-four ballots had been taken, while in 1855-56 one hundred and thirty-three had been cast. But the good humor and spirit of friendly rivalry which marked the contest of the thirty-fourth Congress were superseded by asperity and vindictiveness. Where bribery had been hinted at as the solution of that other contest, now all knew that the present struggle for political existence could not be dominated by personal greed. Where formerly threats of secession had been met with mirthful derision they were now applauded with enthusiasm or greeted with hisses. The cards read poorly for the prospect of a peaceful solution of the country's dangers; the excitement and bitterness in the House

The Mediocrity of the Chair 145

were the national sentiments translated to a smaller field. Non-intercourse, commercial and social, was openly advocated in the South as the "proper prescription for northern fanaticism and political villainy." Indeed, the more affluent northerners, accustomed to avoid the chill blast of northern winters by sojourns in the South, were earnestly advised to deviate from their usual custom and find their solace in Europe or the West Indies that they might escape the insults likely to be visited upon them by the inflamed Southerners.

The manner of victory was a complete surprise to the Republicans. They had pinned their hopes of success upon the possible adoption of the plurality rule, whereas Pennington had been elected by an absolute majority. Yet Clark had succeeded in the avowed purpose of his resolution — had rendered impossible the election of a signer of the Helper compendium.

Pennington now stood with Clay as the only two men in our national history who have been elected Speaker upon their first entrance into Congress. Opposite reasons, however, had conspired to produce the same results. The one had been elected because of his lack of policy, the other because of his very strength of opinion. As Clay stands forth as the greatest of our Speakers, so Pennington by contrast won Cox's appellation "as the most thoroughly unaccomplished man in parliamentary law who ever wielded the gavel." Withal he was respectfully treated and assisted in the discharge of his duties by his more able colleagues on the floor.

Pennington possessed certain traits which commend him to the student of our legislative history. Able as a lawyer, he combined a splendid presence with great talent for humor; was possessed of undoubted integrity and ever manifested scrupulous impartiality — although these traits were tempered by a certain dull mediocrity of intellect. His committee appointments, in which he had the grace to accept the counsel of older heads, were just and able. A fair presiding officer, he suffered from a painful ignorance of parliamentary procedure and of the usual practice of the House. Either through ignorance or personal conviction he did not bend his office to the advancement of partisan ends. He took no advantage of the political opportunities which his position afforded him, and was at times over zealous in his determination not to be, by any possibility, influenced by corrupt cliques which continually sought his ear. He was by the very combination of ignorance, inexperience, and personality merely a moderator. A forceful man in his position would have blundered into strength, a less honest one would have become the willing and easy tool of political corruption. He contributed no strength to the office, he wrote no syllable of power into its story.

For nearly half a century now, each Congress had raised the poisoned chalice of slavery to its lips and staggered under the numbing potion. As far back as 1820 they believed that in the Missouri Compromise they had at last found a Nepenthe for their troubles. But all slavery legislation was as permanent as though it had been stamped on the running stream.

Practical politicians seem never to comprehend the significance of momentum — of that political momentum which instead of remaining constant, rationally increases.

The Mediocrity of the Chair 147

They always legislate on the theory that any force which they set in motion will cease where they will it. They seek a certain end but never grasp the more remote and collateral results of their action.

When railways were first introduced in Spain peasants standing on the track were frequently run over, and the engineers were always blamed, simply because these ignorant country people had no conception of the momentum of a large object moving at a high speed. The analogy between these benighted peasants and politicians of expediency is clear. An apt illustration of that same policy of legislation that inspired Congress in this half century is found in the pauper legislation of England. When steps were contemplated to encourage the production of children by offering financial assistance to the poor — when Pitt declared "Let us make relief in cases where there are a number of children a matter of right and honor instead of a ground for opprobrium and contempt," it was not anticipated, nor intended that the poor-rates would be quadrupled in a half century; that prostitutes with a score of illegitimate children would be chosen over virtuous women as wives, and that thousands of taxpayers would be degraded into the ranks of pauperism. Neither was it anticipated in the United States that the slave issue would resolve itself into a final combat of lead and steel. The North believed the institution to be intrinsically wrong; the South believed it to be right — they could not see that it was as some deadly virus lowering the moral health of the whole body politic.

While the South was sincere in its defense the North was too anxious to conciliate and compromise. Webster, Clay, and Douglas for weary years palliated the wrong and never once faced the real question on its merit. Which suggests whether it is not better to be conscientiously wrong than supinely right.

But the disease became chronic — and it is always easier to cure the acute than the chronic ailments. You rally all the strength of body and spirit to fight the unexpected attack; but you lose heart when it comes on insidiously sapping your energies, turning cheeks of roses to parchment yellow, before you realize that it has you in its clutches.

CHAPTER V

GROW AND COLFAX DOMINATED BY THADDEUS STEVENS

ON the 4th day of July, 1861, Congress assembled in extra session. Through the self-effacement of the southern States the Senate and House of Representatives were overwhelmingly Republican.

Hannibal Hamlin presided over the Senate as the regularly elected Vice-President. In the House the leading candidates for the Speakership were Galusha A. Grow of Pennsylvania and Francis P. Blair, Jr., of Missouri. The Democratic minority, fearing the brand of disloyalty, deemed it inexpedient to hold a caucus and therefore declined to present a party candidate. On the call of the roll Mr. Grow received 71 votes, Mr. Blair 40, with 48, principally Democratic, scattering. Before the announcement of the ballot many of Blair's supporters changed their votes and the official result gave Grow 99 votes — a majority of all the members.

Grow had entered the House of Representatives in 1851, and was then the youngest member of that body. From the Wilmot district in the northern portion of Pennsylvania he seemed the incarnation of abolitionism. Born in Windham County, Connecticut, a community which had given deep of its blood and treasure to our Revolution, he was rich in the heritage of patriotism and sturdy, freedom-loving ancestry. In 1857 he had been the Republican candidate for the Speakership, and in 1859, on the first ballot he divided the votes of his party with the less magnetic Sherman. With Sherman now in the Senate, and because of his strong anti-slavery sentiments and his admitted aptitude for the duties of that position, Grow was chosen Speaker. In 1863 Grow retired for nearly a third of a century from the field of national politics; in 1894, after thirty years, he was elected member-at-large from Pennsylvania and served for a period of ten years amid old surroundings but new companions where his reminiscences of bygone days rendered him a popular as well as an efficient member. In the spring of 1907 his long and eventful career terminated in death. Connected with a glorious past, decorated with the badges of service, he remained to the present generation like some noble genius transmitted from a former age to watch over the course of a later century. He seemed the counterpart of that signer of the Declaration of Independence, the revered Charles Carroll of Carrollton, who appeared to speak to children of the third generation with the voice of Washington, Hamilton, Jefferson, and the other departed heroes of that era.

As Speaker, Grow gave rich fulfillment of the promise of talent and ability. Firm of decision and keen of discernment he seldom erred; with the greatest of all American parliamentary leaders, Thaddeus Stevens, to guide the debate on the floor, the House seemed always responsive to his will.

Grow himself was the first Speaker to descend from the rostrum and take part in the discussion on the floor even when the House was not in Committee of the Whole. In

Grow and Colfax

this manner he led the fight for the Homestead Bill whose paternity he proudly boasted. Holman in an admirable and terse characterization declared, "No man who was ever Speaker more largely or more beneficially influenced the general course of our legislation. He was a born leader among men."

Thus Grow, active, alert, of inspiring presence and great natural endowments, was the first Speaker of the new era — that of legislative aggrandizement. It was a "War Congress" with a helpless Democratic minority constantly menaced by the dread specter of treason.

In the philosophy of politics there has been evolved a maxim — national perils produce great men. Genius at any rate seems subject to the general economic law of supply and demand. The quantity may be diminished by restrictions or multiplied by bounties. Possibly this can be transposed into the assertion that great men have lived and died unheralded and unsung because of lack of opportunity. Emerson says "times of terror are generally times of heroism."

Our Civil War has produced its heroes of the battlefield, Grant, Sherman, Sheridan, Lee, Jackson, and Johnston, but it produced as well its stirring leaders of legislative combat. Their glory may have been less picturesque, less entrancing, but it is equally enduring. Of all these legislative heroes one man stands pre-eminent — Thaddeus Stevens.

If we are to know, even vaguely, the history of the Civil War, and the advance in the power of the Speaker during the eighth decade of our federal government we must picture at least roughly this most unique character of our history. Three great parliamentary leaders demand the attention of the student of American politics — Clay, Douglas, and Stevens. Only one of these ever became Speaker of the body which he dominated — ever received the name as well as the substance of authority. Thus indeed another political maxim — greatness is not a matter of titles. True this volume concerns alone the Speakers of Congress, but when those Speakers have become manikins may we not with propriety study the mechanism behind the scenes and see what manner of man holds sway?

In the House of Representatives there never was before nor since such an exercise of individual power as that of Thaddeus Stevens. The Republicans were driven in leash by one man; if any one more daring than others broke from control he was politically blacklisted; he always crawled back, humbly presenting an apology which was accepted with grim epigrammatic humor by this wondrous Jehu and then his wrath was suspended as some Damocletian sword over the head of the luckless offender.

What made possible such an amazing mastery over the unwilling minds of the able men whom Stevens dominated? First of all an indomitable will — he never flinched from what he held to be his duty, was never cowed, never retreated. Clay too had such a will, but with it he possessed the art of persuasion and the attribute of personal attraction to an extent unequaled probably by any leader in our history. So great was this magnetism that those who, from principle, openly defied him secretly cultivated his friendship. His friends counted no question of right or wrong if it involved the leadership of their idol. Yet this marvelous man never possessed anything like the power in the House of Representatives that was daily wielded for seven years by this most unpopular man on the floor, Thaddeus Stevens.

Again Stevens manifested a perfect contempt for either applause or censure. He never read the thermometer of public sentiment. With grim tolerance he battled for principle careless of every incidental consequence. He had the undoubted virtue of thinking more of his subject than of himself and no public man was ever less of an egotist.

He was governed by principle — it is difficult to classify it accurately; it may have been moral principle, or the principle of consistency, or even the principle of expediency. At any rate, his attention was riveted upon the slavery question as the great and only issue of the day and to the solution of this problem he applied his unequaled ardor and enthusiasm. Integrity of action is possible even in the furtherance of vicious schemes by unprincipled men. His personality was completely engulfed in his convictions; as to their nature no man need ever have had the slightest doubt. His love of power was the master passion of his soul. He was a Cæsar — grim and imperious. During his ante-bellum service in Congress Stevens achieved no great prominence. He was regarded simply as a diligent member in the committee rooms. But during the war he came into his own and during that period of usefulness his pre-eminence continued unquestioned. It reached its highest point in the second year of the contest. He was essentially the type of man the crisis called for — men who did not hesitate, who did not stop to calculate the material chances of the struggle, but who were controlled by and through moral faith.

Stevens at no time in his career manifested any constructive ability; but he was ever a ready and energetic advocate of measures conceived by others. The fertility of his mind was not so much in ideas as in expedients.

That his relations with Lincoln were at all friendly was due entirely to the President, who always sought to appease the party leaders lest the great cause suffer. When the stubbornness of Johnson had succeeded the conciliation of Lincoln the breach came between the Capitol and the White House. Lincoln's patience and his careful forbearance irritated Stevens, who conceived a low estimate of the President's ability. He was hostile to the renomination of Lincoln at the end of his first term.

Yet Stevens had urged Lincoln to the issuance of the Emancipation Proclamation and championed every war measure with an unflinching tenacity, with consummate mastery of parliamentary tactics and with the remarkable power of his sulphurous philippics. If at times his political methods were unscrupulous, to him the end justified any obliquity of means.

His limitations became at once apparent in the era of reconstruction. He revealed a pitiful ignorance of the basic principles of political economy in his famous bill which sought to make greenbacks equal in value to gold, by inflicting a penalty upon the trading of gold at a premium. His vindictiveness, his obstinacy, and his partisanship combined to make his power a curse during the years of reconstruction. His plan of mild confiscation by which he proposed to liquidate the national debt and provide farms for the negroes from the southern estates revealed his mental limitations. He lacked the power of imagination so essential to the success of the constructive statesman. He lacked the ability to place himself in the position of those for whom, or rather against whom, he sought to legislate. He believed it his religious duty to fasten the supremacy of the Republican party upon the country with such chains that they could not be broken for an indefinite period. He chafed under the conservatism of Lincoln's reconstructive policies. Because of the radical nature of his reconstructive theories and the frequency of their reiteration, he was regarded by many as a fanatic; this estimate was confirmed, no doubt, by his bodily deformity as well as his lack of amiability and his cruel bluntness of expression. At least he was an insoluble enigma — a grotesque assemblage of incongruous qualities.

His position, too, as chairman of the Committee on Reconstruction endowed him with a degree of control over legislation which his failing health, exaggerated by his increasing mental defects, translated into a national misfortune. For his reprehensible conduct in the impeachment procedure the Republican party was far more censurable than he.

In those last years his hatred of Johnson became his cloud by day, his pillar of fire by night. In the National Union Convention of 1864, he had opposed the nomination of Johnson for Vice-President. He said to A. K. McClure, "Can't you find a candidate for Vice-President in the United States without going down to one of those damned rebel provinces to pick one up?"

Stevens could find no forgiveness for the men who opposed him. But in Johnson he found an enemy who by temperament was likely to become a Nemesis. Stevens' wasp-like satire and coarse manners greatly embittered the conflict which, except for his resentful and angry leadership, would never have reached its tragic culmination.

Stevens' hatred of Johnson was so generous in its proportions as to embrace all who were lukewarm in their antipathy to the President. On this theory Stevens at first supported Salmon P. Chase for the presidential nomination in 1868; the Chief Justice of the Supreme Court was far more radical in his anti-southern prejudices than the commander of the army. Later Grant won his support after conforming to the creed of hostility to Johnson.

During these years Stevens' failing physical strength seemed to be sustained only by the tonic of hate. Seated in a chair he was carried from his home to the House by two Irish attendants that he might defeat Sherman's bill to restore the States lately in rebellion to their original antebellum status. In summing up the evidence at the impeachment trial of Johnson, in April, 1868, Stevens started to read his speech — even this a concession to his failing physical vitality. But the iron will at last had met its master; he had proceeded but a few minutes when, too weak to stand, he secured permission to continue while seated. Thus he continued for half an hour; when his voice became too feeble for utterance he handed his paper to Butler, who finished it. On account of his increasing infirmities the management of the trial fell largely to Butler; perhaps this was a national blessing, for

Stevens in his prime would probably have carried it to success.

Blaine correctly rated Clay, Douglas, and Stevens as the three most distinguished parliamentary leaders of this country. Each alike possessed to a wonderful degree the mystic power of command. "In the give and take of daily discussion, in the art of controlling and consolidating reluctant and refractory followers, in the skill to overcome all forms of opposition and to meet with competency and courage the varying phases of unlooked-for assault or unexpected defection it would be difficult to rank with these a fourth name in all our congressional history."

But Clay was the perihelion of compromise, Douglas and Stevens, men of war. Clay fathered the Missouri Compromise, which meant peace; Douglas secured its repeal, which inspired war; Stevens in his Reconstruction Acts reopened the wounds and poured in the vinegar of retribution. Such was this Bismarck of blood and iron, this Gambetta of flaming oratory, this Mirabeau of integrity and vengeance, whose career was at once a national blessing and a public curse.

December 7th, 1863, the thirty-eighth Congress convened at Washington. On the first ballot Schuyler Colfax of Indiana was elected Speaker — Galusha Grow having been retired to private life — by a vote of 101 out of 181. Samuel S. Cox of Ohio received 42 votes, the largest number given to any member of the opposition. However, on purely war issues, the administration commanded a greater strength than these figures suggest.

A young newspaper man of South Bend, Indiana, Colfax had organized a village debating club and framed a moot state legislature of which each member represented some imaginary district. Here he mastered the alphabet of parliamentary law and procedure. Elected to Congress for the first time in 1855 he served continuously in the House of Representatives until 1869, when he became Vice-President under Grant.

As a Speaker he ranks with Clay for enduring personal popularity. But his popularity was that of weakness. He belonged to the class which biologists term invertebrates. He led a gelatinous political existence. Men of firm convictions and strong character never attain that peculiar type of general popularity bestowed upon the colorless man who lacks decision and strength. While the latter may never have enemies who pursue, yet he seldom has friends who follow. The great men of history have always been storm centers. Colfax's name always suggests to the historian the mellow warmth of a summer afternoon. Yet his very strength lay in his weakness. He was a man of slender and undermedium height, with brown hair, a well-chiselled brow, soft blue eyes, a frank face with a mouth denoting kindness of heart and a certain degree of firmness but lacking strong lines of character.

Colfax possessed neither will nor mind of his own. Thaddeus Stevens furnished him with these mental attributes. The fact that Stevens permitted him to remain Speaker for six years furnishes the best index of his character. He was the *alter ego*.

Colfax possessed a certain celerity of thought which made him something of a mental gymnast; he had a talent for the rapid administration of details coupled with an authoritative manner while in the Chair which enabled him to curb

Grow and Colfax 159

the House even in its most turbulent moods; and to preside over that body with distinctive grace and ease. This in itself was a talent, for, with the probable exception of the Wall Street Exchange, the Chicago Wheat Pit, and the Donnybrook Fair, our House of Representatives is quite the most boisterous body in the world.

Colfax was a man of great tact, eminently proficient in the knowledge of human nature. His personal popularity extended even to the ranks of his political opponents. He lacked entirely the self-assumed importance so common among great men. He had a certain familiarity of manner which appealed to the people. It is said that more children were named for Colfax than for any public man since Clay.

Colfax's Speakership was essentially political in its character. He assumed the position of the leader of the House at the very opening and sought to dictate the policy to be pursued by his party. In his speeches he formulated and published their policies. He seemed to announce the passage of a partisan measure as if it were some personal triumph rather than the mere official statement of a ballot.

Colfax took a prominent part in the debates of the House. As Grow before him had done, he frequently descended from the Chair to take a hand in the proceedings even when the House was not in Committee of the Whole. In April, 1864, Long of Ohio, the House being in committee, made a speech advocating the recognition of the Confederate States. On the ensuing day, April 9th, Colfax left the Chair and from the floor moved the expulsion of Long. In the course of his speech he explained his attitude. "I recognize that there is a double duty incumbent upon me; first to the House of Representatives, to administer the duties of the Chair and the rules of the House faithfully and impartially to the best of my ability and judgment. But I feel that I owe still another duty to the people of the ninth congressional district of Indiana, who sent me here as their Representative to speak and act and vote in their stead. It is in conforming with this latter duty to those who cannot speak here for themselves, and who, I believe, would indorse the sentiment of this resolution, that I have felt it my duty to rise in my place as a member of Congress from the State of Indiana and offer this resolution."

In the ensuing debate of the resolution, while there was no objection raised to the Speaker taking a hand in the proceedings of the House, yet Colfax was severely criticised for descending from the Chair to move the expulsion of a member.

There are certain superficial points of resemblance between the Speakership of Colfax and that of Clay. Both declared their intention of retaining the rights of membership while exercising the duties of the Chair. They possessed alike certain personal traits. Both were exceedingly tactful, genial, and pleasant in their manner while never yielding their point; both practiced a conventional impartiality; both were immensely popular with the House — the one probably from merit, the other from lack of it; to both it was the prelude of greater honors. Clay became peace commissioner and later Secretary of State, while Colfax was elected Vice-President.

During his second term Colfax received a vote of thanks at the end of the first session (1866), an unusual tribute.

The legislative storms of the year had been severe and this tribute was paid to his manner of guiding the congressional life-boat. The resolution of thanks of 1869 was more elaborate than customary; it praised him for his "skill in parliamentary law, dignity, and impartiality and promptness." He left the Chair with the record that in six years of service no decision had ever been reversed.

But Colfax, unlike Clay, was a man of mediocre ability. He leaned on others and without their advice and assistance must have failed miserably. His nature impelled him to seek the popular side — to veer with the wind. From every difficulty he emerged with that inimitable smile — in the later days of political nonentity they dubbed him "Smiler" Colfax. His ideas of parliamentary law were so crude that he employed a parliamentary tutor to solve for him the labyrinth of its perplexities. The strength of Colfax's Speakership was derived not from the nominal leader but from the stern support and unflinching power of Thaddeus Stevens.

In the parliamentary organization of the House upon the opening of the thirty-ninth Congress, the Clerk — at the dictate of the Republican caucus, which meant Stevens — had included in the roll of members-elect only those from the loyal States, ignoring the Representatives from the States which had been reconstructed either by Lincoln or Johnson. On the opening day (December 4, 1865), in accordance with law the Clerk read the roll; inspired by Stevens, then in the zenith of his autocracy, the Clerk ignored the heated protest of a member-elect from Tennessee and refused to entertain motions made by two Democrats requiring him to place upon the rolls the members-elect from Tennessee. Stevens promptly got out the black snake whip and these objections were defeated; all attempts at debate were prohibited by points of order, a motion to proceed to the election of a Speaker, and a demand thereon of the previous question. The Republican majority of two-thirds stood as a solid phalanx with Stevens, and Colfax was again elected to the Chair, this time by a vote of 139 to 36 cast for James Brooks of New York.

Colfax in his inaugural address departed from the usual custom of merely returning thanks for his election and, assuring the House of his impartiality and good intentions, launched forth into a political address on the attitude of the Republican party toward the South — an accurate reflection of Stevens' idea of "thorough reconstruction." His text was taken from the perversity of the "rebels" in electing Democratic members in the already reconstructed States.

Stevens immediately offered a resolution for the appointment of a "joint committee of fifteen members — nine from the House and six from the Senate — who shall inquire into the condition of the States which formed the so-called Confederate States of America and report whether they, or any of them, are entitled to be represented in either House of Congress, with leave to report at any time by bill or otherwise," that "until such report shall have been made and finally acted upon by Congress, no member shall be received into either House from any of the so-called Confederate States," and that "all papers relating to the representation of the said States shall be referred to the said committee without debate."

The Democrats offered valiant objection and Stevens

Grow and Colfax 163

moved a suspension of the rules to enable him to introduce the resolution, in which he was supported by the required two-thirds, like driven cattle; then he demanded the previous question. The suggestion of a Democrat that the measure go over until the receipt of the President's message was greeted with the familiar sneer, and the resolution was put through to the music of the whip. Stevens was named as chairman of the House Committee, and Fessenden of the Senate Committee. The Senator became chairman of the joint committee.

In 1866 another "salary grab" was passed. However it produced very little censure despite the fact that it was retroactive, that it was fraudulently coupled with another measure, and that it was railroaded through Congress with suspicious and indecent haste. This salary act increased the annual pay of congressmen to five thousand dollars but reduced the mileage to the more reasonable rate of twenty cents a mile by the nearest route.

The honorable members of that Congress simulated courage, and for once the two hostile parties joined hands in ingeniously dividing the responsibility for the act that neither might be held responsible — a very wholesome and salutary precaution. They concluded, after casting the political horoscope, that the increase would soon be forgotten in the fierce heat of sectional and reconstruction passion, or, at most, that it would be catalogued with the ordinary public and political scandals occasionally to be visited upon the masses. The leaders judged the public pulse correctly, for so indifferent were the people, despite the lurid maledictions of a hostile press, that the managers of the "foray" were later heard to boast that only one member had scorned to pocket his share and that his over-sensitive conscience was rewarded by a defeat for re-election.

The thirty-ninth Congress was a legislative body of marked political ability; but its members were far too partisan to give scientific study to the problem of "the combination in one social organization of two races more widely different from one another than all the other races." They seemed ignorant of the aphorism that color will not yield to legislation and that mental attitude is not subject to resolution or enactment. Yet this same body presents an interesting study of the conservative and radical in politics. The first session apparently listened to reason, the second was ruled by passion. In the first session Trumbull and Fessenden dominated — measures were carefully drawn and thoroughly debated. In the second Stevens held the reins and lashed on the steeds. Bills were enacted first and considered afterwards. Trumbull and Fessenden were forced into the ranks by this new commander whose radicalism and bitterness grew with each rising sun. Johnson by his headstrong obstinacy and intemperate behavior; Stevens by his vengefulness and parliamentary autocracy; and Sumner by his perverted benevolence, all combined to enhance the southern distress. It is difficult to estimate accurately whether the South suffered more, mentally and physically, from the years of war or the years of reconstruction.

The various Reconstruction Acts of this session literally ground the South between the upper and nether mill-stones; and the "Tenure of Office" Bill reduced the President to a state of vassalage without precedent in our national history and suggestive of Charles I and Louis XVI.

Enfranchised ignorance was enthroned in the late Confederacy while disfranchised intelligence was reduced to political and social serfdom.

Upon the assembling of the fortieth Congress, in 1867, a peculiar legislative condition was apparent. As soon as the Clerk of the House had completed the roll-call and announced that a quorum had answered to their names, Brooks of New York arose and directed attention to the fact that there were seventeen States without representation. Ten of these were of the Confederacy and were not called at all; the remaining seven — Connecticut, Rhode Island, New Hampshire, Kentucky, Tennessee, Nebraska, and California — had presented no credentials of members, since under their various laws Representatives to the fortieth Congress had not yet been elected.

The absentees numbered eighty members. Brooks in behalf of his political colleagues presented to the House a formal protest signed by every Democratic member present, declaring "against any and every action tending to the organization of this House until the absent States be more fully represented." He requested that this protest of the minority be entered upon the journal. Under the advice of Stevens the Clerk refused to receive or submit the paper for consideration, and the House at once proceeded to the election of its Speaker. Again Colfax was elected, receiving 127 votes as against 30 cast for Samuel S. Marshall, a conservative Democrat from Illinois. And again Colfax held forth in a political strain in his speech of acceptance and denounced "unrepentant treason " and declared anew for "bloody shirt " reconstruction.

On the 3d of March, 1869, Colfax resigned the

Speakership preparatory to his inauguration as Vice-President on the ensuing day. His successor for the remaining hours of the session was Theodore M. Pomeroy of New York. On the fourth day of March, 1869, Colfax had reached the pinnacle of his career. One of the most popular men in the country, of unquestioned personal morality, he had added strength to the Grant presidential ticket. But his fall like that of Lucifer was tragic and bereft of hope. In December, 1867, and later during his Speakership, certain bills were introduced in Congress to regulate the rates of transportation and otherwise control the Union Pacific railroad, then in process of construction under the aid of government grants. Oakes Ames, a member from Massachusetts, undertook the distribution among members of Congress of a large amount of stock in the Credit Mobilier Company, the construction company of the Union Pacific. His purpose was clearly manifest in his contemporary letters which were later exposed in the congressional investigation — to protect the road from inquisitorial and critical legislation. By January 30, 1868, he had completed his financial operations; in a private letter he wrote: "I don't fear any investigation here — I have used this (the Credit Mobilier shares) where it will produce most good to us, I think." Ugly charges, ingeniously denied, were preferred during the presidential campaign, the facts were suppressed and the public wantonly deceived. When the congressional investigation of 1872 was inaugurated the same miserable stupidity prevailed and again concealment and prevarication were attempted. But the disclosures could not be smothered and political disgrace was the natural result.

Colfax as Speaker of the House at the time had agreed to take twenty shares of the Credit Mobilier stock. Before the Poland investigating committee he admitted contracting for the stock but declared that on more mature consideration he had rescinded the agreement. He swore under oath that he had never received any dividends. But the testimony and books of Ames showed a payment of one thousand two hundred dollars to Colfax as a dividend on Credit Mobilier stock held in Colfax's name. Colfax made a poor witness in his own behalf and floundered pitifully in his efforts to explain a bank deposit of one thousand two hundred dollars made on the date in question.

In the course of his testimony it was revealed that George Nesbitt of New York had donated four thousand dollars as a contribution to his personal expenses for the vice-presidential campaign of 1868. The evidence further disclosed the startling fact that Nesbitt was a large stationer and, while Colfax was chairman of the Post Office Committee of the House, had obtained large contracts for government envelopes. While a frank confession might have saved Colfax, as it did others, his miserable prevarications and subterfuges brought him execration. On the 4th of March, 1873, he left Washington humbled and disgraced. Later he was asked by Grant to become Secretary of State in case Fish persisted in giving up that portfolio; and after Greeley's death he was offered the editorship of the *New York Tribune*, which he declined. From a presidential possibility he became a popular lecturer without influence or voice in the councils of the nation. The Schuyler Colfax of the sixties as Speaker, became the "Smiler" Colfax of the seventies and eighties and in the cartoons. In 1885, at the age of sixty-two, he died in obscurity.

The American public makes heroes of its great men but it has no mercy for its shattered idols.

CHAPTER VI

JAMES G. BLAINE

ON the 4th of March, 1869, James G. Blaine of Maine was elected Speaker. As Clay had been the incarnation of the American spirit in the first half of the nineteenth century, so in the second half Blaine came to be viewed as the first and typical American. A newspaper editor, he was elected to the legislature of Maine in 1858, and from then to the day of his death, almost without exception, held public office. In the legislature his fearless, persistent, and aggressive manner coupled with native ability gave him high rank, and after two years he was elected Speaker. Never had a man seemed naturally better endowed for the position. He showed not alone a knowledge of parliamentary rules and an ability to apply them fearlessly and quickly, but he revealed a thorough comprehension of their basic theories.

He became chairman of the Maine State Committee and by his marvelous genius for organization brought uninterrupted successes to the Republican party. A surprising patience of detail left nothing undone. His organization spread through every county, township, city, street, and block — his finger was at all times on the popular pulse and he quickly responded to its political variations. This was the secret of his wonderful political dictatorship. He had a genius for politics as clever as that of Talleyrand for diplomacy or Napoleon for war. He understood the science of politics; to him the political world was a machine to be operated, not a mere vague, speculative theory. He mastered its principles, its laws, its interdependence of parts. He also possessed to a remarkable degree that talent which enables a man to recognize every person he meets, whether he knows him or not; and to inquire, with perfect composure, after wives and children, no longer in existence.

Then Blaine entered the national councils where his peculiar attributes were quickly recognized. He was an able man who acquired power in a Congress of mediocrity. Stevens was now dead, Colfax was Vice-President; Butler was there with his ability, the ability of a political buccaneer.

Blaine's career of leadership in Congress fell in years when there was little required beyond party management. The war was completed; reconstruction had been set well under way by the demoniacal Stevens and the period of political stagnation was on, in which there was nothing of moment — except to keep the Republicans in power and the Democrats out. To this task Blaine set himself with customary vigor, consummate ingenuity, and that facile lack of scruple which did so much to mould his peculiar reputation.

One needs to know something of the personnel of Congress during these six years of Blaine's control, which culminated in the election of Hayes and the retirement of Grant. In the first place the moral tone was low, not alone in Congress but in all public offices. The people were still intoxicated with patriotism. In the North the question seemed to be not a man's fitness for congressional service, but whether he had shouldered a musket in time of war and how loudly he could rant of patriotism and how bitterly he could assail the South.

From the South came a motley crew, "carpet-baggers" so called. One example will suffice to characterize them. John T. DeWeese, a member from North Carolina, sold a cadetship to the naval academy for five hundred dollars and was "found out." To avoid expulsion he resigned. Even his confrères, his fellow carpet-baggers, bitterly denounced him, not because of his dishonesty; not even because of his clumsiness in being detected; but because he had hurt the market. They had been charging, and receiving too, from one to two thousand dollars for each cadetship. He had cut the rate.

The floor leader of the Republicans during these sessions was Ben Butler of Massachusetts. He was worthy of his hire. To speak charitably he was a spoilsman of the lowest order.

The President himself was a failure; but for that the Republican party was largely to blame. They forced him into a position for which he was totally unfitted by temperament and training. He was ignorant of politics and a poor judge of men. He made miserable appointments; diplomatic and cabinet offices were treated as political spoils to be apportioned to the faithful. General Robert Schenck, returning from a trip to Europe, saw at Paris a woman's hat so beautiful that he purchased it as a present for Mrs. Grant. The President named Schenck as minister to the Court of St. James. Gould, "Jim" Fiske, and their type of corrupt financiers seemed to stand in high favor — and brought him merited criticism. In financial matters and questions that called for an exercise of worldly wisdom he was unsophisticated. There is every reason to believe that he viewed the Presidency as a reward for his part in the Civil War and it is said that he felt the reward a mean one. He is declared to have stated significantly the exact rewards, financial and political, which England had heaped on the Duke of Wellington. At the end of his first term it was tragically said: "The wreck of General Grant's fame is a national misfortune."

A carnival of corruption seemed to dominate the government service. The Credit Mobilier scandal ruined Colfax. Nor was he alone; Blaine, Dawes, Henry Wilson, Garfield, Scofield, Bingham, Kelley, Ames — were involved. What had been whispered in the ear was now proclaimed from the housetops. Public suspicions could not be allayed and more open rumors went unanswered. When Congress assembled in 1872, Blaine, as Speaker, called "Sunset" Cox to the Chair and from the floor moved a committee of investigation. Cox appointed Luke P. Poland of Vermont, Banks of Massachusetts, Geo. W. McCrary of Iowa, Wm. E. Niblack of Indiana, and Wm. M. Merrick of Maryland as the committee. Its personnel was unquestionable. The committee after hearing the evidence reported Februrary 18, 1873, that, with three exceptions, the accused members were free from "any incorrect motive or purpose" and expressed the moral conviction that the accused members had no idea that they have been "guilty of any impropriety or even indelicacy in becoming purchasers of stock."

Ames was declared guilty of selling Credit Mobilier shares to members of Congress at a discount, for the purpose of influencing their votes in matters affecting the

Union Pacific railroad, and his explusion was recommended. James Brooks of New York was also declared guilty of corruption, both as a member of Congress and as a government director of the railroad and his expulsion was recommended. Both of these resolutions were changed by the House to votes of censure — an act deserving severe condemnation. Corruption in public office should be visited with the extreme penalty — party considerations, political expediency, and personal friendship should not be factors in the equation.

The vote of censure was passed February 27th, 1873, Brooks died April 30th and Ames May 8th of the same year — in their graves to find physical immunity.

A senatorial investigating committee in February, 1873, declared Senator James W. Patterson of New Hampshire guilty of "corruption and false swearing" and recommended that he be expelled from the Senate. Five days only remained of the session and as Patterson's term expired on March 4th the resolution was permitted to die.

Through all these charges of prevarication and disgrace one man came unscathed. His conduct at that time and his subsequent career furnish a striking testimonial to the fariness of the American people and their appreciation of honesty and truth. Wm. B. Allison of Iowa had received ten shares of the Credit Mobilier stock from Ames. In his testimony, without any attempt at evasion, he frankly explained the whole transaction — his acceptance of the shares, his dividends, and his return of the stock when he realized the sinister questions involved. His frankness and fearlessness stand as a monument to future generations. To this day his name is never connected with the Credit

Mobilier scandal, and continuously from 1873 until his death in 1908 he was returned to the Senate by an appreciative constituency.

The people probably did not question the native honesty of Bingham, or Garfield, or Dawes, but their faith in the sagacity of these men was shaken. That they should have been suspected of corruption was enough to arouse public sentiment. Garfield stood successfully for re-election and devoted his attention during the campaign to explaining these charges. But he did not entirely escape suspicion; the saving grace of martyrdom served in his case, as in others, to protect his name to coming generations. Colfax was ruined; the public held him guilty of corruption, which they might possibly have forgiven, and of having miserably lied, which they could never forgive.

To those Republicans who felt that the safety of the nation was indissolubly connected with the success of their party the situation was alarming. Nor was it the Credit Mobilier scandal alone.

In 1873, the day before the adjournment of the forty-second Congress, the notorious "Salary Grab" act was passed. The act in itself objectionable was passed in a thoroughly discreditable manner. The retroactive feature by which each member of Congress was subjected to the charge that he had robbed the country of five thousand dollars brought down a veritable cyclone of indignation, similar to that of 1816, which swept from the Atlantic to the Pacific. The cry of thief was taken up throughout the land and so unmistakable was the popular indignation that several members who had drawn the increased salary covered it back into the treasury.

When the forty-third Congress assembled in December, 1873, so persistent had been the cry of "thief," that the salary question was at once taken up in an effort to allay the popular indignation and to offer a bid for personal popularity. In the ensuing debate the three great crimes of the age were declared to be the Missouri Compromise, the firing on Fort Sumter, and the Salary Act of 1873. Public sentiment could not be ignored and in January, 1874, the bill was repealed as of March 4, 1873.

The industrial and commercial panic of 1873, with its Black Friday and its financial paralysis induced by wildcat speculations, the unwarranted construction of railroads, the waste and extravagance that were the heritage of the Civil War, and the enormous fire losses of Chicago and Boston all contributed to the troubles of the Republican party. But with this panic came the consolation that it, possibly, was not wholly due to official dishonesty.

On the last night of the first session of the forty-first Congress, April 10, 1869, a bill was taken up for final passage which renewed the land-grant to the State of Arkansas for the Little Rock and Fort Smith railroad. An amendment was offered which would have emasculated the bill. The friends of the railroad, desperate at the prospect, besought the assistance of the Speaker. Blaine quieted their fears with the declaration that he would rule the amendment out of order, as not being germane to the bill. This ruling he did make, and it was correct and eminently proper, for Blaine, at that time, was not financially interested in the Little Rock road. But within a few months the situation had materially changed. June 29th, of the same year, he wrote, in answer to a proposition from

Warren Fisher, Jr., of Boston, that he would join the railroad forces: "I do not feel that I shall prove a deadhead in the enterprise if I once embark in it. I see various channels in which I know I can be useful." Of itself this phrase is ambiguous; but there was another letter of the 4th of the following October in which he directed Fisher to tell Josiah Caldwell — one of the promoters of the Little Rock road — that he had unconsciously done the company "a great favor" in his ruling of April 10, giving at the same time a detailed statement of the affair.

Blaine enlisted in the cause and his assurances were correct. He certainly proved no "dead-head." On sales of Little Rock and Fort Smith first mortgage bonds to some of his Maine friends he received princely commissions.

The railroad fell into financial trouble, the stock became practically worthless, the interest on the bonds defaulted, and the "Maine friends" grew restless. By all right and precedent, these investors should have received as security on their mortgage holdings the land-grant bonds. These Blaine had retained. An exposure of these suspicious transactions would cause financial bankruptcy and political ruin. And the "friends" were becoming inquisitive. When one reaps dividends he asks no questions; but when his investment fails he wants the situation analyzed. Blaine solved the problem as best he could. He borrowed the necessary money — and was compelled to pay a usurious rate for it — and bought back the bonds from the investors.

In the transaction he at least escaped political annihilation. Evidence, direct and circumstantial, indicates that the interested railroads (the Little Rock and Fort Smith; the Missouri, Kansas and Texas; the Atlantic and Pacific;

James G. Blaine

and the Union Pacific) shouldered Blaine's losses and in return looked to the obligation of gratitude and the opportunity of legislative favors from the Speaker of the House, similar to that ruling of April 10, 1869.

The railroads probably desired not so much positive favors as immunity from congressional interference. These roads all enjoyed land grants and were thus far, at least, subject to the control of Congress. Blaine was openly charged, in December, 1873, with framing his committee assignments to please the railroads.

Rumors and charges circulated freely and the political atmosphere was murky with suspicions. Blaine's first public statement on the question was made in the House of Representatives, April 24, 1876. "For some months past," he declared, "a charge against me has been circulating in private and was recently made public — designing to show that I had in some indirect manner received the large sum of $64,000 from the Union Pacific railroad company in 1871 — for what services or for what purpose has never been stated." Blaine made an indignant and unqualified denial of the charge.

The people at large were inclined to believe him — though the sickening disclosures of the Republican régime conspired to make them suspicious and pessimistic. The charges would not down, and on April 27th, 1876, the accusations again appeared, this time in the *Cincinnati Gazette*, upon the authority of one of the government directors. On the 2d of May the Democratic House ordered its Committee on the Judiciary to investigate.

A sub-committee of three — two of them Democrats — began at once the gathering of testimony which, while not convincing, was at any rate damaging to the ex-Speaker. On the 31st of May a Scotch verdict seemed probable. On that date James Mulligan of Boston — a secretary and accountant for Fisher — casually suggested, in the course of his testimony, that Elisha Atkins, a Union Pacific director, had told him that Blaine gave the seventy-five thousand dollars of Little Rock bonds to Scott, who in turn disposed of them to the Union Pacific railroad for sixty-four thousand dollars. He also stated that he had in his possession at that time some letters from Blaine to Fisher. Blaine thought these had been returned to him, and the effect of this statement was a shock under which he quivered and blanched. He quickly whispered to the Republican member of the committee to move an adjournment. This was of course carried as a matter of courtesy.

A conference was held that afternoon in the Riggs House — Atkins, Fisher, Blaine, and Mulligan attended. Blaine requested that Mulligan surrender the letters in question to him. Mulligan refused and Blaine pleaded in the name of his wife and family, imploring him to permit their destruction as their publication would "sink him immediately and ruin him forever." Mulligan was firm. Blaine then requested permission to read them. This was done and the letters were returned to Mulligan.

Mulligan then left the conference and went to his own room. Blaine immediately followed and again requested permission to reread the letters consecutively. Mulligan, first exacting a promise for their immediate return, handed them to Blaine. In reply to a question as to what use he intended to make of them, Mulligan replied that he would not deliver them to the committee unless requested to, nor would he publish them unless his testimony was impeached. Then Blaine, despite his agreement, refused to surrender them, insisting that since he had written them they were his personal property.

On June 1st and again on the 2d, Hunton, in behalf of the committee, requested Blaine to surrender the papers. Blaine refused and prepared to resist all demands for them to the utmost. Any disclosure would have ruined him. In two weeks (June 14, 1876) the National Republican Convention would meet at Cincinnati and Blaine was the leading candidate for the presidential nomination. Even to leave the question in its present status would defeat him. Some action was imperative. Boldness which would confuse, then as so often, seemed the best weapon. He undertook the most remarkable parliamentary *coup de théâtre* in our legislative history.

Blaine was by temperament romantic, picturesque, impelling — he was just the character to undertake such a course — a man of less resource would have been utterly overwhelmed. By his audacity and his oratorical ability, he made it possible for himself to remain in politics. Rising from his seat in the House on the 5th of June, to a question of personal privilege, he launched forth in a startling epic of audacity. He declared that the resolution of inquiry was aimed at him alone; that, because of his anti-rebel speech of January preceding, the southern members were particularly bitter toward him; that although there were seven Democrats on the Judiciary Committee the chairman in naming the sub-committee had chosen for its majority the two members from the South

(Hunton and Ashe) who had fought in the rebel army. Then he touched upon the sacred rights of private correspondence. "I have defied the power of the House," he continued, "to compel me to produce these letters. But, Sir, having vindicated that right, standing by it, ready to make any sacrifice in the defence of it — I am not afraid to show them. There they are (theatrically waving a package of letters). There is the very original package, and with some sense of humiliation, with a mortification that I do not pretend to conceal, with a sense of outrage which I think any man in my position would feel, I invite the confidence of forty-four million of my countrymen while I read those letters from this desk."

Blaine then read extracts from the letters with a judicious use of asterisks, pleasing comments, and annotations.

Josiah Caldwell, then in London, had been cabled to telegraph Proctor Knott, chairman of the Judiciary Committee, corroborating Scott's testimony. He complied and Knott received the message June 1st, but for some slight reason did not communicate it to the committee. It certainly could not have injured the cause of the prosecution, for Caldwell's reputation was notorious. But Blaine knew the situation and quickly grasped its strategic value. With arrant theatricalism, like the quick thrust of a rapier, Blaine demanded of Knott whether he had received a cable from Caldwell. He asked it with no anticipation of hearing even echo answer. Knott, confused, stammered, hesitated, and then queried, "How did you hear it?" Blaine, quick to grasp the advantage, replied, "I heard you got a dispatch last Thursday morning at 8 o'clock from Josiah Caldwell, completely and absolutely exonerating me from this charge and you have suppressed it." It was superb, theatrical, dynamic. It was a memorable, a magnificent and a profoundly wicked triumph of dramatic art. The applause of the House and the crowded galleries punctuated Blaine's triumph and the confusion of his accusers.

As Proctor Knott testified, it was "one of the most extraordinary exhibitions of histrionic skill, one of the most consummate pieces of acting that ever occurred upon any stage on earth." Blaine's triumph was simply one of audacity. The audience was enthralled and magnetized. But the vehemence of his language could not conceal the poverty of logic. Machiavelli held that it was amusing to deceive the people, and Blaine was apparently quite of the same mind. There was no courting of investigation, no frank explanation, no open confessions which are always connected with innocence. A brief, concise, frank accounting of those Little Rock bonds would have done more to clear his name to posterity than a world of theatrical oratory.

The evidence, and subsequent conduct of Blaine, cannot be reconciled with innocence. The Judiciary Committee were still considering the question. At the session of Saturday, June 10, the chairman of the committee again demanded the production of the Mulligan letters which Blaine had so graciously "read" to the House. But Blaine persisted in his refusal, nor did they ever leave his possession. The committee then adjourned to the following Monday. On the intervening Sunday, while on his way to worship in the enervating heat of a Washington summer, Blaine swooned on the steps of his church. The ensuing illness closed the investigation. Before he recovered Senator Morrill of Maine had been named Secretary of the Treasury and his place in the Senate given to Blaine by gubernatorial appointment. The legislature of Maine ratified his selection and also elected him Senator for six years from March 4, 1877. With that the jurisdiction of the House was an issue. When Congress again convened in December the graver issue of a Presidency was at stake. The committee never reported.

Probably the public at large, certainly the majority of the Republican party, believed Blaine innocent. In fact the charges only increased their devotion to him. They felt that he was being persecuted. Others felt a sympathy for his weakness.

In the ensuing convention Blaine had the largest following and would no doubt have been chosen as the standard-bearer for his party, had not the taint of personal corruption endured. Even the stirring eloquence of Robert G. Ingersoll with his "plumed-knight" speech could not blot it out. And Blaine, brilliant, capable, popular, of wonderful personal magnetism, gave way to Hayes of uninspiring personality, but of sterling integrity. The issue was but postponed eight years. In 1884 the battle was fought and Blaine defeated in a struggle of personal honesty. Small wonder that the convention of 1876 feared Blaine's vulnerability lest he be named as the apostle of corruption. The mere fact that Blaine was nominated in 1884 illustrates how quickly public indignation subsides.

On the 6th of May, 1876, George F. Hoar, then new in national affairs, one of the managers of the House in the

Belknap Impeachment trial, addressed the Senators sitting as a court of trial: "My own public life has been a very brief and insignificant one, extending little beyond the duration of a single term of senatorial office. But in that brief period I have seen five judges of a high court of the United States driven from office by threats of impeachment for corruption or maladministration. I have heard the taunt from friendliest lips, that when the United States presented itself in the East to take part with the civilized world in generous competition in the arts of life the only product of her institutions in which she surpassed all others beyond question was her corruption. I have seen in the State in the Union foremost in power and wealth four judges of her courts impeached for corruption, and the political administration of her chief city become a disgrace and a by-word throughout the world. I have seen the chairman of the Committee on Military Affairs in the House rise in his place and demand the expulsion of four of his associates for making sale of their official privilege of selecting the youths to be educated at our great military school. When the greatest railroad of the world binding together the continent and uniting the two great seas which wash our shores, was finished, I have seen our national triumph and exaltation turned to bitterness and shame by the unanimous reports of three committees of Congress — two of the House and one here — that every step of that mighty enterprise had been taken in fraud. I have heard in highest places the shameless doctrine avowed by men grown old in public office that the true way by which power is to be gained in the Republic is to bribe the people with the offices created for their service, and the true end for which it should be used, when gained, is the promotion of selfish ambition and the gratification of personal revenge. I have heard that suspicion haunts the footsteps of the trusted companions to the President."

Small wonder that Blaine and other leading Republicans wished to divert attention from such things by waving anew the "bloody shirt."

The tone of Blaine's Speakership was above all political. He was undoubtedly one of the best presiding officers who ever graced the Speaker's Chair; he knew parliamentary law, was always master of himself, calm, dignified, and the soul of courtesy. But he manipulated the rules with perfect *sang froid* to assist his party — and the minority often gasped at the unceremonious treatment accorded them. He had all of Colfax's parliamentary and political skill and tact and he had what Colfax had not — audacity, aggressiveness, and the natural qualities of leadership. He was the first Speaker who manipulated the power of his office to further his presidential candidacy. This attempted control of legislation, together with the hostility of Grant's friends — represented by Conkling — twice defeated his nomination for President (in 1876 and 1880) and in 1884 prevented his election.

His rulings were always adroit and plausible, inspiring Vice-President Wheeler's comment: "Mr. Blaine can always give a good reason for a bad decision. In that regard he has neither superior nor equal."

Blaine saw the infinite possibilities for power in the Speaker's duty of recognition, and developed that function to a degree theretofore unknown. He had to be first assured as to the purposes for which the member sought the floor. If the purpose did not commend itself to him the favor or "right" was denied. In this way he acquired vast power in framing bills, for members were willing to yield something rather than lose all by being denied the floor. Here at least was a new departure.

His traditional dignity was frequently marred by quasi-personal disputes with members on the floor. He and Butler had broken — more credit to Blaine. On the 16th of February, 1871, Butler as chairman of the Reconstruction Committee reported a bill from that committee to the House. He was not able to present his bill, as the Committee on Appropriations occupied the floor. Finally on the 20th Butler was recognized and at his request the Clerk of the House began reading the bill. The official was interrupted and Fernando Wood of New York was recognized. Wood moved to suspend the rules to pass a joint resolution repealing the duty on coal — a measure with which Blaine was in hearty accord. Butler's bill was lost. Blaine sought to justify his conduct on the theory that while the Clerk is reading no one "has the floor."

The forty-second Congress met on the 4th of March of the same year. Butler was again circumvented in his efforts to secure action on his bill. In the meantime Blaine prepared a resolution appointing a committee to investigate the affairs of the South. It was passed at once, debate being killed by the heroic use of the previous question. Butler's anger was scorching hot. He wrote a letter denouncing the scheme as a trick, a bi-partisan conspiracy. The following day the subject was brought up in the House. Blaine called another member to the Chair, and on the floor joined in a rough-and-tumble controversy, which could only mar the dignity of his office. Butler's letter he scored as an "insult to the Speaker" and denounced its "mean inferences and meaner innuendoes." After apologizing for breaking the custom of not engaging in any discussion on the floor, he declared: "The Speaker should, with consistent fidelity to his own party, be the impartial administrator of the rules of the House, and a constant participation in the discussion of members would take from him that appearance of impartiality which it is so important to maintain in the rulings of the Chair. But at the same time I despise and denounce the insolence of the gentleman from Massachusetts when he attempts to say that the Representative from the third district of Maine has no right to seek that, under the rules, that resolution shall be adopted; has no right to ask the judgment of the House upon that resolution. Why, even the insolence of the gentleman himself never reached that sublime height before, and that is the whole extent of my offending, that I wrote a resolution — that I took it to various gentlemen on the other side of the House — that I said to the gentlemen on the other side of the House, 'this is a resolution on which you cannot afford to filibuster; it is a resolution demanding a fair, impartial investigation, and under the rules I desire that this resolution may be offered, and my colleague (Peters) will offer it.'"

Butler, quite unabashed, inquired with effective sarcasm if Blaine spoke for the House under the old theory that "one person shall be Speaker of the House, to speak for the House." Blaine retorted that his "predecessor had

James G. Blaine

also been obliged to descend from the Chair to chastise the insolence of that same member."

There was, however, a certain personal fairness about Blaine's régime that strongly appeals to the sentiments of the historian. A member had incurred popular odium because of charges against his character and Blaine was severely criticised because, upon the convening of Congress, this member was reappointed to the chairmanship of an important committee. Blaine replied that the member had been elected by his constituents, he had not been censured by Congress, and it was assuredly no portion of his function to visit mere popular indignation upon him.

During his first year in the Speaker's Chair the charge of corruption had been established against certain members and a resolution for their expulsion being anticipated, one of their number, DeWeese, heretofore alluded to, had sought to forestall this by resignation. Several members, indignant that the corrupt "carpet-bagger" should thus avoid his merited punishment, declared that the House alone had the power to determine when a member's connection ceased. Blaine ruled against them, and was severely criticised by press and people. Of course it was a matter of regret that this easy avenue of escape offered itself. But DeWeese had formally sent his resignation to the Governor of his State, the Governor had duly accepted it and had notified the Speaker of his action. Certainly it was not the province of the Speaker either to suppress or withhold the resignation. By Blaine's request an appeal from his decision was made. A Democrat moved to table the appeal, which was carried by a large majority.

Blaine's authority in Congress became well-nigh absolute. Appeals from his decisions were seldom taken and never sustained. And yet he upheld the rights of the minority. Their abuses had not reached the climax of later years. When the metamorphosis of the long continued Republican majority into a minority was imminent he resisted the effort to fasten upon Congress such a change of rules as would bind and fetter the majority. He declared that the responsibility of the majority to the nation was a sufficient safeguard to its interests.

Blaine was vulnerable to the charge of unworthy motives in making his committee assignments, though fairness demands the assertion that the material at hand was not all that could be desired. Butler was named as chairman of the Judiciary Committee in 1873. Credit Mobilierists were assigned to places of power and authority. The Civil Service Committee was framed in hostility to Civil Service reform legislation. The Democratic platform of 1876 charged Blaine with "marketing his rulings as a presiding officer." His own personal ambitions, however, seemed the controlling influence.

His régime of six years was a story of increasing Republican disrepute. In 1870, for the first time since 1864, their two-thirds majority was lost. Their number fell from 172 to 135, the majority declining from 101 to 35. Still the Republican leaders, exponents of ephemeral expediency, persisted in placing the purely superficial and transitory interests of their party above the welfare of the nation. The Democrats received a well-merited rebuke for their hybrid campaign of 1872 and Grant's overwhelming re-election was rather a choice of two evils, carrying with it a large addition to the Republican majorities in both the House and the Senate. In the former there were 195 Republicans, 88 Democrats, and 4 Liberals; in the Senate 49 Republicans, 19 Democrats, and 5 Liberals. To the detriment of the party and the sorrow of the nation, the two-third Republican majority was restored.

But the issue could not be downed and in 1874 the great question which no amount of political gymnastics could conceal was squarely before the people: Did Grant's administration and the régime of the Republican party merit endorsement? The southern policy of the party had been a failure; the Credit-Mobilier and Sanborn-Contract scandals; corruption and inefficiency in the executive departments; lack of Civil Service reform; the failure of their legislation; the blighting effects of the panic of 1873; the persistent mention of Grant for a third term by self-seeking and repudiated sycophants — comprise a brief catalogue of the burden under which the Republicans staggered through the campaign. The verdict of the people was unmistakable.

The victory of the Democrats was overwhelming. The two-thirds majority of the Republicans in the forty-third Congress melted into a pitiful minority. The next House stood 168 Democrats, 108 Republicans, and 14 Liberals and Independents. The Senate still remained Republican but by a decreased majority. Carl Schurz, one of its most valued members, was defeated. In the House Butler was relegated to private life. The Democrats carried Pennsylvania, and elected Samuel J. Tilden Governor of New York by 50,000 majority. In two years, from 1872 to 1874, the country had undergone a drastic political revolution. It was not, however, so much a vote of confidence in the Democratic party as a repudiation of the Republicans.

From December, 1875, to December, 1889 — a period of fourteen years — at no time did the Republicans control the Presidency, the Senate, and the House. Shades of Thaddeus Stevens!

And with the fall of the Republican party came the passing of Blaine as Speaker. On the closing day of the session, on March 3d, 1875, he pronounced his valedictory — a wonderful speech, magnetic, inspiring, thrilling — slowly the gavel struck three times and the House was adjourned without day, a wonderful soul-stirring picture it was. The applause was like the rolling of thunder, and down many a hard and furrowed cheek coursed the tears of sympathy and regret. Blaine bowed his acknowledgment, but the members seemed loath to leave the scene of his glory, and at last with slow and uncertain step they gradually deserted the hall of their fame.

Two years later Blaine entered the Senate and from that graduated in a larger sense into the national arena. All through his career he grew. His public life seemed an education; experience, study, power, all seemed to develop his latent qualities. At first he was a politician — a wire-puller and party manager; but in 1892, when he laid down the portfolio of State, he was a statesman. This very development was a tribute to his greatness.

Still through it all he retained the impress of those first years and that early training. During all of his active connection with national affairs he kept his hand on the lever of the regular political machine.

Yet his life was tragic in its disappointments—a study in the psychology of human ambition. The reformers refused to support him. In that bitter campaign of vituperation in 1884 he was declared unfit for the Presidency because he was believed to have used public office as a means of private gain. Even the cohesive ties of party fealty — seldom broken in those days — were not strong enough to prevent an open revolt. Carl Schurz repudiated him. His candidacy gave birth to the "mugwump" and for the first time since the war gave the Presidency to the Democrats. The Democrats hated Blaine for his attack on Davis and the South, eight years before. Conkling had sworn revenge and Grant plotted his downfall. Arthur might well cherish animosity for Blaine's avowed hostility and contempt. Caricature, lampoon, ridicule, were all mustered as allies in the fight. His enemies adopted the precept of Beaumarchais, "Calumniate! Calumniate! Something will always stick." The day of their revenge was at hand.

Comparing Blaine with Clay, that other Speaker of high aspirations and defeated ambition, we find many striking parallels but differences equally striking. Both were men of electric vitality; both possessed the faculty of inspiring enthusiasm; both knew the art of touching men's hearts.

Clay was without question the greater orator. However, Blaine entranced his audiences by his oratorical brilliance. He used few gestures but his language was so chaste and apt and his thoughts so clear and so artistically draped that he enthralled his listeners even when they were not persuaded. Blaine was a more profound thinker and possessed of wider knowledge and was positive and fearless. Clay was a man of compromise.

Both were intensely American — both worshipped at the altar of American glory and national advancement. To both the great prize beckoned — both reached out and failed.

CHAPTER VII

KERR, RANDALL, KEIFER, AND CARLISLE

THE best index of the political revolution which swept the country in 1874 was the forty-fourth Congress which convened at Washington on the 6th of March, 1875. Blaine was again nominated by the Republicans against Michael C. Kerr of Indiana, presented as the Democratic candidate. Kerr was elected by a vote of 173 to 106. Kerr had served in the House for several sessions and was favorably known as one of the Democratic floor leaders. A man of high character, acknowledged ability, and unquestioned integrity, his Speakership was all the more brilliant by comparison with the sordid record of his predecessors, Blaine and Colfax. Of him one of the most conservative and high-toned periodicals said, "Mr. Kerr was, we believe, the only man in public life, investigated during the session, who not only proved that the charges against him were unfounded, but came out of the ordeal with a reputation strengthened by the attacks made upon it."

Naturally this Congress through the infusion of much new blood made some mistakes — but they were the transgressions of ignorance, not of dishonesty and corruption. It introduced to the public many able characters, not before familiar to the nation. All in all the forty-fourth Congress was a welcome relief after those which had debauched the Capitol for the previous six years.

Kerr was an able parliamentarian and though an earnest partisan, his vision was not distorted by the lens of prejudice and he was always fair and just. His very election to the office was an earnest of his character. The first Democratic House of Representatives for fifteen years — since the opening of the Civil War — the nation had chosen them as a rebuke to the profligacy and unfitness of their predecessors. And by that logic they were put to the test. How would they regard the trust? Randall and Kerr were the leading candidates for the Speakership. By virtue of longer service and greater aggressiveness Randall had been the leader of the minority in the House. But he suffered from the withering touch of suspicion — and the Democrats felt, if they were to retain the power entrusted to them, it could be only through the preponderance of the best elements of their party. Kerr was above even a whisper of doubt, and he was chosen that the nation might feel that the pendulum had swung.

He discharged his duties in a manner well calculated to conserve the confidence reposed in him. His committees were carefully chosen and did much to clear the atmosphere of its malarial germs. A Democratic committee ably assisted Bristow in his prosecution of the Whiskey Ring when members of his own party were blocking every step; other committees revealed Blaine's "financial operations," exposed Belknap, and investigated the extravagance and corruption rampant in the Interior and Navy Departments. The House scaled down the list of appropriations nearly thirty million dollars, and would have accomplished even more had it not been checked by the Republican Senate.

But Kerr was not spared to serve the term of his office.

In 1875, already a victim of tuberculosis, he gradually succumbed to its ravages — a martyr to his high conception of public trust. His friends had besought him not to accept the Speakership with its exacting and onerous duties; a rest and a change of climate might have prolonged his career — but he refused to listen either to the appeals of his friends or the counsel of his doctors. Even then his death had not seemed thus imminent. He died during the congressional recess on the 19th of August 1876, at the age of fifty. In a proclamation two days later President Grant paid the following tribute to his memory: "A man of great intellectual endowments, large culture, great probity and earnestness in his devotion to the public interests."

In the following fall ensued the memorable Hayes-Tilden campaign. The issue had been determined the preceding year. Blaine, then the leading candidate for the presidential nomination, with the skilled intuition of the politician, realized that on only one issue could the Republicans take the aggressive — the eternal southern question. The financial issue then prominent — the one on which Hayes had made his successful campaign against "Fog-Horn" William Allen, for the chief magistracy of Ohio — was both dangerous and ill suited to the temperament of the "magnetic man." Although this continued "baiting" of the oppressed Southerners might not, and did not, appeal to the conservatives of the North yet it was apparent that the only prospect of Republican success lay in diverting attention from the shameful disclosures of Republican unfitness then crowding the daily prints.

The passions of war were again inflamed — for such an issue was best suited to the oratory of Robert Ingersoll, Morton, Blaine, and a host of lesser satellites. "We are dealing with a new rebellion," declared Edmunds, as though it were a surprising and dangerous thing that the people should denounce Republican corruption and threaten the defeat of dishonesty. Torchlight processions, camp-fires, drum and fife corps were abroad in the land while Wheeler from the stump sounded the keynote "Let your ballots protect the work so effectually done by your bayonets at Gettysburg." "We confront the old issue," shrieked Wheeler as though there were not a still older issue — that of primal integrity. The result was close — a man of greater physical and moral courage than Tilden would probably have marched triumphant into the White House.

The assembling of the second session of Congress on the 4th of December, 1876, found the House without a Speaker — the only time in our national history that an incumbent of that position had died in office.

Samuel J. Randall of Pennsylvania, who had been Kerr's competitor in the Democratic caucus, was elected to the unexpired term. A member for thirteen years from a Philadelphia district, he had, by the length of his service and his own adaptability, acquired a thorough knowledge of the rules and methods of the House. Strongly partisan, bold and aggressive, he possessed the natural traits of leadership. He imitated Clay and Blaine in impressing his own personality upon the House. In some features of legislative control he exceeded those after whom he had patterned. He even carried this to the point of acting as

House conferee (though informally and as a substitute) on two important appropriation bills.

Randall was on the whole fair-minded toward his political opponents — though obstinately adverse to compromise and never able to forget the interests of the Democratic party. No greater testimonial to his fairness can be found than his rulings during the days of stress and storm which broke after the election of 1876 when, in the following spring, the question of the Presidency was brought before Congress. Randall of course was opposed to Hayes, and under the rules then in vogue the tactics of obstruction could not be circumvented. In 1877 a determined effort was engineered in the House to prevent the completion of the electoral count by those very parliamentary tactics. It is doubtful if Randall would have been accused of remissness in his duty had he permitted these motions to prevail and thus encompassed the defeat of Hayes. He withstood the bitter assaults of his political associates, surrendered his personal preferences and conscientiously obeyed the letter and intent of the Electoral Commission Act, stopping all obstruction on the presidential election.

Although the Democratic caucus had decided that the count of the electoral votes should be permitted to continue, a group of the members determined to retard the work by filibustering tactics. These obstructionists were actuated by different motives. One type, some two score in number and consisting of such men as Blackburn of Kentucky, Springer of Illinois, Mills of Texas, Cox of New York, and O'Brien of Maryland were unwilling to lend any countenance, actual or passive, to what they called "the fraud." The "irreconcilables" they were christened. The others, mostly southerners, were inspired by other considerations.

The majority, convinced that Hayes would be declared elected and persuaded of the futility of further opposition, desired that the count proceed lest civil war or even anarchy be the dread alternative. But before surrendering they wished to rescue some brand from the burning. They believed that by sufficiently alarming the Republicans they could force some assurance that the new administration would not lend military support to the Republican claimants for the State offices in Louisiana and South Carolina.

This movement took definite shape shortly after the decision on the Louisiana vote had convinced the Democrats that the national ticket was lost to them. The brand was to be the State ticket in these States. Legislative conditions promised well for the success of the venture. Filibustering was then flourishing in luxuriance. Randall too was committed to it — for during the preceding Congress had he not occupied the floor for seventy-two consecutive hours and forced the Republicans to abandon their attempt to re-enact the Force Bill? The rules of that Congress were in force, Randall was in the Chair, and the Democrats were in the majority — could they not easily and consistently "filibuster to the millenium?"

For a time Randall held control of the situation but on the 24th of February the hand of rebellion was raised. The "irreconcilables," anticipating certain defeat, determined to filibuster for the remainder of the session. Dilatory motions of every description were offered.

Kerr, Randall, Keifer, and Carlisle 199

The Speaker ignored them. Surprise, anger, consternation, even among the conservative Democrats, greeted this arbitrary display of power. The House was in an uproar. Democrats — even Randall's closest political associates — shouted vociferously, mounted their chairs and gesticulated wildly; others slammed and pounded their desks and many rushed forward to congregate in a seething mass in the open space before the Speaker's desk.

With extreme difficulty a semblance of order was restored. Randall announced firmly that he refused to recognize a certain motion because, though proper in form, it was manifestly offered to delay the progress of legitimate business. The Chair announced his position in the following terms: "The Chair rules that when the Constitution of the United States directs anything to be done, or when the laws under the Constitution of the United States enacted in obedience thereto, direct any act by this House, it is not in order to make any motion to obstruct or impede the execution of that injunction of the Constitution and the laws."

The Speaker was assailed with the expletives of impotent rage. The members of his own party accused him of every variety of crime and venality — they even insinuated corruption and hinted at a financial consideration. But Randall stood firm, like some rock of time against which the waves of anger were dashed to spray. On the first of March the contest waxed with even greater bitterness. The thunder clouds of indignation roared above; the storm broke. The day's session was probably the wildest ever enacted in any American legislative body. The Democrats were determined. In the wild scenes that ensued Randall alone was impassive though his dark face was ashen and his nerves seemed strained to the point of breaking.

James Monroe, a Republican member of the House, has thus described the scene: "He (the Speaker) was subjected to a strain upon voice, and nerve, and physical strength such as few men could have endured. At times he was visited with a storm of questions and reproaches. Would he not entertain a privileged motion? He would not. Would he not put a motion for a recess? A motion for the call of the House? A motion to excuse some member from voting? A motion to reconsider? A motion to lay something on the table? He would not. Were not these motions in order under the rules? They were. Would he not submit some of them to the House? He would not. Was he not then an oppressor and a despot? He was not. Would he not then put some dilatory motion? He would not. Why would he not? Because of his obligation to the law."

The disorder was increased and the clamor multiplied by the presence on the floor of the House of many persons who had no business there, and from the galleries packed with partisans who wildly applauded each demonstration. Growing more and more pale, but never flinching under the cruel assaults, Randall declared firmly that he would submit no longer to the disorder. "If gentlemen forget themselves," he said, "it is the duty of the Chair to remind them that they are members of The American Congress."

Meanwhile the Republican leaders had been approached and *pour parlers* suggested that some understanding could be reached. It might be possible to control the "irreconcilables" if some assurances could be offered that the Federal Government would not interfere with the State elections, particularly in Louisiana; in fact some definite assurances along this line must be given. A conference, private and avowedly unofficial, was called at Wormley's Hotel. The conferees were John Sherman, James A. Garfield, Charles Foster, and Dudley Denison, all of Ohio, in behalf of Hayes; E. J. Ellis and William Levy of Louisiana, and Henry Watterson of Kentucky representing the Democrats. As a weapon the threat of filibustering, with the possible resort to civil war, was effectively used by Tilden's supporters. The Republican members spoke indefinitely and offered only general promises of certain mental attitudes. This was unsatisfactory, and the time was growing short. The Democrats insisted upon a guarantee that the Federal troops would not be employed to support Republican claimants to those State offices by bayonet or sword. The whole question was one of extreme delicacy, for it involved the very existence of the reconstruction policy of the Republican party. At length, however, the Democrats were persuaded that the troops would be withdrawn.

Hewitt, who had insisted from the first upon a peaceful settlement of the controversy and who had been denounced and threatened by his own party associates for his course, suddenly abandoned his attitude of conciliation and allied himself with the "irreconcilables," who now confidently proclaimed their success. No explanation was offered of this unexpected conduct. Hewitt's closest personal and political friends argued with him in vain. The situation seemed hopelessly complicated. Few members on either side of the House understood what was transpiring. Time for the Wormley conferees to agree and opportunity to secure the official approval of Tilden to the abandonment of the contest — for these Hewitt was playing.

Through the entire day and long into the night the battle raged. The "irreconcilables" noticed that the conservative Democrats were voting with them on the Vermont case. Wild with delight they saw victory already won. Suddenly Levy appeared on the floor. Informing Randall of the successful termination of the Wormley conference, word was given to abandon the contest. Levy appealed to his fellow-members to refrain from preventing the completion of the count and thereby protect Louisiana and South Carolina. The radicals rallied from the shock and sought to muster their disorganized hosts. But the gloom of defeat had replaced the hope of victory. The resolution was defeated and the possibility of preventing the completion of the count vanished. With this the strength of the filibusters rapidly deteriorated.

In the early hours of March 2d, Hayes and Wheeler were officially declared elected and the most bitter political contest of our history was ended. The members waited in vain for Watterson's "hundred thousand"; the chapter was closed, written in ink where blood had offered. But for Randall's stern demeanor and the Wormley conference filibustering might have succeeded as the preface to war.

Randall, however, soon found himself the object of an investigation involving his integrity. February 27th, 1879, the charge was formally made in the House that through the machinations of Randall and some of his associates, illegal warrants had been signed for appropriations to continue the operations of the Bureau of Printing and Engraving, "which was directly in the interests of Samuel J. Randall, who is a large stockholder in the paper mill which is alone authorized to supply the Bureau of Engraving with paper."

An investigating committee was appointed which exonerated him from the charge — a welcome diversion from the outcome of certain other investigations — though to be accused, even, was a severe implication of distrust. Again he was classed with Blaine in the intimacy which he maintained with the moneyed men of the nation.

Blaine and Randall helped materially to increase the political importance of the Speakership, though from different motives. Blaine sought to add to its prestige, to make himself personally prominent and popular — in short, attempted to further his presidential ambition by its manipulation. Randall on the other hand merely desired to increase the influence of the Chair by developing it into an essentially governing power.

Blaine's rulings had not only permitted but even encouraged filibustering; the precedent thus established Randall faithfully followed. In fact Randall quite largely owed his election to the successful "filibuster" which he had marshaled — with the assistance of Blaine's advice and rulings — in the forty-third Congress against the Force Bill.

In this manner Randall effectively forced his will upon the House. He believed it his duty to obstruct legislation, rather than to facilitate it, in order to retrench the lavish expenditures then threatening. Ignoring the wonderful growth of the nation in its population and the marvelous expansion and development of its resources he permitted appropriations of only the most economical sort. By these same tactics he succeeded in preventing tariff legislation to which he was opposed.

Even in 1879 it was felt that the rules and parliamentary practice of the House had become intolerable. This situation was even further aggravated by the adoption of the so-called Holman amendment during the second session of the forty-sixth Congress (1880). This rule, for the first time in our national legislative history, authorized riders providing general legislation on the annual appropriation bills. Mr. Kasson of Iowa attacked this innovation vigorously, declaring that it "stripped all other Committees of their rightful powers and jurisdiction and conferred it on the majority members of the Committee on Appropriations and their conferees, of whom the Speaker never lost sight or control." No more vicious or intolerable rule, from the standpoint of sound principles and methods of legislation, was ever even suggested in either House of Congress during the century of their existence. Its effectiveness was destroyed by the vetoes of the President. But as a rule it remained until rejected by an overwhelming vote in 1886 under the leadership of the then Speaker, Carlisle. It was resurrected in the fifty-second Congress by Crisp, who awarded the chairmanship of the Committee on Appropriations to Holman as a personal and political necessity.

The forty-sixth Congress was convened in extra session March 18th, 1879, owing to the failure of the army and legislative appropriation bills caused by the attached riders which President Hayes had vetoed.

The popular demand for some decisive parliamentary reform had become so insistent that Randall was forced to yield. June 19th, 1879, a resolution was introduced by the Committee on Rules authorizing that committee to sit during the approaching recess for the "purpose of revising, codifying, and simplifying the rules of the House."

This committee of the forty-sixth Congress was the most famous Committee on Rules in the entire career of the House of Representatives. Its chairman was Randall; with him were Alexander H. Stephens of Georgia, who had been Vice-President of the Confederate States and had served in the House twenty-six years; Joseph C. S. Blackburn of Kentucky, later Senator from that State for three terms; James A. Garfield, within a year elected to the Senate, and promoted to the White House; and William P. Frye of long and distinguished service as member and President *pro tempore* of the Senate.

Every member had won the laurels of fame as a political leader, as a legislative expert, and as a parliamentary student. Despite this their arduous labors brought only contemptible results. They inaugurated their efforts by adopting a ridiculous and vicious rule that the report should be unanimous. Randall was always ready with his veto, often singly interposed, to suggested remedies for some of the most iniquitous rules of the present code. He seemed inspired at all times with the desire of increasing in every possible manner the power and authority of the Speaker. He justified his attitude on the ground that the Speaker had long since outgrown the swaddling clothes of a moderator; that he had become by virtue of his position the party leader with the avowed duty of favoring partisan interests.

However, the codification and revision of the committee cleared away much antiquated rubbish. But for the solitary objections of Randall most of the reforms incorporated in the rules of the various Houses since 1880 would then have been adopted. The general code had remained unchanged.

Randall was the first Speaker who sought directly to increase the power of his office by changing the rules. Carlisle, Reed, and Crisp followed and outdistanced his example. Randall's conception of the Speakership is best portrayed in his own words, delivered in the House: "Soon after I entered this House, I came to consider that that office (the Speakership) was the highest office within the reach of an American citizen; that it was a grand official station, great in the honors which it conferred, and still greater in the ability it gave to impress upon our history and legislation the stamp of truth, fairness, and right. . . . When it fell to my fortune to occupy the Speaker's chair, I realized how true was my idea of the position."

In the election of 1880 the Republican majority in the House was restored. Blaine was now in the Senate; Reed was serving his second term but had not yet given evidence of those traits which were later to revolutionize congressional procedure. J. Warren Keifer of Ohio, from his intense Republicanism of the old days, and his length of service, was selected as the party candidate for Speaker in the forty-seventh Congress and elected to that office December 5th, 1881. Keifer was a "stalwart" partisan — one of the rabid anti-slavery, anti-Southern type. Re-elected to Congress, in 1905, after a long period of retirement, he still clings to the ideas and garb of other days.

An army-blue suit, cut in the style of the ante-bellum days, swallow tails, low front vest revealing a vast expanse of ruffled snow-white shirt, a narrow string tie, white beard and heavy shock of silver hair — Keifer to-day presents a picture of another age, an earlier generation.

But Keifer's partisanship lacked tone and aggressiveness — it was distinctly weak. He was not a strong character and those who had supported his election soon woke to the realization that he lacked the mental ability with which he had been credited. Further, he manifested an eminent lack of fairness in the discharge of his duties. In a republican form of government the people are always hostile to the practice of nepotism. It is felt to be incompatible with the fundamental institutions of the country. Keifer affronted the public by a marked contempt for popular opinion. One nephew he appointed Clerk to the Speaker at a salary of one thousand six hundred dollars, another nephew Clerk to the Speaker's table at one thousand four hundred dollars, and a few months later made his son private secretary at a salary of one thousand eight hundred dollars. He was bitterly denounced by the public prints when he removed an efficient stenographer of long service and replaced him with a near relative.

Keifer's weakness was again manifested in the nondescript character of his committees. Each committee was appointed as a unit regardless of the necessity for harmony and legislative coherence. The Committee on Elections was the most flagrant example of his remissness in this direction. As constituted that committee consisted of eleven Republicans and two Democrats. Further, Keifer was easily influenced, to-day dominated by one faction and to-morrow by another. The dynasty of the cloak room and the lobby were always dominant and notorious.

In the Chair Keifer displayed a pitiful lack of strength which, coupled with the partisan tone of his rulings, won for him at once the contempt of his party associates and the ill will of his opponents. Like his predecessors, Keifer sought to impose his personal will and impress on the House — but his mental and intellectual disposition prevented his differentiating between political acumen and partisan bias.

In the next Congress when the Democrats again obtained the ascendency, Keifer received the empty honor of the minority nomination. But with it came a sting — for while this naturally involves the floor leadership, he was deserted by his associates and his career as a national figure terminated ingloriously.

However, there is something to commend in his administration of the office. He lacked but little of accomplishing the *coup de théâtre* with which Reed a decade later startled the nation. Keifer's ruling "that the constitutional right of the House to determine the rules of its proceedings cannot be impaired by the indefinite repetition of dilatory motions," was the first and most decisive step toward stamping out filibustering. He was prepared and determined to anticipate Reed and count a quorum of members present but not voting. But Reed, ex-Governor Robinson of Massachusetts, Kasson and other leading Republicans intimated that they would not support the Speaker on an appeal from his ruling, and he was forced to abandon the plan which would have won for him the plaudits later bestowed upon Reed.

Kerr, Randall, Keifer, and Carlisle 209

On the assembling of the forty-eighth Congress, December 3d, 1883, John G. Carlisle of Kentucky was elected Speaker. He served in that capacity for three successive terms until March 3, 1889. Carlisle was essentially a political Speaker but he appreciated better than Keifer had done the proper limitations. In short the political aspect of the office was not offensively paraded. A man of great native ability, one of the country's most eminent lawyers, later United States Senator, and Secretary of the Treasury, yet he too was, as Colfax had been, at times an invertebrate. He seemed always to have his ear to the ground to catch the first whisperings of public sentiment and that once declared he feared to defy it. In his rulings as Speaker while always positive he never seemed arbitrary. His fairness won him the respect and regard of the members of the opposition. He regarded the Speakership in the light of a judicial office and frequently refused to make purely partisan decisions.

His committee assignments were framed with the view of securing the issue on which he had been elected to the Chair, that of tariff reform. Yet until the fiftieth Congress, owing to the effective opposition of Holman and his adherents, Carlisle was unable to force a tariff bill through the House; even then his success was made possible only by partially dismantling the Committee on Appropriations and rejecting the Holman amendments for which he secured Republican assistance. However, his committees reflected more closely the personal views of the Speaker than any other influence.

This seemed the keynote of Carlisle's administration of the office. His theory was that the Speaker was the leader of Congress, that he should have a definite, cohesive legislative policy, and that he should so shape his committees, and so grant the favors of recognition as to secure the success of that policy. This constituted the personal Speakership. And yet within the House he never feared the issue nor sought to shift or shirk the responsibility. To secure the success of his policy he frequently defied a large majority on the floor and persistently refused recognition to those who wished to present important business for consideration. For the first time this conception of the office was presented to the nation. It meant not that the Speaker held the balance between the minority and the majority, neither that he represented the policies of the majority, but that the individual dictates of the Speaker were to dominate the House, that the Speaker was the source of authority and the dictator of congressional legislation.

Yet he maintained the confidence of the nation and the respect of the Republican party, for his rulings were at all times eminently fair and marked by a distinctive judicial tone. One or two incidents of his career in the Chair illustrate at once his conception of the office and the opposition he encountered. In 1885 he was accused of maliciously using his power to postpone consideration of the appropriation bills until the last hours of the session (while at the same time confidently assuring the anxious that there would be no extra session), and then forwarding them to the Senate, the only theatre of discussion, so late as to prevent any debate, and forcing a settlement through secret conference committees.

In 1887 a member of the House, for three long hours,

paraded up and down the floor, bill in hand, desperately seeking recognition from the Chair and at the end of his efforts in anger and protest, tearing his cherished bill to bits and throwing it at the foot of the dais, stalked out of the House.

An interesting incident of Carlisle's rule serves at once to indicate the peculiar angles of parliamentary procedure and to reveal the manner of the birth of the United States as a naval power. During the second session of the forty-ninth Congress the naval appropriation bill was brought up for discussion. The House went into Committee of the Whole and Carlisle called James B. McCreary of Kentucky to the Chair. The Secretary of the Navy, William C. Whitney, had stated in his report that the United States did not possess a warship fleet enough to run away or strong enough to fight. The desire for a stronger navy was manifest throughout the House. During the consideration of the naval appropriation bill the chairman of the Committee on Naval Affairs, Hilary Herbert, later Secretary of the Navy, offered an amendment providing for an appropriation to construct one battleship and one cruiser. Wm. Holman raised a point of order against the amendment, citing as authority rule 21, clause 3, as follows: "No appropriation shall be reported in any general appropriation bill or be in order as an amendment thereto unless in continuation of appropriation for such public works and objects as are already in progress."

In the debate on the point of order it was shown that in the previous Congress an appropriation had been made for the construction of a cruiser; McCreary held that the appropriation to construct a new cruiser was the commencement of a new navy, and therefore, under the rule cited, the proposed amendment continued a public work or object already in progress, and therefore Herbert's amendment was in order. Holman immediately appealed from McCreary's ruling but withdrew the appeal when Speaker Carlisle and former Speaker Randall sustained McCreary's decision. Thus the beginning of the "new navy" which through the glories of Manila and Santiago was later to rank with the world's greatest flotillas. The ruling of McCreary has been followed and referred to in the Rules and Practice of the House of Representatives.

During the fiftieth Congress the Committee on Rules, of which Carlisle was chairman, showed no signs of activity. At length a petition signed by every Republican member of the House was presented to the Speaker requesting him to call a meeting of that committee and make a report. The petition was completely ignored — nor did the Rules Committee present any report during the entire Congress.

Yet, despite the strength and tone of Carlisle's rule, he made no effort to check filibustering which flourished fruitfully. During the sessions of the fiftieth Congress, this form of parliamentary tactics reached the perihelion of idiocy. One paper graphically summed it up as "filibustering run mad," and insisted that "a single member on the floor might play the rôle of Czar as successfully as the Speaker." The zenith of this abuse was reached when General Weaver, a member from Iowa, by his own unaided efforts, blocked all business of the House for nearly two weeks and forced Carlisle to accede to his demands. Weaver's *modus operandi* was the continual proposal, in alternating succession, of two or three separate motions, and when one was voted down, or otherwise disposed of, immediately offering another. This situation was largely the result of Carlisle's refusal to change the rules by amendments which might promote general legislation. But the country at large was afflicted by no such qualms of conscience and visited their disgust upon the Democratic party in the ensuing election.

Personally popular, an excellent parliamentarian, Carlisle established a new and stronger conception of the Speakership. A man of strong and winning personality, enforced by intellectual brilliancy, he received an enthusiastic ovation at the end of his term. In Kentucky he was rewarded by election to the United States Senate. He became Secretary of the Treasury during President Cleveland's second administration. In 1896, along with many of the most prominent Democrats of the country, he advocated the gold standard and returned to his native State to expound that doctrine. Those who had delighted to honor him and shout his praises a decade before, now led the mob which hooted his speeches and assailed him with malodorous and contemptible missiles. Taking up his residence in New York City he began the practice of law, and again his native power of command and strong force of purpose, with his acknowledged legal capacity, forced him to a position of leadership. He will live as one of our strongest Speakers — an exponent of the personal power of the Chair.

CHAPTER VIII

"CZAR" REED — THE "REVOLUTION"

DECEMBER 2d, 1889, for the first time in fourteen years the Republicans were fully restored to power. The margin was small, dangerously small, but they controlled, none the less, the Presidency, the Senate, and the House of Representatives. The majority in the House was eight, a number that gave little promise of Republican legislation. Sickness, absence, independence, rebellion would easily translate such a bare majority into a triumphant minority. For the success of party measures, to which the Republicans had pledged themselves at the preceding election, it was necessary to increase the majority to an extent which would insure the easier and more certain dispatch of business. At the opening of Congress, Thomas B. Reed of Maine was elected Speaker.

He had first taken his seat in the House of Representatives in 1877. At this time the Democrats were in the ascendency and the era of the bitter reconstruction debates was past. The great battles were over and had now given way to party skirmishes, a sort of guerrilla political warfare, a continuous clashing and jockeying for position on the less important topics of the day. Reed was naturally equipped for this kind of political activity. As a member of the Potter Committee, appointed to investigate the Presidential election of 1876, he performed a conspicuous service to his party, although along purely partisan lines.

"Czar" Reed — The "Revolution" 215

His clever cross questions, native shrewdness, and keen repartee served, not so much to establish the essential truth concerning the election, as to subject the Democratic candidate to the charge of a thwarted attempt to purchase the office.

In the political skirmishes of the ensuing years Reed soon won distinction. A strong partisan, insistent that the Republican party ought always to prevail, his skill at verbal retort, and shrewdness in debate, combined with other natural qualities to make him an effective leader. A concentrated thinker, probably no other man of his age ever evinced such an aptitude for epigrammatic and clever expression. Aggressive and cautious as a debater he excelled in the ability to condense a whole argument into an epigram, and these were always worthy of the literary artist. They formed his sword of attack and his armor of defense. He seemed to combine happily the wit and sarcasm of Disraeli, the scholarship of Roseberry, and the sturdiness and stubbornness of Gladstone.

His caustic comments are quoted widely even after a decade. "The Senate," he said, "is a nice, quiet sort of a place where good Representatives go when they die." His definition of a statesman as "a successful politician that is dead" will probably live as long as politics continue to absorb attention.

Reed seldom made a set speech, but his impromptu performances, always courageously and defiantly conducted, won for him a position of authority. He certainly did not achieve it by the thorough discussion or study of any great question.

Not more than six times in his whole legislative career

did he deliver a prepared speech. Apparently he never mastered any one particular subject or group of subjects, although he naturally acquired a vast store of miscellaneous and uncatalogued information on the leading issues of the day. Never did he generate any great moral force; it was simply as a party leader that he rose above his associates. Yet for this, some explanation may be found in the exigencies of the political situation. During all but eight years of his service in the House, his party was in the minority and for six of those eight years he was in the Chair. Of course he had much to do with constructing and moulding the legislation passed when his party was in the ascendency.

Reed's success was quite largely that of personality — due somewhat to his unique appearance, somewhat to his inimitable but natural drawl, somewhat to his wit, somewhat to his abundant and ready knowledge.

At the opening of the forty-seventh Congress, Reed was a prominent candidate for the Speakership, in the Republican caucus. After sixteen ballots, Keifer was selected for the honor. The forty-eighth Congress was Democratic and Keifer received the complimentary vote of his party, although this did not carry with it the usual concomitant of the floor leadership of the minority. In the forty-ninth and fiftieth Congresses, both Democratic, Reed was the Republican candidate for the office. Upon the promotion of Frye from the House to the Senate and the election of Garfield first to the Senate and then to the Presidency, Reed had been heralded by common consent as the leader of his party in the House. During those six years on the floor he had carried his party with credit

"Czar" Reed — The "Revolution" 217

through the era of Democratic control. A born debater, resourceful like Blaine, aggressive yet cautious, he always emerged triumphant from the daily verbal hand-to-hand conflicts. An example of his keenness and ability at repartee which goes to show the elements of his success is found in a debate in 1880 on a resolution with reference to the electoral count. Davis, a Democrat from North Carolina, made an earnest, serious speech in support of the measure. Reed rose to the contest. Opening with his inimitable Yankee drawl and nasal twang he made a clever and withal able reply. He was frequently interrupted from the other side of the House; finally Finley of Ohio insisted on a reply to his question. Reed yielded, then in a few words discomfited the intruder with his clever retort, adding, "Now having embalmed that fly in the liquid amber of my discourse, I wish to proceed." Amid wild peals of laughter from both parties, he concluded his speech, for no one again cared to turn upon himself the shafts of such sublime ridicule.

In the campaign of 1888 the Republicans had pledged themselves to such a revision of the rules of the House as would permit the transaction of public business. And although they controlled a majority, still, the margin of power was so uncertain that they could not even adopt the new rules if the minority refused a quorum. A quorum of Republicans alone seemed a physical impossibility. Contests were filed in many congressional districts where Democrats had received certificates of election. When the House convened, December 2d, 1889, the Republicans had a majority of eight, including the five members from recently admitted States. But when the fifty-first Congress adjourned on the 3d of March, 1891, although there had been no intervening elections by the people the Republican majority had increased to twenty-four. A majority of eight in a body of three hundred and thirty members, representing widely separated and variant local interests, was not sufficiently reliable to enable the leaders to inaugurate the policies to which they had pledged the party. Therefore nine Democrats lawfully and regularly elected by the people in their respective districts were ejected from their seats, and in eight of the cases Republicans were seated in their places. In the other case the contestant had died in the interim and the contested seat was declared vacant. A sufficient commentary on the partisan character of the procedure was furnished by subsequent events. The nine ejected members returned to their constituents and with but one exception offered themselves as candidates for re-election. Of these eight who became candidates seven were returned to the next Congress by decisive majorities and in the district where the ejected member did not run, a Democrat was elected. The Republican contestants were seated with questionable and purely partisan celerity until a "safe" majority was secured. The Democratic minority, indignant at their own slaughter, a process which seemed so arbitrary and so widely divorced from legislative fairness, naturally rebelled and made requisition of every possible weapon in the effort to save the seats of their colleagues. The emergency thus presented, when the Democrats with their efficient minority had raided the parliamentary arsenal, required decisive action.

The Speaker postponed the report of the Committee

on Rules and during the consideration of the contested election omitted to follow the usual custom of adopting provisionally the rules of the preceding House. The Speaker conducted the daily business of the House under the plastic code of general parliamentary law until the necessary majority was ensured to adopt the rules which had already been framed. The Democrats found their most effective weapon in refusing a quorum; in practicing that peculiar art of metaphysics which admits of corporeal presence and parliamentary absence. Even parliamentary law has many fictions; but it seemed a self-contradiction to assert that a member may be present for obstruction and not present for business.

January 29, 1890, marked the storming of the parliamentary Bastile. The contested election case of Jackson v. Smith was called up for the consideration of the House. The yeas and nays were demanded on the question of consideration: 161 voted yea, 2 voted nay, and 165 were recorded as not voting. The very members who had demanded the yeas and nays sat serenely silent in their seats confident of their success. Immediately after the vote was announced the objection of no quorum was raised. Speaker Reed thereupon directed the Clerk of the House to record the names of those present who refused to vote. A Democrat, one of those present, but not voting, immediately appealed from the decision of the Chair. Amidst the confusion and turmoil, such as had not been witnessed since the last hot-blooded ante-bellum debates, Reed continued unabashed in his count of those whose presence was apparent. Having concluded his arithmetical calculation he announced the vote with a brief, crisp justification of his ruling. The appeal from his decision was laid on the table by a majority not of the House but of the quorum. On the following morning the battle was renewed. Again Reed counted those present but not voting in order to secure a quorum necessary for the approval of the journal. This time he refused to entertain any appeal from his decision on the ground that the House had already decided that question. Consternation and confusion reigned on the floor of the House. Reed's rulings were wormwood and gall to the Democrats, milk and honey to the Republicans. The members rushed madly about the floor, the scowl of battle on their brows, shouting phrases of swelling affirmation and vociferous denial. The House was lashed as in a tempest. The levees had given way and let loose a mad torrent of eloquent invective; shouts, jeers, hisses mingled with applause; the Democrats exhausted the vocabulary of vituperation in their attacks upon the Chair; "tyrant," "Czar," "despot," were among the milder oratorical projectiles hurled at the Speaker. Reed sat serene and confident. The occasional protest of an individual member could at times be heard above the din. "I deny the right of the Speaker to count me present," shouted McCreary of Kentucky. With that unfailing touch of humor which so often turns wrath into mere protest, Reed replied, "The Chair simply stated the fact that the gentleman from Kentucky appears to be present; does he deny it?" In that phrase of repartee was comprised the logic of the situation.

An "arbitrary, corrupt, and revolutionary action" was the denunciatory comment of Breckenridge of Kentucky. The folly of verbal protests being apparent the physical

"Czar" Reed — The "Revolution" 221

presence but constructive absence theory gave way to the idea of corporeal absence. Members dodged under their desks, behind screens, bolted for the doors. In the mad rush for the exits members lost all sense of personal and official dignity and some incurred physical injuries. Upon the order of the Chair the doors were bolted and with each test of the quorum count the defiant minority spent their anger in madly raving about the chamber, — pictures of furious inefficiency. On one occasion Kilgore of Texas kicked open a door and effected his escape from the chamber. This was the most notable parliamentary scene ever enacted upon the American legislative stage.

The tension of the day was somewhat relieved by General Spinola who, pointing to the painting of the Siege of Yorktown hanging in the hall, gravely accused Speaker Reed of counting the Hessians in the background in order to complete a quorum. This sally softened the bitterness of the minority members and inspired the applause of the majority.

The logic of the situation is clearly revealed by the roll-call on a resolution at the time of Reed's first rulings; 163 members voted in the affirmative; 130 Democrats remained silent though actually present. The negative vote of every Democrat present with thirty-two more could not have defeated the measure. In short, their very silence, according to the theory of the minority, was more efficient than their actual suffrage. One step further in this ingenious system of logic and we see that had any two of the silent 130 voted against the measure their votes would have carried it.

Some very interesting side lights may be thrown on this

parliamentary struggle. On the 29th of January there lay in Reed's desk a proposed code of rules — the report of the Committee on Rules — authorizing the Chair to count, for the purpose of a quorum, those members present but refusing to vote. But this report had not yet been submitted to the House — in fact was awaiting the reduction of the Democratic minority so that its passage might be assured. But the question would admit of no longer delay and Reed determined on another and bolder procedure.

One of the first rules ever adopted by the House of Representatives was one requiring all members to vote. The first member who persistently refused to obey that rule was John Quincy Adams, in 1832 and during the remainder of his congressional career. The initial efforts to compel his acquiescence in the rule failed, and the evil grew rapidly until, in the forties, it became firmly established as a means of effectively blocking business. In the thirty-eighth Congress it was proposed to count those present but not voting so as to constitute the necessary quorums. Speaker Colfax, however, refused to assume the responsibility for so radical a departure from the established custom. On February 24th, 1875, the leaders of the forty-third Congress sought to induce Speaker Blaine to count a quorum when the minority were practicing the actual-presence-but-constitutional-absence theory. Blaine replied to their insistent request, that "it would be an absurdity for the Chair to oppose his opinion to the actual record of the roll-call. The Chair cannot declare a quorum on a yea-and-nay vote," he said. "The moment you clothe your Speaker with power to go behind your roll-call and assume that there is a quorum in the hall, why, gentlemen, you stand on the very brink of a volcano."

In 1879 Tucker of Virginia offered an amendment to the rules conferring on the Speaker the power to declare a quorum whenever those voting and those present but declining to vote should together constitute a majority of the House. His amendment received but little support from his own side of the House and was so vigorously attacked by the Republicans that he withdrew it to ward off defeat. Blaine was one of its most insistent opponents, and delivered a speech defending the filibustering tactics of the Republicans during the sessions of that Congress. The opinion rendered by Blaine that the majority party must furnish the quorum in order to conduct business was quoted as authority. Reed had further declined to support Keifer on an appeal when as a member of the forty-seventh Congress the Speaker had approached the Republican floor leaders with the quorum-counting ruling which he proposed to make. Nor had Reed at any time during his service, when the Republicans were in the minority, hesitated to take frequent and effective advantage of this same technical absurdity to prevent the majority from acting.

While Reed's rulings of the 29th and 30th of January startled the country, yet in various legislative and municipal bodies, as well as decisions of the court, there could be found at once precedent and authority.

In 1874 the Speaker of the House of Representatives of Massachusetts, the Hon. John E. Sanford, ruled that "it is not necessary to a valid decision of a question that a quorum shall vote, if the requisite number be present." In Maine in 1880 the courts had declared legal an act of a board of aldermen whose aims a present, but silent, minority had attempted to block. In Illinois the court said, "There is no propriety in giving to a refusal more potency than to a vote cast." The Supreme Court of New Hampshire declared "the exercise of the law-making power is not to be stopped by the mere silence and inaction of some of the law-makers who are present." In December, 1889, the Supreme Court of Indiana held that: "It is inconceivable that their silence should be allotted greater force than their active opposition. . . . Certainly the most that can, with the faintest tinge of plausibility, be claimed is that their votes must be counted against the resolution. If members present desire to defeat a measure they must vote against it, for inaction will not accomplish their purpose. Their silence is acquiescence rather than opposition."

In 1883 Lieutenant Governor David B. Hill of New York had made a similar ruling in the Senate of that State, and had been upheld by the decision of the courts. The same rulings had been made in Ohio, Kentucky, and twice in Tennessee; and in 1889 the principle of quorum-counting was specifically incorporated into the joint rules of the legislature of Massachusetts.

Reed's ruling has not been vindicated — as is generally supposed — by the United States Supreme Court; but the constitutionality of the rule, as a method of determining the presence of a quorum, was established in the case of United States *v.* Ballin.

The great question which confronted the fifty-first Congress upon its organization was not what it should legislate about, but whether it should even be permitted to legislate at all. In recent years filibustering had grown until it promised to completely check all attempts at legislation. Three methods, generally speaking, were adopted by the minority to prevent action by the majority. Yet, either under the rules formally adopted, or the customs long sanctified for governing all deliberative bodies in the transaction of their business, these practices were permissible. The refusal of a quorum, dilatory motions, and prolonged debate constituted the effective triangle of obstruction.

The Constitution fixes a quorum at a majority of the members of the House and provides that one fifth of those present may demand that the vote on any question shall be taken by the "yeas and nays." If the margin of political ascendency in a legislative body is narrow, it is practically impossible to maintain through every minute of every session a majority quorum on the floor. Therefore the refusal of a quorum by the minority has been at once the most facile and the most effective measure by which the minority could defeat the consideration of any business distasteful to it.

Thus mere inertia had become a match for ballots. This system, so popular and so efficacious in Washington, rapidly spread through the country. Nor was that surprising, for it is far easier to maintain silence than to debate, and more suggestive of repose to yield to the laws of gravitation than to expend physical and nervous energy. Had it been restrained within conservative bounds and had it been employed only as a means of preventing some violent legislative enactment, or calling to the attention of the nation some gross administrative neglect of the majority, it would have long endured and found strong supporters. But in 1882 it was adopted as the method of preventing a vote on contested election cases and in 1889 it effectively established the old Liberum Veto of the Polish Diets by which any single member could negative the vote of all others. It was adopted with acclaim in the State legislatures; it was practiced in city councils and school boards and here it came in direct contact with the people. It even invaded the realm of business and was apparent in the meetings of the boards of directors of private corporations. This pleasant fiction of physical presence and constructive absence might have flourished in the seductive atmosphere of distant Washington but when it invaded the very regions of business the bubble was quickly pricked.

Scarcely less effective than the system of constructive absence was the dilatory motion as a weapon of parliamentary obstruction. Until the fifty-first Congress an individual member could make any motion he saw fit, provided he secured the floor. With the support of but one fifth of the members present — and that was never difficult to secure — he could set in motion the roll-call and he and his associates needed only to respond to their names and renew motions twice in an hour and the legislative assembly of the nation was paralyzed while four fifths of its members were literally shackled and helpless. This one-fifth order for yeas and nays intended by the framers of the Constitution simply to show the constituencies how their Representatives voted, had been prostituted to the use of the filibusters. Until the Reed rules were adopted, a motion to take a recess and to adjourn to a time certain were privileged motions, and, like the motion to adjourn, always in order.

If any member or coterie of members wished to obstruct the dissenting majority, a member of the minority would move to recess or adjourn until eight o'clock; another would move to amend the hour to read to 8.30, and still a third would move an amendment to the amendment to make it 9.30. Thus an endless chain of amendments and roll-calls would be launched and the House would be helpless. Or on bill day, if any disgruntled member wished to forestall legislation he need only offer the Revised Statutes for re-enactment and have them read while no one could restrain him. This was at once the simplest and thus the most brutal weapon in the arsenal of the filibuster.

The third method of parliamentary obstruction and the most common in deliberative assemblies, is that of unlimited oratory invoked simply to defeat action. This can always be anticipated by the adoption of a rule to take a vote at a certain hour, to limit speeches to a certain length, or by what is known in England as cloture or in the United States as the previous question. The previous question had been adopted into the rules of the House of Representatives in 1789, in the English sense, and was so maintained for twenty years. In 1811 the House under Clay decided on an appeal from the Chair that the previous question shut off further debate and secured an immediate vote on the main question.

This rule gave the majority the power to close debate and was necessary at the time of its adoption, when the majority of the House of Representatives were seeking to force through the necessary legislation to inaugurate the second war with England. A gag-rule it was, of course, but yet it was necessary if legislation were to be secured. Yet, effective as it seems, the previous question has been only partially successful in preventing obstruction. It has never been applied in Committee of the Whole; where obstruction is at once most frequent and most effective, nor in the United States Senate, which is now our real deliberative assembly.

On the 14th of February, 1890, the House of Representatives adopted the report of the Committee on Rules afterwards known as the "Reed Rules." The Republican members of that committee were Reed, McKinley, and Cannon.

In this new code five innovations were proposed: —

1. All members must vote unless they have a pecuniary interest in the question at issue.

2. The dignity of the House and the rights of members are given precedence over every question but a motion to adjourn.

3. One hundred shall constitute a quorum in the Committee of the Whole.

4. Members present but not voting may be counted as a part of the quorum in any ordinary session of Congress.

5. No dilatory motion shall be entertained by the Speaker.

With their adoption the cry of impotent rage was renewed against the Speaker. Around the last two of the five enumerated rules waged the storm of bitter criticism and hostile invective. Although the Constitution merely provides that a majority shall constitute a quorum to do business and does not demand that that quorum shall be

"Czar" Reed — The "Revolution"   229

ascertained by a roll-call nor deny that those who refuse to vote are physically present and are constituent portions of the quorum, the Democrats throughout the country assailed Reed as the despoiler of the Constitution and the assassin of democratic government. The quorum-counting rule was fortified by the rule allowing the Speaker to order absentees arrested, brought to the bar of the House and counted as present for the purpose of constituting a quorum in case they refused to vote on the pending question. Against the fifth rule the artillery of abuse was particularly directed. Outside of the following seven motions — to adjourn, to lay on the table, for the previous question, to postpone to a fixed date, to refer, to amend, and to postpone indefinitely — called motions of right and having special privileges — the Speaker was given the power to declare from his own individual judgment that certain motions were intended to obstruct business and thus refuse to entertain them. The press of the nation could not be silenced from the Chair of the Speaker, but those members of the House who protested were promptly disciplined.

"The sacred rights of the minority" constituted the text of the opposition, as though that were some fetich, some sacred combination of words before which all must bow, or as though the rights of the majority were less sacred. Nowhere did these critics preach of the *duties* of minorities. No matter how many fictions may be devised, so many checks and balances are placed about majorities that we are to-day quite largely governed by minorities.

The death-knell of filibustering had been sounded. Until the election of the fifty-first Congress this had not been a partisan question. The country at large, and the leaders of both parties, had wearied of the spectacle of a minority, of even a single member, defying the majority and effectively blocking legislation, and they were united in the belief that a radical reform must be brought about. Yet when the Democrats scanned the election returns and realized that they were in the minority and, further, when they saw that the Republicans intended to legislate radically upon the tariff and the question of the supervision of elections, in harmony with the platform on which the people had elected them, then the question began to assume the tinge of partisanship. The Democrats frankly declared and openly threatened that they would permit no legislation of which they did not approve.

Thus the will of the people was to be set at naught — and it became not so much a question of what laws should be enacted, but whether popular opinion should be ignored. In short, reduced to its last analysis, the question involved the survival of representative government. The issue then was a vital one and no one more correctly gauged it than did Speaker Reed.

Reed later declared in response to a question as to what course he would have pursued had the House refused to support his radical ruling: "I should simply have left the Chair, resigning the Speakership, and left the House resigning my seat in Congress. . . . If political life consisted in sitting helplessly in the Speaker's Chair and seeing the majority powerless to pass legislation I had had enough of it and was ready to step down and out."

In the destruction of one evil, that of filibustering, the field was prepared for another and possibly more dangerous one — the one-man power. Yet during the entire six years of Reed's service as Speaker, no reputable man ever questioned either his absolute integrity or honesty. Nor was there even a single accusation that he refused to entertain any motion offered in good faith. Every member whom he declined to recognize was one who clearly desired the floor simply as a means of obstructing the conduct of business. Those whom he counted in constituting the quorum were actually present in the chamber. He was not misled even when such men as Congressman, later Governor, Flower was violently denouncing him for counting them present at the very time that they were addressing him in their impotent frenzy and declaring themselves constructively absent.

"What becomes of the rights of the minority," they demanded of Reed. He replied as if to mock the question, "The right of the minority is to draw its salaries and its function is to make a quorum."

The charge was widely made and generally credited that the adoption of the Reed Rules would prevent all debate in the House and thus propagate untold dangers. It was asserted that the lock step at the penitentiary would be airy freedom compared with the future congressional procession. It was very clear, however, with the marvelous development of the country, both in physical size and in diverse commercial interests, that the practice of unlimited discussion, even if honestly indulged in, and not for the purpose of filibustering, had become incompatible with the proper progress of business under modern conditions.

Even under the repressive "Reed Rules" there was

ample opportunity for debate. The most conclusive answer to the charge that debate would be strangled is found in the fact that the Congressional Record shows that there was more debate in the fifty-first than in any preceding Congress. In reality, the application of those rules has actually enlarged the principle of freedom of debate. The time formerly consumed in dilatory roll-calls and filibustering is now largely devoted to legitimate discussion.

Reed went to the heart of the situation in a statement on the present status of parliamentary laws. "The whole matter," he declared, "is very simple. You have a representative body to legislate for a great country. Many thousands of bills are introduced at each session. If the House worked night and day it could not give intelligent consideration to one half of these measures. In practice it is found impossible to act upon one tenth of them. What then shall we do? Shall there be no legislation because not all can be done that should be done? If some must be favored for consideration, who shall select these? The committees? Yes; but there are many committees all pressing for legislation which they deem important, and the House has only so much time at its disposal. In order that anything like attention to the most important interests shall be given, there must be a process of selection. This work cannot be well given over. The Speaker alone is responsible to the entire House. He must aim, of course, to carry out the desires of the committees and should he act in an arbitrary or unfair way, he would be very quickly brought to book by them. He cannot exist without their support." This was his reply to the charge that the members no longer deliberate and follow their own convictions but that they simply assemble daily to enact such matters of legislation as have already been decided upon by the Speaker and his trusted associates.

Through all of these trying days of conflict, of personal denunciation, and bitter excoriation it does not appear that Reed wavered once. He had determined upon the course to pursue, and his iron will never faltered. He had prepared himself to assume the consequences and he held his party to the task with a grip that was never once relaxed. He controlled the session absolutely. Individual members were stifled and committee reports were smothered while many bills that had already been agreed upon — particularly bills for public buildings — were withheld from the House at the dictate of the Speaker.

At once Reed became the most conspicuous man in the Republican party and the most prominent figure in public life. His rulings and his conduct were cited with approval or denounced with scorn in every legislative body in the civilized world.

Reed was literally the master of the House. The cartoonist fostered this conception and pictured "Czar Reed" with an imperial crown on his massive brow and a scepter with which he belabored the shrinking crowd around him. His attitude toward the Republican party was the replica of Carlisle's attitude toward the Democratic. He sought not so much to represent his party as to force his own views upon it. One member picturesquely denounced him for "sitting in the chair with his feet on the neck of the Republican party." Like Carlisle, Reed had appointed the chairman of Appropriations, and the chairman of the Ways and Means and the Speaker himself as the majority members of the Committee on Rules. The three most powerful men in the House were thus associated and all legislative power concentrated. He ruled by the force of his will and the strength of his logic, rather than by any art of the diplomat or wile of the politician.

One experience reveals the application of those traits which earned for him the sobriquet of "Czar" Reed. There was a brief lull in the business of the House and the day and hour were opportune. The leader of the minority was known to have ready for presentation a resolution recognizing Cuban belligerency. The floor of the House was almost deserted and the member rising from his seat, and calling "Mr. Speaker," stood out conspicuously. "Mr. Speaker," again repeated the leader of the minority. Meanwhile Dingley of Maine was seated at his desk, paying no attention to the surrounding affairs, and clearly absorbed in some tariff statistics. Reed, ignoring the member insistent upon recognition, gazed into space. Without any further activity on the floor of the House, the nasal drawl of the Speaker could be heard — "The gentleman from Maine moves that the House do now adjourn. Do I hear a second? The motion is seconded. The question is now on the motion to adjourn. All in favor will say 'aye.' Those opposed, 'no.' The 'ayes' have it. The — House — stands — adjourned," punctuated with the sharp rap of the gavel. Dingley, awakened from his study by the noise, looked up with an inquiring air. He had uttered no sound, nor had there been an audible "second." Indeed the Republican members had been so completely unconscious of the proceedings that not over ten voted on the motion. Still the House stood adjourned

"Czar" Reed — The "Revolution" 235

by the unauthorized but deliberate conduct of the man who had been elected merely to give voice to its will. A notable tribute this was to the one-man power. Yet Reed had acted from thoroughly patriotic motives, and he felt that he had averted a great danger and had saved the country from war with Spain.

The only commentary that one may offer is that, should the Speaker in time become either himself corrupt or be controlled by the forces of corruption, his office would be a most powerful fulcrum for the overthrow of democratic institutions. That the cause was worthy and the motive pure alone saved Reed's conduct from being a national calamity.

Another congressional incident of the Spanish war days, while the country seethed with excitement over the destruction of the Maine, is interesting as revealing the manner in which Reed plied the club of power. The clamor for an immediate declaration of war was so insistent that several Republican members, hostile to President McKinley, took advantage of the situation to discountenance the administration. They joined the Democrats in an affort to sustain an appeal from the Speaker's decision in ruling out a resolution to declare war long before the country was ready for the struggle. The insurgent Republicans, adopting the Cuban term "Reconcentrados," met in secret session, and sought to muster enough Republican support to overrule Reed. All manner of inducements, rewards, and threats were suggested in the effort to carry their point. A man of less courage and determination than Reed might have yielded. He, however, stood firm and manifested his ability as a leader and

Speaker by withholding this virtual declaration of war until the President informed Congress that the nation was at length ready for the conflict.

When the resolution was finally offered and the Speaker declared it in order, the "Reconcentrados," who had been clamoring so loudly for hostilities, now threw every possible obstacle in the way of a clear-cut declaration of war by offering amendments to recognize the independence of Cuba, etc. At this juncture the excitement in the House became so intense that every member jumped to his feet, and for an interval Reed lost control of the situation. Charges and countercharges were wildly bandied about; the lie was passed between Bartlett of Georgia and Brumm of Pennsylvania who were standing in what was called the "Cherokee Strip" on the Democratic side of the House; a general rush of members toward the contestants followed this exchange of compliments. Cooler heads and a calmer frame of mind prevailed, Reed soon regained control of the feverish assemblage and the resolution was adopted without amendment.

Yet Reed was entirely out of sympathy with the Republican party in its treatment of the Spanish colonial possessions. He denounced the acquisition of the Philippines as an operation at once un-American and freighted with trouble. "The Senate is arranging to pay two dollars a piece for the little brown bellies, but in the end they will cost us many thousands each," was his observation when told that there were ten million Filipinos in the islands. Within ten years from the ratification of the treaty the sober judgment of the majority of the people is that the Philippines should be disposed of in some manner consistent with the dignity and honor of the United States.

The personality of a man who could effect such a complete parliamentary revolution as that of 1890 is interesting. Reed was a careful student of political history and philosophy, and a man with strong convictions and practical views of public policy. He combined in effective harmony strength of character, force of ideas, and political sagacity. Temperamentally he was aggressive, with a will of iron and nerves of steel, serenity of temper, and cosmopolitan broadness of view.

He presented a striking contrast to McKinley, with whom he saw much political service. Reed was bound by his personal convictions, which were at once so clear and firm as to defy popular clamor or mock public opinion. This probably is a political weakness, but Reed was at all times a statesman rather than a politician. Even his ambition to be President, keen and enduring as it was, could not shake his determination to follow the line of personal conviction. He often marveled at the popularity of McKinley. McKinley was quite the antithesis — a diplomat, a charmer of men by the arts of persuasion and personal contact.

Reed relied rather on the appeal to the head than to the heart — but his faith in the intellectual balance of sentimental America was destined only to mock him.

Reed acquired an imperishable reputation as a wit; it was not, however, so much wit as a cleverness of retort, which a mental aptitude, developed by eighteen years of continuous practice, had given him.

He used to say with keen scorn in his attacks on the

Democratic party — "individual Democrats have principles but the party has none." He believed that the Republican party stood for the only worthy and safe policy and thus he was naturally an intense partisan. This probably accounts in some degree for his indignation that at the opening of the fifty-first Congress, the Republican party should be the victims and the sport of a noisy, defiant, and mocking minority. "The mentor of the Republicans and the tormentor of the Democrats," Lafe Pence characterized him.

As Speaker he was a strict disciplinarian enforcing even the minor rules of the House with religious scruple. He had a high sense of the dignity of his office. He permitted no smoking on the floor of the House. One warm day a member removed his coat and flaunted his shirt sleeves before the nation — Reed promptly dispatched a page to order the coat restored to its proper domain. His clever wit often won obedience where a sterner manner would have inspired defiance. A member with low shoes and white socks one afternoon deposited this combination on his desk in front of him. Reed sent an assistant Sergeant-at-arms with the message, "The Czar commands you to haul down those flags of truce."

The many stories told of Reed illustrate his keen sense of humor coupled with a cleverness of satire which often, in a single sentence, combined a character sketch with a political speech. A member from Louisiana once approached him with a frank request that he be placed on the Committee on Rivers and Harbors. Reed looked at the suppliant very gravely and in a low but decisive tone of voice asked: "How much of a steal do you want?"

The answer apparently not being satisfactory, the request was denied.

On one occasion when Breckenridge of Kentucky had paused in a speech of most mournful and distressing cadences, Reed convulsed the House by pretending to weep; holding his handkerchief to his eyes, he exclaimed aloud to Cannon, while the funereal tones of the orator still echoed in the hall: "Joe, were you acquainted with the deceased?"

The Hon. Robert R. Hitt used to tell with unction of his first meeting with Reed. Hitt had just been elected to his first term in Congress, and on the opening day of the session was on the Pennsylvania Avenue cars bound for the Capitol. Next to him sat the Speaker with whom, however, he was not acquainted. When the conductor requested the fares, Hitt, having no small change, tendered a five-dollar bill. The conductor scowled, handed back the bill, and said he could not make the change. Whereupon Reed handed out the necessary nickel for his associate and the conductor passed on. Turning to Hitt, Reed asked, "Do you work this racket on the conductors as a regular thing?" With this incident began an intimate acquaintance which terminated only with Reed's death.

One morning the redoubtable J. Hamilton Lewis, a picturesque and talkative Beau Brummel from the Pacific coast, resplendent in immaculate array, and still gloved, rushed madly down the center aisle waving on high a copy of the New York *Sun*. "Mr. Speaker," he shouted, "I rise to a question of personal privilege. I have here a copy of this morning's New York *Sun* in which I am referred to as 'a thing of beauty and a joy forever.'" Instantly Reed retorted, "The point is well taken; it should have been a thing of beauty and a jaw forever." Lewis, with the grace to appreciate such spontaneous humor, joined in the applause which followed this sally.

On one occasion a member of the House, on terms of rather close personal friendship with Speaker Reed, asked him his opinion of another member. "Well," said the Speaker in his inimitable manner, "——— is a first rate fellow, and I like him very much; but the trouble with him is that he fails to realize his true relation to the stellar universe."

Congressman Sulzer once applied to Speaker Reed for recognition to pass a pension bill for an old soldier. Mr. Reed took the bill, read it over, and then said to Mr. Sulzer: "This man is not entitled to a pension under the law. I am worried nearly to death with these pension bills."

"I know it," good naturedly replied Sulzer, "but just think of it, Mr. Speaker, if I do not pass this bill it will be the death of this poor old soldier. Recognize me and I will get it through in a few minutes, and I will save two lives, yours and his."

Sulzer had scarcely descended the steps from the Speaker's Chair, when Mr. Reed announced:

"The gentleman from New York is recognized to pass a pension bill. All in favor signify by saying 'Aye'; those opposed 'Nay.' The bill is passed and two lives are saved — the old soldier's and that of the gentleman from New York."

The House laughed, but only the Speaker and Sulzer understood the joke.

"Czar" Reed — The "Revolution" 241

In view of Reed's well-known characterizations of public men, particularly interesting is the comment of Crisp, who was later Speaker of the House, upon the attitude of the Republican members toward the "Czar." "The unquestioning loyalty of the Republican following to Reed," he said, "reminds me of the Hindu who, kneeling in prayer before his idol, consoled himself with the idea that though his god was ugly yet he knew it was great."

The fifty-first Congress, thus dominated and controlled by Reed, passed several measures of an extreme partisan tone. Even with the restraining influence of Reed to head off the forays on the "trough," the appropriations of this Congress reached an enormous total. "The billion dollar Congress" the Democrats called it. "This is a billion dollar country," Reed replied, but even this clever retort failed to convince the electorate of the necessity for such extravagance.

In the elections of 1890 the country was swept by a Democratic landslide and with the fifty-second Congress in 1891, Reed became the leader of an effective minority. So bitter had been the animosities of the fifty-first Congress, that when, upon its adjournment, the customary vote of thanks to the Speaker was moved, the minority voted in the negative. To this farewell Parthian shot Reed made an effective retort in his valedictory speech.

When the Republicans were restored to power four years later Reed was again elected Speaker and served in that capacity during the fifty-fourth and fifty-fifth Congresses. During his six years service as Speaker, never once did the breath of scandal touch him — a remarkable and refreshing record in the murky moral atmosphere of the national Capitol.

In 1899 Reed had ceased to be *en rapport* with the Republican party. His convictions on American colonialism were too strong and his conceptions of political principles too clear to be subordinated to mere acquiescence in party councils. Too much of a patriot and statesman to become a mere disgruntled obstructionist, he conceived that the only good consistent course was to withdraw from public life. Further he had only a very modest fortune and he felt strongly the obligation to give up the meager salary of public service for the more remunerative income of the law. Offered $50,000 a year as his share of the profits of a New York law firm, he accepted the arrangement. At the close of the fifty-fifth Congress on the 3d of March, 1899, Reed withdrew from public life. He died December 2d, 1902.

The greatest monument to his memory and to the value of his work as Speaker was reared by the Democrats long before his retirement from Congress. The fifty-second Congress convened in Washington, December 7th, 1891, with the Democrats firmly in the saddle. In the Democratic caucus a bitter fight had been waged for the Speakership. Carlisle was no longer a Representative or the ballot would have been a mere formality. He had firmly established himself in the hearts of all true Democrats by his success in the Speaker's Chair and his ability as a leader on the floor. But when Carlisle wielded the scepter he permitted no heir apparent. Among the leading Democrats were Judge Charles F. Crisp of Georgia, Roger Q. Mills of Texas, and Wm. M. Springer of Illinois. Of these the best known nationally was Mills who had been the Democratic tariff leader in the fifty-first Congress. But Mills possessed certain temperamental qualities which militated against him — warm tempered and impulsive he frequently lost that self-control and poise so necessary to the presiding officer of a deliberative assembly. Crisp had been rather the political leader of the minority in the general questions of legislation, and particularly in the parliamentary evolutions necessary to secure proper Democratic alignment under the Reed rules. Crisp was moreover a man of marked judicial temperament, calm and deliberative with ability to maintain through trying crises his own dignity and the dignity of his position. But the eternal question of the "pork barrel" was injected into the caucus. The old members advocated the election of Crisp. The new ones saw their chance for desirable committee assignments if they could secure the election of Mills. Springer of Illinois, hero of one of Reed's famous retorts, was the third candidate; his following was mostly of a personal nature, such as a member of ability will attract after long service. During Reed's first term in the Chair Springer, in the course of an appeal, quoted Clay's famous epigram, "I would rather be right than be President." *Sotto voce* Reed's answer could be heard, "The gentleman need not worry for he will never be either." This had clung to Springer and doubtless hurt him in this contest.

Compromise seemed impossible and the triangular fight bade fair to open party sores and engender factional strife. After thirty ballots had been cast in the caucus a majority was finally secured by Crisp.

The Democratic House immediately turned to the welcome task of banishing the "Reed Rules." The defeat of the Republican party in 1890 had been overwhelming, and they found themselves a minority of but one fourth the total membership of the House. The Republicans could offer no effective opposition with such a disparity of strength. With pride of conscious power the successful party set about its task of restoring the old order. During these two years the Democrats were able to conduct business through their overwhelming majority, though it was at all times unwieldy and frequently inefficient.

Although Crisp went back to the Democratic rules of the fiftieth Congress he introduced a new type of parliamentary "tyranny" fully as obnoxious as the Reed Rules, in an amendment reported from the Committee on Rules of the fifty-second Congress. This established the Committee on Rules as the autocrats of legislation in the House. This was a radical departure from the long-established rules and principles of parliamentary law and practice. The tyranny of Reed seemed beneficence when Crisp ruled that not even "the question of consideration could be raised against a report from the Committee on Rules." This committee, dominated of course by the Speaker, became the dictator of the House and the members were forbidden even to question its wisdom or decision by invoking against its report the question of consideration, a fundamental principle of all legislative and deliberative assemblies. Thus the power of the Committee on Rules to force action on any measure effectively precluded dilatory motions.

On the 7th of August, 1893, the fifty-third Congress

was convened in special session. The Democrats had been retained in power, though by a largely reduced majority, and Crisp was re-elected Speaker. With a more evenly balanced political alignment on the floor the Democrats were in danger of being checkmated in their efforts to pass purely party measures. They had two years previously held a Boston tea party over the "Reed Rules" but now by their own impotency they were forced to drag the seas, and resurrect those rules of procedure which had been so ruthlessly thrown overboard. The quorum-counting rule was restored, though in somewhat different shape. In the form in which it was adopted by the fifty-third Congress, when the "yeas and nays" were demanded, the Speaker was empowered to appoint two tellers, one from each party; these were to note those present who refused to vote, and add their names to those who voted so as to constitute a quorum. The rule providing that one hundred members shall constitute a quorum of the Committee of the Whole was also restored as a political necessity by the hard pressed, if inconsistent, Democrats.

Crisp proved a vigorous and aggressive political leader and was credited with the legislation of both the fifty-second and fifty-third Congresses. He was essentially a political Speaker, but, while his parliamentary decisions often displayed a decidedly Democratic tint, he never failed to maintain the respect of his political opponents. Although a good parliamentarian, many of his rulings can scarcely be reconciled with any sound principle of parliamentary law or practice. Yet Crisp never secured control of legislation to the extent that Reed had. Reed conceived this to be at once a political and personal duty.

While Crisp was Speaker of the House in the fifty-third Congress, Senator Colquitt died, and the Governor of Georgia telegraphed Crisp that he would appoint him to fill the vacancy. With a fidelity to duty, a respect for the friends who had elected him Speaker, rarely to be seen in public life, and with a proper appreciation of the great honor and power attached to the Speakership, Crisp gathered his Democratic friends around him, and, after consulting them, said: — "I am thankful for the honor conferred on me by my brother Representatives and I appreciate the position I hold, and having accepted the high honor I will decline the Senatorship, fill out my term as Speaker, and then be a candidate for the Senate." This he did and although successful in his campaign for the Senate he died without entering upon his duties in that body.

One anecdote is told of Crisp which is eloquently expressive of a truth abundantly illustrated in Congressional life. Once Crisp left the Speaker's Chair after getting "order" for a member who was holding the floor but not his audience. The Speaker had pounded the House into temporary quiet, and, yielding the gavel to another, went into the Democratic "cloak-room." He appeared somewhat annoyed — he was of the placid, unruffled order of men — for the "orator" upon the floor had repeatedly called upon the presiding officer to secure "order" for him. As Crisp passed into the cloak-room, he said, "The Chair can get order for a member but it is the fault of the member if the order is lost; a speaker must himself keep order." The truth of this comment is exemplified almost every hour when the House is in session. Only those whom the members desire to hear have order.

Reed, as leader of the minority during the fifty-third Congress, received the rare vindication of seeing his political opponents adopt the very system of rules for which they had so scathingly denounced him. A still greater vindication, however, was in store. In the elections of 1894 the Republicans were restored to power by a vote larger than any they had ever yet received in the two-score years of their party existence. Reed was elected Speaker of the fifty-fourth Congress (and again of the fifty-fifth) which contained the largest Republican majority (133), to that time, ever returned.

Carlisle, Reed, and Crisp had each added largely to the evolutionary development of the Speakership, and yet each had added a different element of strength, each had developed a new method of dominating the body over which he presided. Carlisle had arbitrarily and effectively employed the right of recognition and thereby made himself a power and withal brought upon himself the cudgels of denunciation — a vigorous warning to any who might dare to imitate. Reed had stamped out filibustering and the press of the country appeared with the black borders of despair, and the red type of anger. Crisp had built the Committee on Rules into an effective weapon of power. While each Speaker had initiated some virile reform yet each was the stronger by the development due to his predecessor. The great fact was established — and therein lies the justification of this trinity of arbitrary methods — that the majority could do business, could legislate as they had been instructed by the ballots, and that the minority still existed as an appreciable factor in the equation.

With the retirement of Reed from political life and the

retention of the Republicans in power in the fifty-sixth Congress, by a majority of thirteen, no one man stood out in the limelight as conspicuously deserving the mantle of leadership. General David B. Henderson of Iowa, soldier and patriot, was chosen. The elements which conspired to secure the election of Henderson were entirely personal. He had enjoyed a long term in Congress and was familiar with its rules and usages; he was genial, kindly, and personally popular, and above all he stood out as a representative of the influence of the Civil War as a factor in politics. He had fought and suffered for his country, had lost a leg in its service, and was the personification of military heroism. Henderson was the type always associated with camp-fires, reunions, fourth-of-July speeches, and flag raisings. A man of moderate ability and rather weak of will power, he was dominated at all times by the members of the Committee on Rules, consisting of Payne, Dalzell, and Cannon Henderson as a Speaker betrayed his weak points, not the least of which was a narrow partisanship, and he was a decided disappointment to the country. He was, however, re-elected Speaker of the fifty-seventh Congress but retired to the more fitting scenes of private life after the close of its second session. A man of intemperate habits, probably induced by the suffering from his old wound, the whisper of scandal was frequently heard and his private morals were questioned. It is held, however, by his friends that his retirement was due, not to threatened exposure, but rather to the insidious attacks of mental impairment which were already becoming apparent. Whatever may have been the cause, certainly none were so unsophisticated as to give credence to his avowed reason that he was no longer in harmony with the views of his constituents.

Such remarkable responsiveness to popular sentiment does not accord with the universally accepted tenets of political philosophy. Certainly previous to this General Henderson had never manifested such sensitiveness to any public unrest. However, there is no more mysterious science than the psychology of motive.

CHAPTER IX

JOSEPH G. CANNON — THE PRESENT SPEAKER

November 9, 1903, with the convening of the fifty-eighth Congress, in special session, Joseph G. Cannon of Illinois was elected Speaker. The old fourteenth Congressional District of Illinois sent Cannon to Congress in 1872, when he was thirty-six years of age. He has missed only two of the last thirty-six years as the Representative of this district.

His service, beginning when Grant was President and Blaine Speaker, has brought him into contact for a generation and more with all branches of the government and all the prominent statesmen of the time. He was soon appointed to membership on the Committee on Post Offices, where by diligent and persistent application he became an acknowledged authority on postal and subsidiary questions, thereby commanding a certain respectful consideration and earning promotion to more important assignments.

Cannon typifies the West — not the far West of mountains and prairies, and cowboys and Indians, nor the middle West of to-day, but the frontier West of half a century ago, the country of Douglas and Lincoln, and even Benton and Clay.

A study of Cannon's personality is interesting, not alone in its psychology but also in the insight which it gives into the impelling forces which dominate his life. Lincoln

Joseph G. Cannon — The Present Speaker 251

is his ideal of an American statesman and this ideal he has apparently sought to imitate in certain superficial traits of speech, dress, and habit. He is studiously democratic in his tastes, and remarkably abstemious in his habits and desires. At no time has he ever been subjected to moral or financial criticism.

His ideals are not exalted; he lacks imaginative or artistic genius. His mental attitude reveals the lack of such broadening influences as education, culture, and travel in early life; he has an honest and sincere contempt for art, architecture, and refinements generally. Cannon is probably the most unimaginative man in public life to-day. The new office buildings of the Senate and House of Representatives, strongly suggestive of institutional and military structures, are enduring monuments to this attitude of the present Speaker.

A superlatively intense partisan, he believes firmly in but two ideals — his party and his religion. To him all things of Democratic origin are inherently culpable. He clings with religious tenacity to the political ideals prevalent in the post-bellum days when he first entered Congress. His admiration is reserved for the man who votes the straight ticket. For the "mugwump" — the man who scratches his ticket — he feels only contempt.

Cannon is inherently a Tory, and withal an honest one. In Congress he fights for "vested rights" as conscientiously as Sir Pitt Crawley fought against the reform of the Rotten Boroughs.

The gentleman who nominated Mr. Cannon in the Republican caucus preceding the opening of the sixty-first Congress, referred to the present Speaker as "the Iron

Duke of American Politics." It is interesting to recall in this connection that the original Iron Duke, Wellington, was a notorious Tory and reactionary, the sworn enemy of all popular reform; that his victory over Napoleon retarded the progress of democratic ideals in Europe for at least a third of a century; and that Wellington battled as bravely in London as at Waterloo, and with all the vigor and valor of the old military squares against the efforts of the British people to gain adequate representation in Parliament. One does not forget, either, that in 1831 Apsley House, the residence of Wellington, was stormed by the London populace, that every window of the structure was broken in the fury of their attack, and that as a protection from future outbursts of that same hatred the Iron Duke erected iron blinds before his windows, and in this barricaded mansion the general of Waterloo spent his final years. Yet, it seems by times as though Speaker Cannon, this "Iron Duke of American politics," enjoys something of that same sort of popularity which was thus visited upon Sir Arthur Wellesley, the Duke of Wellington. On the whole the comparison may not have been inaccurate, for Wellington was also a constitutional conservative, with a hearty contempt for mere popular opinion.

Cannon is in all ways temperamentally a conservative. He constitutionally opposes any change from the existing order. It has been well said that had he attended the caucus on Creation he would have remained throughout loyal to Chaos. However much you may quarrel with his standards, judged by those standards Cannon is a man of remarkably strong character. His integrity has never been questioned though he has for years occupied a

Joseph G. Cannon — The Present Speaker 253

position where temptations might be manifold and his name easily associated with scandal.

His studied unconventionality is his chief personal characteristic; medium sized, with a quaint, ruddy face lighted generally with a kindly smile, chin whiskers, and thin white hair and piercing gray eyes; at banquets he drinks champagne from his water glass, tilts his chair back against the wall and smokes the finest cigars in the style popular at the cross-roads store.

As a legislator, he was from the first noted for his capacity for work, the foundation of all genuine success. An industrious student of fiscal problems, as chairman of the powerful Committee on Appropriations, he became adept at appropriation figures, mastered the details of our government, watched the daily balances of the Treasury, and fought expenditures with such zeal as to gain the title "watch-dog of the Treasury." He has a rare and courageous indifference to public opinion. At all times his frankness, even brutal bluntness, has commanded a certain measure of respect if not admiration. This honesty, this proud sincerity, are in refreshing contrast with the truckling tactics of the ordinary politician. He does not hesitate to announce his opinions or to fight for them in the face of bitter opposition. He scorns to quibble, he has no sympathy with those who dissemble.

Cannon's forensic ability developed from his common sense and his earnestness. Entirely lacking in eloquence, as we understand that term, with no wealth of figure or allusion, with no power of vocabulary, without the epigrammatic talent of McKinley or the quaint sarcasm of Reed, with a voice that is harsh and unattractive, Cannon is none the less a powerful speaker. Phraseology simple in its texture, a quaint philosophy and a homely supply of simile combined with a spirited earnestness, serve to drive home his remarks. His delivery is powerful, full of fire, and suggestive of the blows of the pugilist. In debate he presents an interesting figure. His oratorical attacks while on the floor of the House suggested physical rather than verbal combats. He would begin his speech with waistcoat open, and his coat sleeves pulled well up, his eyes sparkling with fire, even his hair and beard rising in partisan hostility. His speeches made, then as now, little impression when read, but owed their value to their effective delivery.

His words seemed to carry conviction, to impress his audience with his sincerity and his inherent honesty. He has been ever a foe to verbosity. He strips all speeches of oratorical underbrush. He possesses a keen contempt for mere oratory, the profligate waste of words. He seldom makes pretentious speeches, confining his efforts largely to a mere running fire of quips and satire.

At the Republican National Convention of 1908 Cannon presented just such an interesting oratorical figure when he appeared on the platform to second the nomination of Mr. Sherman for the Vice-Presidency. Clad in a black alpaca coat, the thin sleeves of which were held above his cuffs, with one leg of his wrinkled trousers caught on his shoe top, his vest unbuttoned, his hair tousled and thin arms waving, he made a remarkable speech, combining biblical quotation with the vernacular of the street. His appearance aroused the convention to cheers of laughter and applause, and secured for him a marked

Joseph G. Cannon — The Present Speaker

ovation. Yet Cannon was a source of constant embarrassment to the Republicans in the ensuing campaign. Cannon, not Bryan, was Taft's greatest impediment in the middle West. The spellbinders were constantly forced to apologize for his convention speech and explain or ignore his congressional record.

In 1908 a determined effort was made to defeat him for re-election to Congress. But his home town of Danville is proud of the fame he has bestowed upon it. With a magnificent federal building, a soldiers' home, a liberal and wise distribution of local patronage, and a superabundance of pensioners to his credit, his local organization was invulnerable and he was elected by a handsome majority.

Continued and valuable service in the House and his position as chairman of the Committee on Appropriations enabled him to secure the election as Speaker upon the retirement of General Henderson. While fighting the battles of his party on the floor of Congress for a third of a century he had made few personal enemies. Although regarded as a somewhat narrow-minded and deeply prejudiced partisan and a very mediocre parliamentarian, he possessed certain elements of good fellowship that made him popular on both sides of the chamber; homely and unconventional, free and intimate of speech, able to call half the members by their first names, his personal popularity was a powerful factor. But none considered him a great man — none ever classed him with Reed or Crisp or Carlisle.

An aggressive man, disposed to be arbitrary and addicted to having his own way, the rules of the House of Representatives have been a powerful instrument in his hands, and through them he has been able to stamp upon all legislation the impress of his peculiar personality.

When the Reed Rules were adopted parliamentarians realized that they would become a dangerous weapon in the hands of an undesirable Speaker. When Cannon with his conservative convictions made use of these rules to thwart the will and desire of the country at large, the people for the first time awakened to the dangers of the situation and their criticism was divided against the rules themselves and the man who applied them.

The power of Cannon is twofold; it is personal and it is legislative. His committee assignments are made with a particular view to securing legislative action in accord with his personal ideas. An industrious use of the Committee on Rules enables him to dominate at all times. No Speaker has more violently abused the power of personal recognition. If by some chance a member arises without having first consulted Cannon and manages to secure recognition by the very audacity of his act, the Speaker will say: — "For what purpose does the gentleman rise?" The member is thus forced into the humiliating and ridiculous position of explaining why he should be recognized. This explanation invariably being unsatisfactory, the Speaker raps sharply with his gavel, and answers: — "The Chair recognizes the gentleman from New York (some other member) to offer a motion." The member thus ignored can only resume his seat amid hilarious confusion.

Previous to the amendments of the sixty-first Congress on the days set aside for the enactment of purely local bills of a minor character by unanimous consent, the

Joseph G. Cannon — The Present Speaker 257

Speaker was able again to reward his friends and punish those inclined to rebellion. Often on the success of these bills would depend the re-election of many men to Congress. Each member was compelled first to consult the Speaker and secure his consent to recognition. The Speaker on these days had before him a list of the members to be recognized and this order was scrupulously followed. Thus the Speaker's power was neither to be ignored nor defied. His smile and assent made and unmade members, accordingly as he bestowed or withheld those powerful benefices.

The House of Representatives is to-day a parliamentary body with a general order of business which is scarcely ever followed but which is constantly displaced by the action of the Committee on Rules. The Speaker not only dominates this committee but, rather, is the committee itself. All legislation must be presented to the House through its various committees; in order to present their reports before the recent amendments these committees were compelled to go to the Committee on Rules and secure from this committee a special order or rule.

These special orders are usually secured for purely partisan measures. The following is an excellent example of a special order reported from the Committee on Rules and adopted by the House during Cannon's Speakership: — "Resolved that immediately upon the adoption of this resolution the House shall proceed to debate for a period not exceeding one hour the bill to further regulate commerce, with the amendments thereto recommended by the Committee on Inter-State and Foreign Commerce, as set forth in their report on the said bill; and at the end of the debate a vote shall be taken on the said amendments and on the bill to its final passage, without intervening motion."

Such an order permits only one hour of debate; it does not permit individual members to offer amendments but confines the voting to such amendments as may be offered by the committee; prohibits all appeal; and prevents the presentation of any motion, even the privileged motion for adjournment.

The greatest abuse of the functions of this committee is the presentation of orders prohibiting amendment. This has developed into a glaring evil. For example, a "sundry-civil" appropriation bill may contain several vicious sections and yet under such a rule it must be adopted or rejected *in toto*. It forces members who object to certain items of the bill, but approve of others, to support the entire measure. The result is that the bill may be laden with objectionable "riders."

Thus it happened that until the sixtieth Congress practically no bill came to the floor except by unanimous consent or under a special rule or order limiting the time it should be debated and regulating the fashion in which it could be amended and frequently the manner in which amendments should be voted upon. Discussion and amendments were permitted in the Committee of the Whole House and the final adoption of the measure by the House itself became a legal formality. Roll-calls could be demanded, however, on whether the House should go into Committee of the Whole, on the amendments accepted by the Committee of the Whole after the bill came up for formal adoption by the House, and on the formal passage of the bill itself by the House. A roll-call could also be demanded on the question of adjournment.

Toward the close of the first session of the Sixtieth Congress the Democrats organized a concerted filibuster. This filibuster consisted in demanding as many roll-calls as possible and in offering all manner of amendments in order to increase the opportunity for roll-calls. Also a roll-call was demanded every night on the question of adjournment.

The Rules Committee prepared to meet the issue and the House took an automatic recess at five o'clock each day on the word of the Speaker, although to do this it was necessary to continue indefinitely the legislative day. Other special orders throw the House automatically into Committee of the Whole on the presentation of an appropriation bill and limit the number of final roll-calls on the measure to two, one covering all amendments in a lump, and the other on the bill's passage. In a word the result of the procedure adopted by the Rules Committee has been gavel legislation by the Speaker. Small wonder it is, then, that Mr. Cannon has declared that he was "responsible" for such bills as are passed on the one hand or defeated on the other.

The methods of legislation to-day in the House of Representatives are quite the most arbitrary of any legislative body in the world. The personality of Cannon and the development of the function of the Committee on Rules have contributed to this end. The right to name all committees, the power to grant recognition, let alone the other great powers of his office, have been sufficient to sustain the Speaker in every action of parliamentary rule or procedure. It is practically impossible to force any committee to report a bill to the House for the reason that the other committees consider this an invasion of their rights and, standing together in their power, defeat such a motion. Previously even when a committee was prepared to report it rested entirely with the Speaker to determine arbitrarily whether the bill should be called up or considered. If it was denied a special order from the Committee on Rules, it was lost in the volume of other measures.

The question naturally arose, Why not abolish all this? Could not the members eliminate it by their votes? This seemed plausible and was a part of the defense which Cannon offered to all criticism. But it was against all the laws of human nature to suppose that any member would defy the Speaker, or would vote against him, when the very next day he might be forced to seek some committee assignment or secure recognition under the unanimous-consent rule.

To maintain equitable discipline on both sides of the House, the Speaker loans to the leader of the minority a certain portion of his power although it is occasionally to the interest of the Speaker to connive at a rebellion in the ranks of the dissenting party.

An incident of unpleasant notoriety shows the folly of Cannon's defensive claim that the majority rules. During his term in the chair a public-building bill prepared by the proper committee was ready to be reported to the House; a petition addressed to the Speaker, and signed by a majority of the members requested permission to consider the bill. The petition was laid upon the Speaker's desk, or thrown into the waste basket — the bill was never considered nor even reported out.

Cannon defends the system now in vogue with religious fervor. It is said that these special orders of the Committee on Rules are practically never used in the matter of private bills and are requisitioned scarcely more than ten times out of five hundred bills of a public nature. It is noticeable, however, that this system of procedure has been resorted to in bills of commanding public interest — such, for example, as the railroad rate bill and the employers' liability act.

The rules are most frequently used, it is asserted, to prevent amendment of partisan measures by members of the minority or by disgruntled members of the dominant party. Cannon's friends declare that the Committee on Rules is an evolution of, or supplement to, the old party caucus. That whereas in the days of old "King Caucus" a member read himself out of his party by offering amendments, so now he is glad to seek refuge from the indignation of disappointed constituents behind a rule. In reality the Committee on Rules is an evolution of the old motion to suspend the rules which required an affirmative vote of two thirds of the members. A rule which serves the same purpose can be carried by a scant majority vote.

There is no question that the criticism of the present rules and procedure has been intensified by the construction and application given them by the present Speaker. Until Cannon's elevation to the Chair the Speakers were content to work inside the legislative and parliamentary machinery and preserve the fiction that the majority, possessing the votes, naturally rule. But Cannon has been too frank, too impatient, too arrogant to pay homage to such pretense. Preceding and during the sessions of Congress Cannon states frankly what legislation will be enacted and what bills will be defeated. This is a part of his mental constitution — his party pride, his frankness, his dislike of pretense and sham. No other Speaker has done so much to educate the people of the country to the real power of his office; so to speak, he has conducted them back of the legislative scenes and explained to them the mechanism which controls the spectacle. Then too he has been more persistent in wielding the lash of his office upon the House. It seems an imperious assertion of power for a Speaker to ignore a petition signed by a majority of the members. He and his intimate legislative friends have been more arrogant and more contemptuous of public opinion than any of their predecessors.

Cannon's defense of his conduct is always at hand, and is entirely technical. He claims the members have the power to control absolutely all legislation and by the rule of the majority dethrone the Speaker; that he need not be impeached to be eliminated; that he can be deprived of his power at any time by a majority resolution. If Cannon is approached concerning the fate of a bill which has not been reported out of the committee to which it was referred, he will answer guilelessly that it is in the hands of the committee and that it is quite out of his power to be of assistance. This may be true but it ignores the fact that the committee was so appointed that a majority would be hostile to the measure.

The humor and picturesqueness of the man have served often to remove the bitterness naturally consequent upon

Joseph G. Cannon — The Present Speaker 263

his legislative conduct. On one occasion a motion was offered by a member of the minority. On the vote a swelling chorus of "Ayes" was followed by a few straggling "Noes." Cannon in his peculiarly grotesque manner announced "the 'Ayes' make the most noise, but the 'Noes' have it." Of course this was not essential as such a vote was merely preliminary to a division and roll-call. It, however, gave the "whips" opportunity to summon to the floor the absent members. None the less the incident clearly typifies the domination of Speaker Cannon.

On another occasion, many of the Republicans being away from their seats, the Democrats seized the opportunity thus offered to call up a measure in which they were interested. They proceeded to carry the measure to a vote as speedily as possible. Cannon dispatched messengers to summon the Republicans and resorted to all manner of parliamentary tactics to delay the voting. In final desperation he was forced to order a third roll-call in violation of all known precedent. A dozen enraged Democrats sprang to their feet: — "Why does the Chair call the roll a third time?" was their passionate query. Without hesitation Cannon replied: — "The Chair will inform the gentlemen that the Chair is hoping a few more Republicans will come in." The Democratic anger was lost in a storm of laughter and applause.

At one time while Cannon was presiding, a motion was made by a Democrat for the purpose of putting the majority on record, though with no hope of its adoption. A rising vote being demanded it was put to the House. Some five or six members rose in the affirmative and then half the House stood in the negative.

Cannon began to count, "One, two, three," he said: "four — oh, hell! a hundred," and thus the vote was recorded.

A message of President Roosevelt to Congress was forced to wait some twenty-four hours before it was read to the House. Cannon explained that this was the result of a parliamentary tangle but the impression prevailed, none the less, that it was a studied effort to rebuke the Chief Magistrate. Indeed there seems plenty of occasion for the humor of the member who, being requested by a constituent to secure for him a copy of the rules and regulations of the House, sent the man a picture of Speaker Cannon. And yet Cannon has not followed General Henderson's manner of handling the minority like galley-slaves. At all times he has treated them with fairness and generosity, at least by his own standards. Still in judging Cannon we must not lose sight of the fact that our political ideals have all undergone revolution since the days when he first acquired political leadership. Even in a short decade we have renounced the standards of popularity by which we were accustomed to judge public officials. Those who most criticise Cannon as a legislative force, like him as an individual.

Yet when all has been said it is still true that there never has been a man in the House of Representatives more the master of every parliamentary trick and technicality than Joseph G. Cannon, who is so fond of saying to his critics that he is but one member of the House, that he has but one vote and that the law making is in the hands of its members.

Popular dissatisfaction and political unrest under the

Joseph G. Cannon — The Present Speaker 265

legislative absolutism of Cannon reached the climax of revolt during the last days of the sixtieth and the opening hours of the sixty-first Congresses. Confronted with a hopeless ambition to defeat the Illinois Tory for re-election the parliamentary insurgents centered their efforts upon securing reforms in the rules and procedure of the House. To make the assault upon the entrenched forces of Cannonism required the rarest type of bravery — political heroism.

At the opening of the sixty-first Congress Cannon was re-elected to the Speakership for the fourth consecutive term, being the second Speaker in our history to whom such an honor has been awarded. Andrew Stevenson alone shares that distinction with Cannon. By a combination of members of the dominant party with the minority several changes in the existing rules were secured.

These amendments are of particular interest. First they established a calendar for unanimous consent, the apparent effect of which is to enable a member to bring a proposition before the House without having to consult the Speaker and secure from that official the promise of recognition. It is likely that under the new code it will be more difficult to force a bill through the House under unanimous consent. Instead of having only the Speaker to satisfy all the members must be shown the wisdom of the proposed legislation, probably unimportant to the public, but of manifest interest to specific localities.

The calendar Wednesday secured at the close of the sixtieth Congress is protected by requiring a two-thirds instead of a majority vote to set it aside. On calendar Wednesday the roll of committees must be called. Theoretically this gives every member an opportunity to demand consideration on any bill which has been favorably reported by a committee. Practically it is likely to mean that in the future bills will expire in the committee instead of on the calendar. The right has been secured to vote upon bills which reach the calendar, but the query suggests itself, What of the bills that never reach the calendar? Legislation can be killed by non-action in committee without either debate or roll-call on the floor of the House. Thus the right to name the committees constitutes a veto power in the hands of the Speaker.

The Speaker can no longer name the Committee on Rules, this function being exercised by the caucus of the dominant party. On a motion to recommit a bill after a rule from the Committee on Rules, subsequent to the demand for the previous question, the Speaker is directed to give preference in recognition for this purpose to a member who is opposed to the bill.

It is difficult, of course, to presage the probable result of an hitherto untried law of parliamentary procedure. The best that can be suggested is to point out its defects and the opportunity which may be afforded for ignoring its dictates. The establishment of a calendar for unanimous consent bills and the rule requiring a two-thirds vote for dispensing with calendar Wednesday may both be dismissed with but a single word of comment. It is true that the Representative may no longer be compelled to sue for recognition to secure unanimous consent for the enactment of some bill. It is equally true that the regular calendar is more strongly protected. But the Speaker still retains the power of appointing all committees, except the

Joseph G. Cannon — The Present Speaker 267

Committee on Rules. A little more discretion in appointing these committees, a thorough understanding with the prospective members of these committees before their appointment and it is reasonable to suppose that the calendar will be less clogged. In short, the logical result will be the death of more bills in committees. Moreover, calendar Wednesday may be defeated by the very simple legislative feat of recessing from the preceding day instead of adjourning under the regular custom.

After a bill which has been favorably reported shall have been upon either the House or the union calendar for three days any member is now permitted to file with the Clerk of the House a notice that he desires the bill placed upon the unanimous consent calendar. Then in due form and at the proper time, under the amended rules the Speaker is required to direct the Clerk to call the bills upon this calendar. Should objections be raised to the consideration of any bill thus called it is immediately stricken from this calendar and cannot regain a place thereon. It is apparent that the intervention of any of the lieutenants of the Speaker will be sufficient to deprive any bill of the sanction of unanimous consent. The bill is then *ipso facto* permanently removed from the calendar.

Conferring upon a caucus the power to name the members of the Committee on Rules is likely to prove equally meaningless. Unless a candidate for the Speakership controls a majority of a caucus he cannot be elected Speaker. But controlling that majority he can dictate his confrères on the Committee on Rules as completely as though the power of their appointment rested, as before, absolutely in his hands.

In short these amendments to the presents rules are reforms more in name than in fact. Against an hostile and determined Speaker they could avail naught.

The remaining amendment presents, however, an opportunity for some difference of opinion. One cannot do better than to quote the most distinguished authority on parliamentary law in this country, the Hon. Asher C. Hinds, who is the parliamentary clerk of the House and to whom Speaker Cannon constantly defers. Mr. Hinds in a personal letter under date of March 24, 1909, makes the following observations upon the amendment concerning the motion to recommit: — "This amendment is difficult to understand unless one has considerable knowledge of parliamentary law. Most important bills are considered in Committee of the Whole where the votes of individual members are not recorded. In this committee all sorts of amendments are offered, and are usually voted on by members in accordance with views formed from the instruction of the debate, although the member may know that a considerable element in his district who do not have his advantages of instruction may have views at variance with his vote. When the bill is reported from the Committee of the Whole the previous question is at once ordered on it, thus preventing the offering in the House of amendments voted down in Committee of the Whole. There has been, however, one motion to commit with instructions, which is in order after the previous question is ordered. But it has been the practice to recognize a member of the majority party to make this motion. Mr. Fitzgerald's amendment will force the Speaker to prefer a member of the minority party, and this

Joseph G. Cannon — The Present Speaker 269

will enable the minority to force the members of the House to go on record by 'yea' and 'nay' vote on a proposition which they have already rejected in Committee of the Whole on an unrecorded vote. The minority will have the same power as to bills considered under special orders. In other words members will be forced to record their positions on more questions than hitherto. The new amendment breaks up a system that has existed in the House for many years. It will force the member to record himself on many immature questions, and perhaps will tend to hasten the country into projects which have not been sufficiently searched in public discussion. In a time when it is the general belief that the House is too slow in responding to public opinion this new rule will be commended; in a time when the general belief is that the House is too precipitate and reckless in yielding to temporary clamor, the rule will probably be condemned. The minority party will probably profit by the new system, as Mr. Fitzgerald evidently expects."

The recent revolt in the House of Representatives was aimed not so much at the rules and procedure, as at the system which Speaker Cannon had perfected for their application and enforcement. This system in reality made him more powerful than the President of the United States. Without his consent and assistance, legislation was practically impossible. The President might recommend, but the Speaker dictated, legislation. He not only decided what legislation should be permitted, but he even shaped the form of that legislation to comply with his own personal ideals. Responsible to but one congressional district for his conduct, Cannon has in practice apparently represented the entire three hundred and ninety-one districts of the United States.

When we sum up the results of the insurrection we find: that Cannon was re-elected, though above courageous protest by certain members of his own party; that the old rules were readopted; that the amendments to those rules do not in reality touch the root of the evil; that the Speaker still has the power to pack his committees; that the Speaker and the Committee on Rules still have the power to seal or pronounce the fate of all legislation. So much for the concrete results. But in all fights there is a moral factor, frequently as potent as the physical elements concerned. And in this contest the moral effect of the insurrection is probably quite efficient and we may look to see the dominant factors in the House of Representatives chastened and subdued, with the result that we will have a more liberal administration of the rules in the future.

The slight reforms already secured may mean the beginning of a real revision. At least they constitute the most marked change since the Reed Rules were adopted in the fifty-first Congress. The results are already noticeable in the fight on the Payne Tariff bill before the special session of the present Congress. The rule from the Committee on Rules fixing the date for voting on this bill was passed by a narrow margin of sixteen votes, while the Republicans controlled the House by a majority of forty-seven. Cannon and his lieutenants in order to secure the adoption of the rule were forced to surrender positions which they had previously declared they never would abandon. In the debate on the duty on petroleum, the Speaker himself left the Chair and made a personal plea to save the provision of the

Payne Bill, but he was unable to stem the tide and though fighting courageously was decisively defeated.

Members who have hitherto been lacking in courage may now join hands in a determined effort to secure for the House its pristine freedom of action.

Admittedly in such a numerous body as our national House of Representatives it will always be necessary to have some machinery by which the majority may be able to transact the necessary legislative business despite any factional obstruction.

Cannon says: — "The Committee on Rules is a piece of machinery necessary to assist the majority of the House of Representatives in working its will." But the chief trouble with the Committee on Rules is that it is not a tool of the majority so much as a private instrument of the Speaker's authority. Cannon insists that the committee does not issue orders to the House, but this is merely a technical and theoretical exposition of its practice. True the committee can be overruled by the House, but this is a theoretical possibility only. In actual practice nothing of the sort occurs, nor is likely to occur, for few members of the majority have the audacity or courage to oppose the ruling powers of the House. This brings us back, then, to the Speaker and his power of appointing committees which is really the keystone of the whole structure of his autocratic authority. If the Speaker were deprived of such power the Committee on Rules would be a comparatively harmless and even useful institution.

Cannon again remarks that the criticism of the rules has been largely "due to lack of knowledge, misapprehension, and to demagogic editorials and press reports." In this he may be correct. For the rules may in some measure facilitate the manner in which the Speaker now dominates the House and its conduct, but they are not the real source of his power. It has been the personal force of the Speaker himself, backed by the strength of the group about him which he has made powerful, that has constituted the chief element of his dictatorship. Only the most radical revision could destroy this edifice.

During Speaker Cannon's régime Congress revised the pay of its members. Congressional salaries of five thousand dollars a year had endured for a third of a century, not so much from a conviction of the justice of that figure as from a wholesome respect for popular sentiment. Shortly before the close of the fifty-ninth Congress a Salary Act was passed, increasing the compensation of the Speaker of the House of Representatives, the Vice-President and the members of the Cabinet to twelve thousand dollars per annum, and raising the salaries of Senators and members of the House to seven thousand five hundred dollars. The conservative portion of the public and the less radical daily prints generally admitted the justice of this salary increase. Then, too, it was divorced from the disagreeable features of retroactiveness and partisanship which had inspired the particularly bitter condemnation of the Salary Acts of 1816 and 1873. Made effective for the ensuing Congress, beginning March 4, 1907, it was the first Congressional Salary Act in our history which did not increase the stipend of the enacting Congress.

CHAPTER X

RÉSUMÉ. THE ENGLISH AND THE AMERICAN SPEAKERS OF TO-DAY

THUS then in the cycle of a hundred years we have seen the evolution of the Speaker. Originally a moderator, registering merely the opinions of the House, non-partisan in his rulings, he was without particular power or prestige. During the first Congress the House selected its own committees by ballot. This was found to be both cumbersome and unsatisfactory and in January, 1790, that power was vested in the Speaker.

This then was the first accession of strength though it was not employed as a means of securing definite legislation until 1811, when Clay, as Speaker, so framed his committees as to force an English war. While the number of committees remained small and unimportant, this power of the Speaker was rather administrative than political. Naturally with the growth of influence among the committees, the prestige of the Speaker and the ability to bestow honors upon his political friends increased equally. In another score of years this great power was clearly acknowledged. In the first place the committees might shape legislation, or they might even prevent legislation by declining to report bills towards which the House might be favorably disposed. Through this machinery the Speaker soon dominated legislation. We recall that in 1848 a candidate was on the threshold of election to the Speakership when it was discovered that he had promised to frame certain committees contrary to the wishes of his party associates.

Naturally, when this theory of the control of legislation through committees had been once completely affirmed, the Speaker ranked next only to the President in power and authority. At the opening of the session he could absolutely decree what measures should be submitted to Congress, and he could further mould those measures to his own ideas before their submission. Under Clay, also, through the necessity of blocking interminable debate and suppressing the redoubtable John Randolph, the previous question was drafted as a means of compelling the necessary enactments.

Clay was the first Speaker who really dominated the legislation of Congress, even as the Speakers since the Civil War have placed their impress upon the activity of the House.

The Speakers who presided over the House of Representatives before the period of the Civil War were mostly men of inferior ability. There were but four able leaders — Clay, Banks, Cobb, and Winthrop, all strong men. Macon, Sedgwick, and Stevenson were of a mediocre type though probably the best to be obtained in the not too illustrious Congresses over which they presided. There was during it all a certain narrow political tone in the conduct of the Chair — not so much a building up of power as a diverting of authority to the ends of political expediency.

With the growth and development of the nation and the

resultant increase in membership of the House of Representatives, certain evils naturally developed. The House became unwieldy; parliamentary obstruction was invoked as a means of defeating the will of the majority. "Long-distance" speechmaking was indulged in. But to this there were obvious objections. It involved an extreme of physical exertion and nervous exhaustion. Dilatory motions and time-consuming roll-calls offered an alternative, and animate as well as inanimate objects promptly seek the line of least resistance. On the Kansas-Nebraska Bill in 1854 this art was exercised to the extent of one hundred and one roll-calls. As the size of the House increased this became a still greater, a still more effective, weapon of the obstructing minority. To-day it requires thirty minutes to call the roll on a single vote. A simple numerical calculation will reveal the number of roll-calls necessary to waste an entire session of Congress.

The third device of the minority was that of refusing a quorum. The venerable John Quincy Adams introduced the practice into the House not with the intention of developing obstructive tactics, but from motives of conscience. One of the rules passed by the first Congress, in 1789, demanded that every member should vote on all questions in which he was not personally interested. Nor had this obligation been questioned or ignored until 1832, when a resolution to censure Stanberry of Ohio for improper reference to the Speaker was before the House. When the "yeas" and "nays" were ordered on the adoption of the resolution, Adams requested that he be excused from voting. His reasons for this unusual request were presented in writing. The House refused to excuse him, and the call of the roll proceeded. Adams declined to respond to his name, declaring, however, that he was not moved by any spirit of defiance, but was impelled to his course by purely conscientious scruples.

A protracted debate followed on a motion to reconsider the vote declining to excuse Adams from voting. The infinite possibilities of establishing such a precedent were prophetically outlined. Foster declared that, if any member might persist in his refusal to vote, legislation would be impossible. In the absence of a quorum composed entirely of the majority party, in order to defeat any action the minority members need only maintain silence and the measure must fail. The motion to reconsider was lost; the Speaker read the rule requiring all members to vote upon every measure, and the Clerk was directed to again call the name of Adams. But Adams persisted in his course and made no reply.

Drayton thereupon offered a resolution for the appointment of a committee to consider some method of procedure in this breach of rules by the offending Adams. After some discussion the whole matter was tabled. After the failure of this first effort to compel a vote by an obstinate member, the House was uniformly unsuccessful in its effort to enforce that rule. Again and again Adams refused to vote, particularly on measures relating to slavery, despite the persistent efforts of the House to compel his obedience.

In the forties, a refusal to vote was the accepted method of obstructing legislation. During the Civil War the Republican party enjoyed such an overwhelming majority that filibustering became largely a lost art. But with the

Résumé

recrudescence of the Democratic party in the Reconstruction days, the custom was revived.

The question was always non-partisan — either party that happened to constitute the minority employed it with equal effect. The leaders of both parties united to condemn the practice, only the next day to lead the forces of obstruction along the same line. The abuse grew apace and the whole structure rested simply upon a forced interpretation of the constitutional phrase "a quorum to do business." The claim was made that "business" meant each separate item of business taken as a unit, and not the continuous business of a daily session. The Constitution provides for compelling the attendance of members for the purpose of securing a quorum. What could this avail, if, when present, those members, by remaining silent, could enforce the doctrine of constructive absence and defeat a quorum?

Clever parliamentarians had found that by employing rules of procedure intended to protect the rights of the minority and ensure freedom of debate, they could not only retard but could even prevent legislation. Framed, in theory, to promote the proper transaction of business, these rules had come to mock the purpose of their creation, had developed simply into an intricate system calculated to prevent legislative action. As they had gradually developed, or evolved, these rules became unwieldy and highly technical, with the result that only a few of the members really mastered them. And by those they were prostituted to unworthy ends. And thus to-day the House of Representatives is governed by a complicated and artificial system of rules so hard to be understood that many clever men of national renown serve long terms in that assembly without even professing to comprehend the laws by which it is governed.

There was no longer majority legislation, but only minority rule. In the fiftieth Congress obstruction culminated. It was patent that under the prevailing rules and procedure no measure could pass which did not have practically unanimous support. The evil reached such an extreme that minorities ceased to be political classes and indeed came to consist of one or two men. These few wishing to defeat some bill, or force the House to the consideration of their measures — for it was possible to secure a positive as well as a negative result — picked up the cudgel of filibustering. In 1889 the climax was reached. Weaver of Iowa, in an attempt to secure consideration of the bill organizing the Territory of Oklahoma, through the adroit use of points of order and dilatory motions, kept the House continuously engaged in roll-calls.

The fiftieth Congress, in continuous session longer than any Congress in our history — such was the pernicious activity of the filibusters — passed but one great party measure which went through simply because the opposition waived their obstruction. The majority was helpless; the minority without power.

Responsibility was a thing of the past. The majority were defied and chained like Prometheus to the rocks while the minority vulture feasted on its heart. Reed with one fell swoop broke the shackles. The question then became partisan and a thundering storm of abuse swept the land. The right to filibuster, declared the dissenters, is necessary to protect the minority from serfdom to the majority. But they ignored the axiom that the primary duty of a legislative body is to act; that the surest method of securing intelligent consideration for legislation is to make it impossible for the minority to block the way by parliamentary obstruction.

Action had given away to debate. The two contributing elements to this condition were the vastly increased amount of business which the development of the nation had thrown upon Congress; and the perpetuation of a set of rules and a system of parliamentary procedure which lacked sufficient elasticity to expand with the demands of modern legislation. From the first session of Congress in 1789 until the second session of the forty-sixth Congress in 1880, there had been no thorough and complete revision of the rules of the House of Representatives. A partial revision had been made in the thirty-sixth Congress in 1860, but this still retained several rules long obsolete and antiquated. Nor did the revision of 1880 offer any effective veto to the efforts of the obstructionists. The reforms of Speaker Reed in no manner justified the fears that congressional debate must now be impossible. The practical result is greatly to lessen filibustering and thus enable Congress to transact a much larger volume of business. Yet there is no refuting the assertion that "counting a quorum" may mean minority legislation. For thus we may have the artificial enactment of a statute by one fourth of the House plus one vote, when approximately three fourths of the House may be opposed to it.

The Committee on Rules is the particular feature of the present parliamentary procedure of the House which attracts the most vigorous criticism. The origin of this system of control is a matter of evolutionary interest. In 1883, during the Speakership of Keifer, the Republicans endeavored to enact a tariff bill. As a result of a bare majority their control of the House was precarious. When the tariff bill was reported out by the Committee on Ways and Means it seemed doomed to ignominious burial on the House calendar. To make it a special order and thus secure its consideration before final adjournment required a two-thirds vote. This the Republicans could not secure. Accordingly, the Committee on Rules reported a resolution providing that, on its adoption, the rules should be suspended and the tariff bill made a special order. This resolution was immediately carried by a majority vote and thenceforth the necessity of a two-thirds vote for a suspension of the rules was superseded. Thomas B. Reed was a member of the Rules Committee at that time. This method of procedure became immensely popular during Speaker Carlisle's régime. Even the English House of Commons has borrowed from us this parliamentary weapon though in that body our name of "special orders" has given way to the more suggestive title of "guillotines."

Since the Civil War, with one exception, the Speakers have all been men of commanding power. Keifer alone was weak. Every Speaker has conserved and magnified the political and personal influence of the office. The only pronounced partisan in the Chair before the war had been Andrew Stevenson, who so studiously played the Cassius to Jackson's Cæsar. Since that period the office has been viewed entirely through the political telescope with only the refractive lens of moderation. The general centralization of power during the Civil War left its indelible influence upon the character of our government. A part of this influence is manifested in the development of the Speakership. Since that date it has been the growth of evolutionary necessity.

To-day the autocrat of Congress, the Speaker, possesses a power which seems scarcely second to that of the President of the United States. Official rank and lack of patronage alone make him a lesser planet. He is the absolute arbiter of the destiny of every member of Congress. He may elevate into prominence or relegate to obscurity by committee assignments, and by referring bills to hostile committees. An able man and a clever politician in the Chair owns the House of Representatives body, soul, and conscience. In theory the Speaker should give the opportunity for the proper presentation of every argument which can be mustered on any question. But there are many difficulties which render impossible the attainment of this theoretical perfection. And to-day the Speaker invariably gives the advantage in recognition to the members of his own party.

The dream of reformers in the House of Representatives has been a series of rules for the order of business which would carry through to final consideration the most important and desirable measures without the favor or control of the Speaker or any similar agency. What we probably need, after the present amendments, is not so much a revision of the rules of procedure, as it is the election of Speakers in sympathy with the people, men who will employ the present rules, not as an implement to defy but rather as an engine to advance the popular demands.

Yet another precaution is exercised — even now the

member desiring recognition must first "consult" the Speaker and submit his intention to the approval of that dignitary. In this way another arrow is added to his quiver, and by the able use of his various privileges and prerogatives of framing committees, referring bills and extending recognition, he becomes the absolute arbiter of legislation. From his decision there is neither appeal nor relief. In the hands of an unscrupulous man the power now vested in the Speaker would become a serious menace to the stability of the nation. The only safety lies in securing Speakers of unquestioned integrity.

On all sides the question is propounded, wherefore the immense loss of prestige of the House as compared with the Senate? What is the reason for this declension from the power of the days of Madison, Clay, Randolph, Adams, Douglas, and Stevens, when Representatives gave free utterance to their views and in some real measure were mouthpieces for their constituents? Is there to-day any member of the Senate who would imitate the example of Clay who had been elected to that body and might have remained there throughout his life, and yet preferred the House?

It is of interest to note that out of thirty-five Speakers of the House of Representatives only one, Polk, ever became President. Why did not Clay, Blaine, Carlisle, Reed, and Cannon realize their final ambition? Has it been because the nature and function of their office has bequeathed to the public a perverted idea of the personal attributes of the incumbents? Is it because their committee assignments and their parliamentary decisions have rankled in the hearts of their powerful colleagues? Is it that with their elevation to the Speakership they have been removed from the debates of the floor and the opportunity of leaving their personal impress upon public measures? Reed was Speaker but the McKinley tariff bill made a President of the member whose name it bore.

With the immense growth of the country and the constantly increasing volume of business transacted by the lower House it is impossible to extend that freedom to the members which marked the days of two generations since. In the sixty-first Congress there are 391 members in the House of Representatives. By way of illustrating the necessity for some form of selective control it is interesting to note that 29,394 bills and resolutions were introduced in the sixtieth Congress. Of these 2,326 were reported back to the House, of which 646 were considered and passed. Besides these about 60 public bills became laws in omnibus bills, and about 7,000 private bills, mostly pension bills, also became laws in omnibus bills, the President having objected to the labor of signing so many acts. The others remained in the pigeon-holes of the various committees to which they had been referred. Not only the members of the minority but also the members of the majority are thoroughly gagged and shackled until they are the mere simulacra and shadows of legislators.

To-day the Senate is the real deliberative body, for there we find no rules of cloture, no shackling of self. Before the Civil War this freedom of speech and manner was secured upon the hypothesis that each Senator was an accredited Ambassador from a sovereign State and should be entitled to speak without restriction. This theory, destroyed by the war, has given way to the idea that in one assembly the right of full discussion must be assured. In the House members have served through a full session, in many cases through two sessions, without even once securing recognition from the Chair. Even if the new member be so fortunate as to secure the floor to partake of what Matthew Arnold once called the "Thystean banquet of clap-trap" the effect is not wholly inspiring.

With unlimited right of debate, with no cloture and with scanty rules the Senate has customarily transacted as much business during a session as the House and that, too, more efficiently. But with the close of the first session of the sixtieth Congress a strong filibuster in the Senate inspired a technical construction of the rules of even that body. The Vice-President announced that it was within the province of the Chair to count a quorum and that he would refuse to order a roll-call if a quorum were actually present. The Senate, by vote upon a point of order submitted to it by the Vice-President, determined that the question of "no quorum" could not be raised until after intervening business if the previous roll-call had disclosed a quorum present; and that debate was not such intervening business. Further, they invoked a rule of the Senate, which in practice had long lain dormant, prohibiting a Senator from addressing the Senate upon any question more than twice in any one day. The senatorial traditions of a century were thus overthrown. From this interpretation of the rules it is impossible to prolong the debate indefinitely and in this way filibustering is strangled where the end of the session is indeterminate. This precedent gives a Speaker no opportunity for intermission except by yielding the floor and after surrendering twice, under the rule, he would not be permitted to speak further on that day. By refusing to adjourn and thus continuing the legislative day until the measure should be enacted it is only a matter of time until any filibustering contingent could be completely exhausted.

Nowhere are the institutional, political and social conditions of England and the United States more sharply contrasted or more clearly portrayed than in the Speakership of their lower legislative bodies. The Speaker of the House of Commons, without material power, yet inaugurated into office with pomp and display; the Speaker of the House of Representatives, second only to the President in prestige, yet surrounded only by democratic simplicity. In England, with true monarchial subservience to form, the custom of centuries long dead still prevails. The English Speaker is originally a member of the House of Commons, and is selected by the leader of the House — oftentimes, but not necessarily, the Prime Minister — from among his own partisans. Personal character, dignity, and skill in parliamentary procedure are essential prerequisites. Usually he is elected unanimously by the House but he must be approved by the King. While this approval is now bestowed as a stereotyped formality it still remains the symbol of the former legislative subserviency.

The English Speaker is purely a moderator. Whatever may have been his political predilections, or party affiliations before his election to the Speakership, he ceases to belong to any party or to entertain political preferences from the moment he first steps upon the dais. He barters political freedom for the wig and gown of office, and as he ascends to the Chair he doffs the vivid colors of party and assumes instead the modest tint of neutrality. Ancient friend and former enemy, bitter partisan and devoted ally, cruel opponent and faithful companion must all receive that same meed of impartial ruling. His duty is largely to preserve order, facilitate the business of the House, enforce the rules and indicate the member who is recognized, when several have arisen at the same instant. Naturally these are duties of no little importance and in their fulfillment carry a weight of dignity but they neither suggest nor predicate political power. With such non-partisan duties the personality of the Speaker weighs but little in the political scales of England. It matters little to either party whether the Speaker be from their own ranks or from the number of the opposition.

In England custom forbids the Speaker to render any assistance even by personal advice to his own party. His knowledge of parliamentary procedure is equally at the disposal of either party or any member of the Commons. Upon his election he forfeits — actually, though perhaps not theoretically — his rights and privileges as the representative of a constituency in the House. His constituents then choose between the honor of returning the Speaker and the disadvantage of being unrepresented in Parliament. He is practically disqualified from speaking in the debates and is permitted to vote only in case of a tie. In sharp contrast again to the American functionary the English Speaker has no power to appoint committees, that function being exercised by the House of Commons itself. Without the ability either to advance or suppress bills he can neither promote nor retard legislation.

The English Speaker's daily entrance into the House

Résumé

of Commons is at once a picturesque and impressive ceremonial. The pristine pomp and formality seem all to have been conserved through the varying mutations of the centuries. Shortly before two o'clock of the afternoon all the attendants of the House, in evening dress, gay with their gilt chains and badges, and the police, take their position in two columns in the members' lobby. The inspector of the police at the head of the parliamentary detail stands facing the corridor which leads to the Speaker's rooms and the members' quarters. When he catches sight of the procession as it turns the distant corner, he announces in impressive and stentorian tones "Hats off! Speaker." All present then uncover and stand silent in two rows at right angles from the entrance to the corridor to the entrance to the House.

The Speaker's procession advances impressively. First a policeman, then an attendant, then the Sergeant-at-arms of the House, in wig, court dress, and sword, carrying over his shoulder the great gold mace, surmounted by a crown. Immediately following him comes the Speaker with powdered peruke, clad in a black lace coat, black satin knee-breeches and stockings, and buckled shoes, with a full robe of black silk, the train borne behind him by a page. Following him, walking side by side, are the Speaker's Chaplain and Secretary, or legal adviser, the former clad in ecclesiastical robe and white gloves, the latter decked in morning dress.

Slowly, with measured tread, and military precision, in absolute silence, marked by even footfall, the procession passes into the lobby, proceeds to the exact center, wheels at a right angle — everybody bowing as the Speaker passes — and enters the House, the door being closed at their heels.

As they enter the chamber, the Sergeant-at-arms steps quickly aside, the Speaker assumes the custody of his robe and proceeds up the floor between the two rows of benches filled with the standing members of the House. He stops and bows three times to the members who in turn acknowledge the salutation. The Speaker then passes to the left of the Clerk's table, the Chaplain to the right; for a moment they pause, bow low to each other, and then step up to the table. In the meantime the Sergeant-at-arms has placed the mace below the table. The doors having been locked upon their entrance, he casts a personal glance about the House to discover the possible presence of strangers. None being seen, the Chaplain is requested to read the statutory prayers of the Church of England. The prayers, couched in the impressive and solemn Elizabethan verbiage, last exactly five minutes. The Speaker then mounts the dais to his massively carved chair, the Chaplain bowing three times withdraws backward, and the Sergeant-at-arms advances up the floor and lays the mace in its appointed place upon the table. The doors are thrown open and the House of Commons is in session.

In striking contrast to this impressive ceremonial — the heritage of an ancient day — is the method of opening the American House of Representatives. Wearing no distinctive garments, the American Speaker enters the House informally in the same manner as any other member. At the hour of twelve, noon, he quietly mounts to his chair and with one sharp rap of the gavel calls the House to order. After brief prayers by the Chaplain the House is ready

Résumé 289

for business; nor is the presence of strangers felt to profane the dignity of the occasion. One bit of ceremonial alone remains to suggest other days. As the Speaker calls the House to order the Sergeant-at-arms raises the silver mace — the Roman fasces, except that it shows the emblematic eagle in place of the Latin battle-axe — and deposits it in a marble column at the right hand of the Speaker, where it remains during the session of the House. This mace, representing the authority of the Speaker, the Sergeant-at-arms carries before him whenever called upon to quiet any disturbance in the House, and its mystic influence suggests strongly the enduring influence of tradition and form. It is wonderful how, despite the iconoclasm and materialism of the present age, the imagination may be excited by artificial appliances. It is manifest in every page of history; the hideous war paint of the savage used to frighten his enemy, the mace of the Speaker, the Bambino amid a Sicilian rabble, a sacred icon among the Russian peasantry.

There are many other interesting contrasts between the English and American representative bodies. The Speaker of the House of Commons is held in much higher respect than the American Speaker and is a person of the highest official dignity. In the House of Commons the slightest reflection upon the Speaker's actions or character is a grave breach receiving immediate and serious reproof. In the United States, in times of intense party feeling, the Speaker is often bitterly assailed and his fairness openly challenged. He is not a moderator like the English prototype, but rather the leader of the majority, a powerful partisan and as such is subjected to what an Englishman would declare brutal indignities.

The House of Commons is, from many points of views, quite the most decorous legislative body in the world — a contrast to our House of Representatives, which partakes of the attributes of a riotous mob. In the House of Commons it is out of order to peruse a newspaper or read a book; to stand while another member is addressing the Chair; to address personally another member, all remarks being couched in the third person and addressed to the Chair; to pass between the Chair and the member who is speaking. Strange anomaly, it is deemed perfectly proper, as long as a member is seated, to wear the hat, tilted at any angle no matter how rakish; but if the member rises even for a moment, he must uncover. Nor would any member dare commit so flagrant a violation as to pass between the Speaker and the table, or between the Speaker and the mace either when it is deposited on the table or when it is in the hands of the Sergeant-at-arms. In passing to and from their seats members never fail to make obeisance to the Speaker.

In the House of Representatives, on the other hand, members stand around singly or in groups discussing any and all questions, sit about reading the daily prints, write letters, pass in and out of the House and circulate about generally without the slightest regard for the Speaker. One reason for this is probably to be found in the arrangement of the chambers in which these two bodies meet. In the House of Commons they have the rather meager accommodations of forbidding benches; in the House of Representatives each member has his individual desk and comfortable swinging chair. All of which suggests the anomalous idea of form without power, and shadow without substance. The one has the appearance, the other the actuality, of authority. In one particular at least, our legislative manners recommend themselves heartily — no member thinks of offering himself with his hat on. In England it is quite in order, if the member be an occupant of the front bench, to recline flat on one's back with the feet perched on the table in front of the Speaker offering the soles of the shoes to the contemplation of the Chair and one's associates. Commend us again to American legislative etiquette.

In the House of Commons there is neither the bell of the French Chamber of Deputies nor the gavel of the American House of Representatives. The mere repetition of "Order, order" by the English Speaker seems far more effective in quelling disturbances on the floor than the violent ringing of the bell of the President of the French assembly, suggesting always a lively auction; or the vigorous pounding of the gavel by the American Speaker, suggesting the prosperous carpenter shop.

The method of procedure in the event of a death in the personnel of the English and American Houses reveals again a marked contrast. If a member of the House of Representatives dies, his desk is draped with crepe; a delegation from the House and Senate is named to escort his body to his native state and to attend the obsequies; the House adjourns for a day; another day, a month or so later, is devoted to eulogies of the deceased; these are printed in costly pamphlet form with his portrait engraved therein.

When a member of the House of Commons dies, the incident for the time is wholly ignored. A week or so later, the chief whip makes the following formal motion: "That the Speaker do issue his warrant to the Clerk of the Crown to make out a new writ for the electing of a member to serve in this present Parliament for the borough of ——— in the place of Mr. ———, deceased." Unless sentiment is to be counted out as a factor in our public life, the American custom seems at least more humane.

The English Speaker also receives marked social consideration. He ranks as the first commoner of the Kingdom: his invitations to dinner are royal commands not to be ignored or treated lightly; and court dress is always worn by members who dine with him officially.

To raise him beyond any possible personal interest in legislation, the Speaker of the Commons receives an annual salary of five thousand pounds and the use of a palatial house which forms a part of Westminster Palace. The American Speaker in contrast receives an annual salary of twelve thousand dollars out of which he furnishes his own residence. The American Speaker holds office but two years, when he is subject to re-election or defeat, being ever the sport of political storms. The English Speaker retains office, no matter how often the politics of the ministry may change, through any number of successive administrations, until either his health has failed or he resigns. In the event of his retirement he receives a yearly pension of from five thousand to six thousand pounds for the remainder of his life; and the sovereign bestows upon him a peerage carrying with it a seat in the House of Lords.

When the Speaker of the House of Representatives retires, he becomes a private citizen dependent upon the whims of fortune.

APPENDIX

THE PRESIDENTS OF THE CONTINENTAL CONGRESSES AND THE CONGRESS OF THE CONFEDERATION (1771–1788)

1774, Sept. 5–Oct. 22, 1774,	PEYTON RANDOLPH, of Virginia.
1774, Oct. 22–Oct. 26, 1774,	HENRY MIDDLETON, of South Carolina.
1775, May 10–May 19, 1775,	PEYTON RANDOLPH, of Virginia.
1775, May 19–Oct. 31, 1777,	JOHN HANCOCK, of Massachusetts.
1777, Nov. 1–Dec. 9, 1778,	HENRY LAURENS, of South Carolina.
1778, Dec. 10–Sept. 28, 1779,	JOHN JAY, of New York.
1779, Sept. 28–July 10, 1781,	SAMUEL HUNTINGTON, of Connecticut.
1781, July 10–Oct. 23, 1781,	THOMAS MCKEAN, of Delaware.
1781, Nov. 3–Nov. 2, 1782,	JOHN HANSON, of Maryland.
1782, Nov. 4–Nov. 1, 1783,	ELIAS BOUDINOT, of New Jersey.
1783, Nov. 3–June 3, 1784,	THOMAS MIFFLIN, of Pennsylvania.
1784, Nov. 30–Nov. 4, 1785,	RICHARD HENRY LEE, of Virginia.
1785, Nov. 23–June 6, 1786,	JOHN HANCOCK,[1] of Massachusetts.
1786, June 6–Nov 3, 1786,	NATHANIEL GORHAM, of Massachusetts.
1787, Feb. 2–Oct. 30, 1787,	ARTHUR ST. CLAIR, of Pennsylvania.
1788, Jan. 22–Nov. 1, 1788,	CYRUS GRIFFIN, of Virginia.

SPEAKERS OF THE HOUSE OF REPRESENTATIVES (1789–1909)

1789, April 1–March 3, 1791,	FREDERICK A. MUHLENBERG, of Pennsylvaina.
1791, Oct. 24–March 3, 1793,	JONATHAN TRUMBULL, of Connecticut.

[1] Hancock was sick and unable to preside during this term.

1793, Dec. 2–March 3, 1795,	FREDERICK A. MUHLENBERG, of Pennsylvania.
1795, Dec. 7–March 3, 1799,	JONATHAN DAYTON, of New Jersey.
1799, Dec. 2–March 3, 1801,	THEODORE SEDGWICK, of Massachusetts.
1801, Dec. 7–March 3, 1807,	NATHANIEL MACON, of North Carolina.
1807, Oct. 26–March 3, 1811,	JOSEPH B. VARNUM, of Massachusetts.
1811, Nov. 4–Jan. 19, 1814,	HENRY CLAY, of Kentucky.
1814, Jan. 19–March 3, 1815,	LANGDON CHEVES, of South Carolina.
1815, Dec. 4–Nov. 15, 1820,	HENRY CLAY, of Kentucky.
1820, Nov. 15–March 3, 1821,	JOHN W. TAYLOR, of New York.
1821, Dec. 4–March 3, 1823,	PHILIP P. BARBOUR, of Virginia.
1823, Dec. 1–March 3, 1825,	HENRY CLAY, of Kentucky.
1825, Dec. 5–March 3, 1827,	JOHN W. TAYLOR, of New York.
1827, Dec. 3–June 30, 1834,	ANDREW STEVENSON, of Virginia.
1834, June 30–March 3, 1835,	JOHN BELL, of Tennessee.
1835, Dec. 7–March 3, 1839,	JAMES K. POLK, of Tennessee.
1839, Dec. 14–March 3, 1841,	ROBERT M. T. HUNTER, of Virginia.
1841, May 31–March 3, 1843,	JOHN WHITE, of Kentucky.
1843, Dec. 4–March 3, 1845,	JOHN W. JONES, of Virginia.
1845, Dec. 1–March 3, 1847,	JOHN W. DAVIS, of Indiana.
1847, Dec. 6–March 3, 1849,	ROBERT C. WINTHROP, of Massachusetts.
1849, Dec. 22–March 3, 1851,	HOWELL COBB, of Georgia.
1851, Dec. 1–March 3, 1855,	LINN BOYD, of Kentucky.
1856, Feb. 2–March 3, 1857,	NATHANIEL BANKS, of Massachusetts.
1857, Dec. 7–March 3, 1859,	JAMES L. ORR, of South Carolina.
1860, Feb. 1–March 3, 1861,	WILLIAM PENNINGTON, of New Jersey.
1861, July 4–March 3, 1863,	GALUSHA A. GROW, of Pennsylvania.
1863, Dec. 7–March 3, 1869,	SCHUYLER COLFAX, of Indiana.
1869, March 3–March 3, 1869,	THEODORE M. POMEROY, of New York.
1869, March 4–March 3, 1875,	JAMES G. BLAINE, of Maine.
1875, Dec. 6–Aug. 15, 1876,	MICHAEL C. KERR, of Indiana.
1876, Dec. 4–March 3, 1881,	SAMUEL J. RANDALL, of Pennsylvania.

Appendix

1881, Dec. 5–March 3, 1883,   J. WARREN KEIFER, of Ohio.
1883, Dec. 3–March 3, 1889,   JOHN G. CARLISLE, of Kentucky.
1889, Dec. 2–March 3, 1891,   THOMAS B. REED, of Maine.
1891, Dec. 7–March 3, 1895,   CHARLES F. CRISP, of Georgia.
1895, Dec. 2–March 3, 1899,   THOMAS B. REED, of Maine.
1899, Dec. 4–March 3, 1903,   DAVID B. HENDERSON, of Iowa.
1903, Nov. 9–   JOSEPH G. CANNON, of Illinois.

INDEX

"A. B. Plot," 54.
Adair, John, of Kentucky, 62.
Adams, Charles Francis, of Massachusetts, 124.
Adams, Henry, 29.
Adams, John, 23, 29, 36.
Adams, John Quincy, 59, 98, 121, 282; Randolph opposed to, 39; associated with Clay, 43; Taylor's loyalty to, 51; Russell's opposition to, 52; candidate for Presidency, 55; supported by Clay, 56; administration of, opposed by Jackson, 60-61; power of, in Congress, 62, 64, 72; opinion of, of Bell, 67; engages in slavery discussion, 68-70; solves New Jersey question, 75-77; diary of, relative thereto, 79; opinion of, of Hunter, 80; labors of, for abolition, 83, 84; secures repeal of gag-rule, 87; refusal of, to vote, 222, 275-276.
Aiken, William, of South Carolina, candidate for Speakership, 110-111; defeated by Banks, 112-114.
Alabama, 55, 64, 69, 139.
Alleghanies, the, 34.
Allen, William ("Fog Horn"), 195.
Allison, William B., of Iowa, 173.
Ames, Fisher, of Massachusetts, 24.
Ames, Oakes, of Massachusetts, connection of, with Credit Mobilier, 166-167, 172-173.

Anthony, Henry B., of Rhode Island, 123.
Appalachian Mountains, 32.
Archer, William S., of Virginia, 62.
Arkansas, 109, 113, 175.
Arnold, Matthew, 284.
Arthur, Chester A., 191.
Ashe, Thomas S., of North Carolina, 180.
Atkins, Elisha, Union Pacific director, 178.
Atlantic and Pacific Railroad, 176.
Austinburg, Ohio, 84.

BACON, Ezekiel, of Massachusetts, 40.
Banks, Nathaniel P., of Massachusetts, 294; candidate for Speakership, 102-111; stand of, on slavery question, 108; elected Speaker of thirty-fourth Congress, 112-114, 144; conduct of, in Chair, 116-118, 274; on Poland Committee, 172.
Barbour, Philip P., of Virginia, 294; elected Speaker, 51-53; candidate again in 1827, 60.
Bartlett, Charles Lafayette, of Georgia, 236.
Bayard, James A., Jr., of Delaware, 123.
Bayard, James A., Sr., of Delaware, 43.
Belknap, William W., 183, 194.

298 Index

Bell, John, of Tennessee, 294; member of twenty-second Congress, 62; of twenty-third Congress, 65; as Speaker, 67-68; opposes Polk, 70, 71; age of, when Speaker, 90.

Benjamin, Judah P., of Louisiana, 123.

Benton, Thomas Hart, of Missouri, 250.

Bibb, William, of Georgia, 33.

Bingham, John A., of Ohio, 172, 174.

Bingham, Kingsley S., of Michigan, 123.

Binney, Horace, of Pennsylvania, 64.

Blackburn, Joseph C. S., of Kentucky, 197, 205.

Blaine, James G., of Maine, 250, 294; on Clay, Douglas, and Stevens, 157; elected Speaker in 1869, 169; character of, 170; involved in Credit Mobilier scandal, 172; charges against, in Little Rock affair, 175-182; conduct of, in Chair, 184-185; breaks with Butler, 185-186; fairness of, etc., 187-188; Republican party under, 188-190; career of, 190-192; defeated for Speakership, 193; in forty-fourth Congress, 194; in Hayes-Tilden campaign, 195-196; imitated by Randall, 196; compared with Randall, 203; in Senate, 206; compared with Reed, 217; discountenances parliamentary reform, 222-223; ambition of, to become President, 282.

Blair, Francis P., Jr., of Missouri, 149.

Blair and Rives, public printers, 86.

Bocock, Thomas S., of Virginia, candidate for Speakership, 125, 133, 137.

Boston, 37, 116, 175, 176, 178.

Botts, John W., of Virginia, 85.

Boudinot, Elias, of New Jersey, 20, 24, 293.

Boutwell, George S., of Massachusetts, 91.

Boyd, Linn, of Kentucky, 294; serves as Speaker, 100-101.

Bragg, Thomas, of North Carolina, 123.

Branch, Lawrence O'B., of North Carolina, 135.

Breckenridge, William C. P., of Kentucky, 220, 239.

Briggs, George, of New York, 144.

Bristow, Benjamin H., 194.

Broderick, David C., of California, 136.

Brooks, James, of New York, 162, 165, 173.

Brown, John, 122, 142; raid, 131, 133.

Brown, William J., of Indiana, 96.

Brumm, Charles N., of Pennsylvania, 236.

Bryan, William J., 255.

Buchanan, James, 137.

Bunker Hill, 33, 87.

Burgess, Tristam, of Rhode Island, 62, 64.

Burlingame, Anson, of Massachusetts, 124.

Burnett, Henry C., of Kentucky, 140.

Burr, Aaron, 27.

Butler, Ben, of Massachusetts, conducts trial of Johnson, 156; in Congress with Blaine, 170, 171, 188; breaks with Blaine, 185-186; defeat of, in 1874, 189.

CALDWELL, Josiah, 176, 180.
Calendar Wednesday, 265-267.
Calhoun, John C., of South Carolina, 60, 78, 110, 121; in Congress of 1811, 32; compared with Clay, 35; on Foreign Relations Committee, 40; opposes Taylor, 52; member of twenty-ninth Congress, 87.
California, 118, 136, 165.
Cambreling, Churchill C., of New York, 60, 62.
Cameron, Simon, of Pennsylvania, 88.
Campbell, Lewis D., of Ohio, candidate for Speakership, 102-103, 112; under Speaker Banks, 117.
Canada, 33.
Cannon, Joseph G., of Illinois, 295; member of "Reed Rules" Committee, 228; dominates over Henderson, 248; elected Speaker of fifty-eighth Congress, 250; personality of, 250-254; in campaign of 1908, 254-255; power of, as Speaker, 255-260; defensive claims of, 260-262; humor and picturesqueness of, 239, 263-264; revolt against absolutism of, 265-272; salaries revised under, 272; ambition of, to become President, 282.
Carlisle, John G., of Kentucky, 295; Clay imitated by, 48; Holman amendment overthrown under, 204; change of rules under, 206; Speaker of forty-eighth Congress, 209; conduct of, in Chair, 210-213, 242; Reed compared with, 233; development of Speakership under, 247; Cannon contrasted with, 255; control of legislation by "special orders" under, 280; ambition of, to become President, 282.
Carroll, Charles, of Carrollton, 150.
Cass, Lewis, of Michigan, 88.
Charles I., 164; struggles of, with House of Commons, 8-12.
Charles II., troubles of, concerning Speakership, 13-14.
Chase, Salmon P., 156.
Cheves, Langdon, of South Carolina, 294; in Congress of 1811, 32; serves on committees under Clay, 40; succeeds Clay in Speakership, 43.
Chicago, Wheat Pit, 159; fire, 175.
Choate, Rufus, of Massachusetts, 62, 64.
Cincinnati, 179.
Cincinnati Gazette, 177.
Clark, John B., of Missouri, offers Helper book resolution, 125-128, 138, 139, 145.
Clarke, Matthew St. Clair, 65, 83, 86.
Clay, Henry, of Kentucky, 63, 71, 116, 121, 147, 250, 294; in Congress of 1811, 32; chosen Speaker, 33; career of, 34-37; relations of, with Randolph, 38-39; assumes control of committees, 39-40; has control of the House, 40-41; methods of, 41-42; in War of 1812, 42-43; retires from Speakership, 43; reëlected Speaker, 44; salary bill under, and its effect, 45-47; greets Lafayette, 47; power of, 47-48; parliamentary ability of, 49; controls Madison, 49-50; opposition of, to Monroe, 50; retires in 1820, 51; returns in 1823, 53; candidacies of, for the Presidency, 53-54; attitude of, in "A. B. Plot," 54-55; "American Sys-

tem" of, 55; defeated for Presidency and supports Adams, 56; appreciation of, 56–58; position of, among ante-bellum Speakers, 59; Stevenson compared with, 66; attempts to control Tyler, 83; White's partiality to, 85; age of, when Speaker, 90; Pennington compared with, 145; Stevens compared with, 152; Blaine's rating of, 157; Colfax ranked with, in popularity, 158–159; Colfax compared with, 160–161; Blaine compared with, 169, 191–192; imitated by Randall, 196; parliamentary rules under, 227; quoted by Reed, 243; dominates legislation, 273–274; prefers House to Senate, 282.

Cleveland, Grover, 213.

Clingman, Thomas L., of North Carolina, 110, 113.

Clinton, De Witt, of New York, 52.

Clymer, George, of Pennsylvania, 24.

Cobb, Howell, of Georgia, 110, 294; in twenty-eighth Congress, 86; age of, when Speaker, 90; candidate for Speakership, 95–96; elected, 98; conduct of, in Chair, 99–100, 274.

Colcock, William F., of South Carolina, 97.

Colfax, Schuyler ("Smiler"), of Indiana, 193, 294; member of thirty-sixth Congress, 124; exposes McQueen plot, 139; elected Speaker of thirty-eighth Congress, 157; appreciation of, 158–159; moves expulsion of Long, 159; comparison of, with Clay, 160–161; reëlected Speaker of thirty-ninth Congress, 162; of fortieth Congress, 165; Vice-President, 166, 170; connection of, with Credit Mobilier, 166–168, 172, 174; Blaine compared with, 184; Carlisle compared with, 209; discountenances parliamentary reform, 222.

Collamer, Jacob, of Vermont, 123.

Colquitt, Alfred H., of Georgia, 246.

Columbia, District of, abolition of slavery in, 69, 95, 97, 108.

Congressional Globe, 102, 137.

Congressional Record, 232.

Conkling, Roscoe, of New York, 124, 184, 191.

Connecticut, 24, 25, 149, 293; agitation in, against salary bill of 1816, 46; not represented in fortieth Congress, 165.

Corwin, Thomas, of Ohio, member of twenty-second Congress, 63; of twenty-third Congress, 64; of twenty-ninth Congress, 87; of thirty-sixth Congress, 124; candidate for Speakership, 141.

Covode, John, of Pennsylvania, 124.

Cox, Samuel S. ("Sunset"), of Ohio and New York, member of thirty-sixth Congress, 124; on Pennington, 145; candidate for Speakership, 157; appoints Credit Mobilier Committee, 172; in Hayes-Tilden dispute, 197.

Crawford, Martin J., of Georgia, 132, 140.

Crawford, William H., of Georgia, faction of, controls House, 52–53; acquitment of, from charges, 54–55; candidate for Presidency, 55, 56.

Credit Mobilier Company, shares of, distributed among Congressmen, 166–167; scandal of, 172–174, 188, 189.

Index 301

"Creole" case, 84.
Crisp, Charles F., of Georgia, 295; resurrects Holman amendment, 204; change of rules under, 206; characterizes Reed, 241; elected Speaker of fifty-second Congress, 242-243; "Reed Rules" under, 244-245; conduct of, in Chair, 245-246; development of Speakership under, 247; Cannon contrasted with, 255.
Crockett, Davy, of Tennessee, 65.
Cuba, 236.

DALZELL, John, of Pennsylvania, 248.
Danville, Illinois, 255.
Davis, Henry Winter, of Maryland, 124, 144.
Davis, Jefferson, enters Senate, 93; leader therein, 123; attacked by Blaine, 191.
Davis, John, of Massachusetts, 62.
Davis, John W., of Indiana, 294; elected Speaker, 88.
Davis, Joseph J., of North Carolina, 217.
Davis, Reuben, of Mississippi, 133.
Dawes, Henry L., of Massachusetts, 172, 174.
Dayton, Jonathan, of New Jersey, 294; Speaker of fourth and fifth Congresses, 26; appreciation of, 30-31.
Delaware, 46, 51, 293.
Denison, Dudley, of Ohio, 201.
DeWeese, John T., of North Carolina, 171, 187.
Dickens, Charles, 120.
Dingley, Nelson, Jr., of Maine, 234.
Disraeli, Benjamin, 87, 215.
Donelson, Andrew J., 61.
Donnybrook Fair, 159.

Douglas, Stephen A., of Illinois, 102, 107, 135, 140, 148, 152, 250, 282; member of twenty-eighth Congress, 86-87; in Senate, 123; rated by Blaine, 157.
Drayton, William, of South Carolina, 276.
Dromgoole, George C., of Virginia, 70.
Duer, William, Jr., of New York, 97.

EDMUNDS, George F., of Vermont, 196.
Edward III., 1.
Edward VI., 7.
Edwards, Ninian, of Illinois, 54.
Eliot, Sir John, 9.
Elizabeth, Queen, resists House of Commons, 5-6; revives "rotten boroughs," 7; House of Commons under, 8.
Ellis, E. J., of Louisiana, 201.
Emerson, Ralph W., 151.
England, 7, 14, 15, 17, 21, 22, 172, 227, 228; Hancock opposes war with, 19; war with, demanded in Congress, 33, 39-40; pauper legislation in, 147; Clay forces war with, 273; "Guillotines" in House of Commons of, 280; Speakership in, contrasted with American Speakership, 285-292.
Essex, Earl of, 5.
Etheredge, Emerson, of Tennessee, 124.
Europe, 145, 171, 252.
Everett, Edward, of Massachusetts, 60, 62, 64.

FESSENDEN, William Pitt, of Maine, 123, 163, 164.
Fillmore, Millard, 34, 64, 91.
Finch, Sir John, 8, 10.

Finley, Ebenezer B., of Ohio, 217.
Fish, Hamilton, 167.
Fisher, Warren, Jr., 176, 178.
Fiske, "Jim," 171.
Fitzgerald, John J., of New York, 268, 269.
Florida, 33.
Flower, Roswell P., of New York, 231.
Floyd, John, of Virginia, 54, 55.
Forney, Johr W., 112.
Foster, Charles, of Ohio, 201.
Foster, Thomas F., of Georgia, 276.
France, 27, 291.
Franklin, Walter S., 65.
Frye, William P., of Maine, 205, 216.
Fuller, Henry, of Pennsylvania, candidate for Speakership, 102, 104-109; stand of, on slavery question, 107, 108; defeated by Banks, 112.

GALLATIN, Albert, 43.
Garfield, James A., involved in Credit Mobilier scandal, 172, 174; in Hayes-Tilden dispute, 201; on Rules Committee, 205; succeeded in House by Reed, 216.
Garland, Hugh A., of Virginia, action of, on New Jersey question, 74-75; overruled by House, 77-78; succeeded by Clarke, 83.
Georgia, 24, 33, 54, 62, 86, 87, 95, 132, 205, 236, 242, 294, 295; agitation in, against salary bill of 1816, 46; Crisp declines Senatorship from, 246.
Germany, 22.
Gerry, Elbridge, of Massachusetts, 24.
Gettysburg, battle of, 196.
Ghent, treaty of, 43, 44.

Giddings, Joshua R., of Ohio, 121; presents anti-slavery petition, 84; anti-slavery activity of, 91, 94, 95; part of, in defeating Winthrop, 99.
Gilmer, John A., of North Carolina, 124, 129, 133.
Gladstone, William E., 215.
Globe, the, 79.
Gorham, Nathaniel, of Massachusetts, 293.
Grant, Ulysses S., 151, 158, 166, 250; support of, by Stevens, 156; asks Colfax to become Secretary of State, 167; administration of, 170-172, 188, 189; enemy of Blaine, 184, 191; pays tribute to Kerr, 195.
Great Britain, 40, 49, 67.
Greece, 39.
Greeley, Horace, 131, 167; fears for Union, 88; on contest over Speakership, 109-110; attacked by Rust, 113; denounced in House, 133; supports Sherman for Speakership, 143.
Griffin, Cyrus, of Virginia, 20, 293.
Grimes, James W., of Iowa, 123, 136.
Grow, Galusha A., of Pennsylvania, 157, 159, 294; candidate for Speakership, 122; member of thirty-sixth Congress, 124; candidate for Speakership, 125-126; declines challenge, 135; elected Speaker in 1861, 149; career of, 149-150; as Speaker, 150-151.
Grundy, Felix, of Tennessee, 32, 40.

HALE, John P., of New Hampshire, 123.
Hamilton, Alexander, 24, 150; aids Speaker Dayton, 27; Clay compared with, 34.

Index 303

Hamlin, Hannibal, of Maine, 123, 149.
Hammond, James H., of South Carolina, 136.
Hancock, John, of Massachusetts, 19, 20, 293.
Hanson, John, of Maryland, 20, 293.
Hare, Sir Nicholas, Speaker under the Tudors, 5.
Harper's Ferry, 122, 142.
Harrison, William Henry, 80.
" Hartsell's Precedents," 49.
Haskin, John B., of New York, 135.
Hawes, Albert G., of Kentucky, 68.
Hayes, Rutherford B., in Hayes-Tilden campaign, 170, 182, 195-196; disputed election of, 197-202, 214; vetoes appropriation bills, 204.
Helper, Hinton R., discussion in House concerning book by, 125-133, 139, 142, 145.
Henderson, David B., of Iowa, 295; Speaker of fifty-sixth Congress, 248-249; succeeded by Cannon, 255, 264.
Henry IV., 6.
Henry VIII., 6.
Herbert, Hilary, 211, 212.
Hewitt, Abram S., of New York, 201, 202.
Hickman, John, of Pennsylvania, 124.
Hill, David B., of New York, 224.
Hinds, Asher C., 268.
Hitt, Robert R., of Illinois, 239.
Hoar, George F., of Massachusetts, 182.
Hobart, Sir Miles, 9.
Holles, Denzil, 9.
Holman, William S., of Indiana, characterization of Grow by, 151;
the Holman amendment, 204, 209; opposes McCreary's ruling, 211-212.
Houston, George S., of Alabama, 139.
Houston, Samuel, of Texas, 123.
Hungerford, Thomas de, 1.
Hunter, Robert M. T., of Virginia, 123, 294; elected Speaker, 78; character of, 80-81; age of, when Speaker, 90; imitated by Winthrop, 93.
Huntington, Samuel, of Connecticut, 293.
Hunton, Eppa, of Virginia, 179, 180.

ILLINOIS, 54, 86, 102, 124, 132, 135, 165, 197, 242, 243, 250, 265, 295; court decision on quorum rule in, 224.
" Impending Crisis of the South — How to Meet It," 125.
Indiana, 88, 96, 124, 127, 157, 160, 172, 294; supreme court decision on quorum rule in, 224.
Ingersoll, Robert G., 182, 196.
Ingham, Samuel D., of Pennsylvania, 60.
Iowa, 136, 172, 173, 204, 212, 248, 278, 295.
Iverson, Alfred, of Georgia, 132.

JACKSON, Andrew, Clay's antagonism to, 35; candidate for Presidency, 55, 56; party of, in power, 59-60; administration of, 61-62; Stevenson subservient to, 65-67, 280; attempted assassination of, 121.
Jackson, James, of Georgia, 24.
Jackson v. Smith, 219.
James I., first parliament of, 8.
Jay, John, of New York, 20, 24, 293.

Jefferson, Thomas, 34, 150; administration of, 28–29.
"Jefferson's Manual," 49.
Jenifer, Daniel, of Maryland, 79.
Johnson, Andrew, of Tennessee, enters Congress, 93; opposition of Stevens to, 154–156; part of, in reconstruction, 161, 164.
Johnson, Cave, of Tennessee, 65.
Johnson, Reverdy, of Maryland, 87.
Johnson, Richard M., of Kentucky, member of Congress of 1811, 33; introduces salary bill, 45; member of twenty-second Congress, 63; of twenty-third Congress, 64.
Jones, John W., of Virginia, 294; elected Speaker, 85; contest over right of, to membership, 85–86.

KANSAS, 101, 108.
Kansas–Nebraska Bill, 110, 111, 116, 117, 118; contest over, 101–103, 107–108; number of roll-calls on, 275.
Kasson, John A., of Iowa, 204, 208.
Keifer, J. Warren, of Ohio, 295; Speaker of forty-seventh Congress, 206, 216; conduct of, in Chair, 207–208, 280; Carlisle compared with, 209; parliamentary reform proposed by, 223.
Keitt, Lawrence M., of South Carolina, 131.
Kelley, William D., of Pennsylvania, 172.
Kellogg, William, of Illinois, 135.
Kentucky, 33, 45, 64, 83, 100, 102, 123, 197, 201, 205, 209, 211, 220, 239, 294, 295; Clay's popularity in, 35, 36; nominates Clay for Presidency, 53; not represented in fortieth Congress, 165; elects Carlisle to Senate, 213; quorum rule in, 224.

Kerr, Michael C., of Indiana, 294; elected Speaker of forty-fourth Congress, 193, 196; conduct of, in Chair, 194; death of, 195.
Key West, 33.
Kilgore, Constantine B., of Texas, 221.
Kilgore, David, of Indiana, 127.
Kimbolton, Lord, 10.
"Kitchen Cabinet," 62.
Knott, J. Proctor, of Kentucky, 180, 181.

LAFAYETTE, Marquis de, 47, 121.
Lamar, Lucius, of Mississippi, 124, 133.
Laurens, Henry, of South Carolina, 19, 20, 293.
Leake, Shelton F., of Virginia, 130.
Lecompton Constitution, 122; anti-Lecompton Democrats, 135, 138.
Lee, Richard Henry, of Virginia, 293; presides over Continental Congress, 17, 20; newspaper attack upon, 19.
Lenthall, William, 12.
Letcher, John, of Virginia, 104.
Levy, William, of Louisiana, 201, 202.
Lewis, Dixon H., of Alabama, 64, 69.
Lewis, J. Hamilton, of Washington, 239, 240.
Lewis, Major William B., 61.
Lexington, battle of, 33.
Lexington district, 35.
Lincoln, Abraham, Clay compared with, 34–35; first appearance of in Congress, 92–93; relations of, with Stevens, 154–155; active in reconstruction, 161; imitated by Cannon, 250–251.
Little Rock and Fort Smith Railroad, Blaine's connection with, 175–176, 178, 181.

Livingston, Edward, of Louisiana, 55.
Logan, John A., of Illinois, 124, 135.
London, England, 180, 252.
Long, Alexander, of Ohio, 159.
Louis XVI., 164.
Louisiana, 55, 238; Clay cheated out of votes in, 56; in Hayes-Tilden contest, 198, 201, 202.
Lowndes, William, of New York, 33.

McArthur, Duncan, of Ohio, 55.
McClernand, John A., of Illinois, 124, 144.
McClure, A. K., 155.
McCrary, George W., of Iowa, 172.
McCreary, James B., of Kentucky, 211, 212, 220.
McDuffie, George, of South Carolina, 60, 62.
McKean, Thomas, of Delaware, 293.
McKinley, William, member of "Reed Rules" Committee, 228; Spanish policy of, opposed, 235-236; contrasted with Reed, 237, 283; Cannon contrasted with, 253.
McLane, Louis, of Delaware, 51, 52.
McMullen, Fayette, of Virginia, 104.
McQueen, John, of North Carolina, 140.
Machiavelli, 181.
Macon, Nathaniel, of North Carolina, 294; candidate for Speakership in 1799, 27; elected Speaker in 1801, 28; conduct of, in Chair, 29-30, 31, 274; superseded by Clay, 33; tolerates Randolph, 38; subserviency of, 66.

Madison, James, in first Congress, 24, 282; control of, by Clay, 40, 49-50.
Maine, 74, 169, 176, 182, 186, 214, 234, 294, 295; quorum rule in, 223-224.
Maine, battleship, 235.
Mallory, Robert, of Virginia, 140, 141.
Manila, 212.
Mann, Horace, of Massachusetts, 98, 99.
Mare, Sir Peter de la, 1.
Marshall, Humphrey, of Kentucky, 102.
Marshall, Samuel S., of Illinois, 165.
Marshall, Tom, of Kentucky, 65.
Mary, Queen of Scots, 5, 7.
Maryland, 51, 87, 118, 124, 144, 172, 197, 293; agitation in, against salary bill of 1816, 46.
Mason, John Y., of Virginia, 62, 71, 123.
Massachusetts, 24, 26, 27, 30, 49, 55, 62, 64, 89, 90, 93, 102, 113, 114, 117, 124, 166, 171, 172, 186, 208, 293, 294; quorum rule in, 223, 224.
Maynard, Horace, of Tennessee, 124.
Merrick, William M., of Maryland, 172.
Mexico, 33, 54; war with, 87-89.
Middleton, Henry, of South Carolina, 293.
Mifflin, Thomas, of Pennsylvania, 20, 293.
Mills, Roger Q., of Texas, in Hayes-Tilden contest, 197; candidate for Speakership, 242-243.
Millson, John S., of Virginia, 128, 129, 137.
Minnesota, 124.
Mississippi, 124, 133.

Index

Mississippi River, 34.
Missouri, 125, 149.
Missouri Compromise, 113, 146, 175; Randolph's opposition to, 39, 49; Clay's success in, 50, 56, 157; Taylor's attitude on, 52.
Missouri, Kansas, and Texas Railroad, 176.
Mobile, 33.
Monroe, James (President), 50, 51.
Monroe, James, of Ohio, 200.
Moore, Sir Thomas, 4.
Morrill, Justin S., of Vermont, 124.
Morrill, Samuel P., of Maine, 182.
Morris, Isaac N., of Illinois, 132.
Morton, Oliver P., of Indiana, 196.
Muhlenberg, Frederick A., of Pennsylvania, 293, 294; Speaker of first Congress, 22–25; reëlected in 1793, 26; appreciation of, 30–31.
Muhlenberg, Peter, 22.
Mulligan, James, 178, 181.

NAPOLEON, 169, 252.
National Intelligencer, 27.
Navarre, Henry of, 85.
Nebraska, 165. *See also* Kansas-Nebraska Bill.
Nesbitt, George, of New York, 167.
New England, 37, 74.
New Hampshire, 64, 173; delegates from, in pre-constitutional assemblies, 18; not represented in fortieth Congress, 165; quorum rule in, 224.
New Jersey, 24, 26, 39, 124, 141, 143, 293, 294; New Jersey question, 73–79.
New Orleans, battle of, 43, 56.
New York, 28, 33, 51, 55, 59, 62, 64, 74, 97, 124, 135, 139, 144, 162, 165, 166, 167, 173, 185, 189, 197, 224, 240, 256, 293, 294; "Bucktails" of, 52.
New York City, 23, 45, 213, 242.
New York Sun, 239.
New York Tribune, 167.
Niblack, William E., of Indiana, 172.
Nicholson, Alfred O. P., of Tennessee, 123.
North Carolina, 24, 27, 28, 30, 106, 123, 124, 125, 129, 133, 135, 140, 171, 217, 294; delegates from, in pre-constitutional assemblies, 18.

O'BRIEN, William J., of Maryland, 197.
Ohio, 55, 63, 64, 84, 86, 91, 102, 124, 125, 157, 159, 195, 201, 206, 217, 275, 295; agitation in, against salary bill of 1816, 46; quorum rule in, 224.
Oklahoma, 278.
Oregon question, 87.
Orr, James L., of South Carolina, 294; candidate for Speakership, 109, 111; accepts election of Banks, 113; elected Speaker of thirty-sixth Congress, 122.
Owen, George W., of Alabama, 55.

PALFREY, John G., of Massachusetts, 91, 94.
Paris, 171.
Patterson, James W., of New Hampshire, 173.
Payne, Sereno E., of New York, 248.
Payne tariff bill, 270–271
Pence, Lafe, of Colorado, 238.
Pendleton, George H., of Ohio, 124.
Pennington, William, of New Jersey, 294; contrasted with Clay, 39; member of thirty-sixth Con-

gress, 124; candidate for Speakership, 141, 143; elected Speaker, 144; conduct of, in Chair, 145–146.

Pennsylvania, 22, 23, 24, 25, 64, 88, 102, 122, 124, 125, 135, 141, 149, 150, 189, 196, 236, 293, 294; agitation in, against salary bill of 1816, 46.

Peters, John A., of Maine, 186.
Phelips, Sir Edward, 8.
Philadelphia, 23, 196.
Philippines, 236.
Pierce, Franklin, 64, 102, 111.
Pinckney, Henry L., of South Carolina, 68, 70.
Pinckneys, the, 24.
Pitt, William, 15, 147.
Pocahontas, 37.
Poland, Luke P., of Vermont, 167, 172.
Polk, James K., of Tennessee, 294; member of twenty-second Congress, 62; of twenty-third Congress, 64; candidate for Speakership, 67; election of, over Bell, 68; reëlection of, 70; as Speaker, 71–72; campaign cry of, 87; age of, when Speaker, 90; Cobb's defense of, 99; presidency of, 282.
Pomeroy, Theodore M., of New York, 166, 294.
Porter, Peter Buell, of New York, 33, 40.
Potomac River, 28.
Potter Committee, 214.
Powell, Lazarus W., of Kentucky, 123.
Prentiss, Sergeant S., of Mississippi, 71.
Pryor, Roger A., of Virginia, 133.
Pym, John, 11.

Quincy, Josiah, of Boston, 37, 40.

Raleigh, Sir Walter, 5.
Randall, Samuel J., of Pennsylvania, 294; candidate for Speakership, 194; succeeds Kerr, 196; in Hayes-Tilden disputed election, 197–202; charges against, 202–203; compared with Blaine, 203; revision of rules under, 205–206; sustains McCreary ruling, 212.
Randolph John ("Baron of Roanoke"), 282; Macon's subjection to, 30; character of, 37–38; relations of, with Clay, 38–39, 41–42, 274; supports salary bill, 45; tricked by Clay, 49; on Crawford investigating committee, 55; powerful in Jackson party, 60; calls Clay "blackleg," 56, 121.
Randolph, J. M., of New Jersey, 73, 74.
Randolph, Peyton, of Virginia, 17, 20, 293.
Reed, Thomas B., of Maine, 295; Clay imitated by, 48; change of House rules under, 206, 208, 270; elected Speaker of fifty-first Congress, 214; cause of success of, 215–216; leader in House, 216–217; Republican majority under, 217–219; forces parliamentary reform, 219–224; rules of House before Speakership of, 224–228; adoption of "Reed Rules" under, 228–233; power of, in House, 233–236; personality of, 237–238; stories told of, 238–241; career and retirement of, 241–242; retort of, to Springer, 243; "Reed Rules" under Crisp, 244–245; development of Speakership under, 247; Cannon contrasted with, 253, 255–256; reforms of, 278–279; helps control of legisla-

tion by "special orders," 280; ambition of, to become President, 282-283.
Rhode Island, 62, 64; delegates from, in pre-constitutional assemblies, 18; not represented in fortieth Congress, 165.
Richard II., 1.
Richardson, William A., of Illinois, candidate for Speakership, 102-109, 111; stand of, on slavery question, 107, 108.
Robinson, George D., of Massachusetts, 208.
Rodney, Cæsar A., of Delaware, 51, 52.
Roosevelt, Theodore, 264.
Root, Erastus, of New York, 63.
Rosebery, Lord, 215.
Ruffin, Thomas, of North Carolina, 106.
Russell, Jonathan, of Rhode Island and Massachusetts, 43, 52.
Rust, Albert, of Arkansas, 109, 111, 113.

St. Clair, Arthur, of Pennsylvania, 20, 293.
Salary bill of 1816, 44-46; of 1856, 118-119; of 1866, 163-164; of 1873, 174-175; of 1907, 272.
Sanborn-Contract scandals, 189.
Sanford, John E., of Massachusetts, 223.
Santiago, 212.
Schenck, Robert C., of Ohio, 86, 171.
Schurz, Carl, of Missouri, 189, 191.
Scofield, Glenni W., of Pennsylvania, 172.
Scott, Thomas, of Pennsylvania, 24.
Sedgwick, Theodore, of Massachusetts, 294; member of first Congress, 24; candidate for Speakership in 1793, 26; elected Speaker in 1799, 27; career and retirement of, 27-28, 31, 274.
Seminole question, 56.
Sergeant, John, of Pennsylvania, 60.
Seward, William H., of New York, 123, 133, 142.
Seymour, Sir Edward, Speaker under Charles II., 13-14.
Sherman, James S., 254.
Sherman, John, of Ohio, 150; candidate for Speakership, 125-134, 138, 141-143; position of, as to Helper book, 129-131, 139; bill of, opposed by Stevens, 156; in Hayes-Tilden dispute, 201.
Sherman, Roger, of Connecticut, 24.
Sickles, Daniel E., of New York, 124.
Slade, William, of Vermont, 71.
Slidell, John, of Louisiana, 123.
Smith, Samuel, of Maryland, 51, 52.
Smith, Samuel A., of Tennessee, 111.
Smith, William, of South Carolina, 26.
Smith, William, of Virginia, 140.
Smith, William N. H., of North Carolina, candidate for Speakership, 140-143.
South Amboy election, 79.
South America, 33, 39, 50.
South Bend, Indiana, 157.
South Carolina, 26, 32, 43, 62, 68, 69, 96, 97, 109, 110, 114, 131, 293, 294; agitation in, against salary bill of 1816, 46; in Hayes-Tilden contest, 198, 202.
Spain, 147, 235.
Spinola, Francis B., of New York, 221.

Springer, William M., of Illinois, in Hayes-Tilden contest, 197; candidate for Speakership, 242–243.
Stanberry, William, of Ohio, 275.
Stanly, Edward, of North Carolina, 96.
Stephens, Alexander H., of Georgia, in twenty-eighth Congress, 86; opposition of, to Whigs, 94, 95; advocates rebellion, 97; on contest over Speakership, 110; member of Rules Committee, 205.
Stevens, Thaddeus, of Pennsylvania, 170, 190, 282; member of thirty-sixth Congress, 124; urges consideration of slavery question, 127; debates with Keitt and Crawford, 131–132; supports Sherman for Speakership, 141; leader in House, 150, 151; power of, 151–154; relations of, with Lincoln, 154–155; opposition of, to Johnson, 154–156; rating of, by Blaine, 157; controls Colfax, 158, 161; offers resolution respecting Confederate States, 162–163; hostility of, to same, 164, 165.
Stevenson, Andrew, of Virginia, 294; compared with Clay, 43; elected Speaker in 1827, 60; reëlected, 61; Speaker of twenty-second Congress, 62, 63; of twenty-third Congress, 64, 65; subservient to Jackson, 65–66, 280; appointment of, as ambassador, 66–67; Polk compared to, 68, 71; compared with Cannon, 265; rank of, 274.
Story, Joseph, of Massachusetts, 34.
Stuarts, the, Speakers of House of Commons under, 7, 8, et seq.

Suffolk, 6.
Sulzer, William, of New York, 240.
Sumner, Charles, of Massachusetts, 91, 164.
Sumter, Fort, 175.
Sumter, Thomas, of South Carolina, 24.

TAFT, William H., 255.
Talleyrand, 169.
Taylor, John W., of New York, 294; succeeds Clay as Speaker, 51; defeated for Speakership, 52; declines candidacy, 53; on Crawford investigating committee, 55; Speaker in 1825, 59; defeated for reëlection, 60.
Taylor, Zachary, 93, 99.
Ten Eyck, John C., of New Jersey, 123.
Tennessee, 32, 64, 65, 68, 93, 111, 123, 124, 294; Polk governor of, 71, 72; members from, refused place upon rolls, 161–162; not represented in fortieth Congress, 165; quorum rule in, 224.
Texas, 197, 221, 242.
Thompson, Waddy, Jr., of South Carolina, 69, 70.
Tilden, Samuel J., elected Governor of New York, 189; in Hayes-Tilden campaign, 195–196; subsequent dispute, 197–202, 214.
Toombs, Robert, of Georgia, member of twenty-ninth Congress, 87; opposition of, to Whigs, 94, 95; advocates rebellion, 97; in Senate, 123.
Train, Charles R., of Massachusetts, 124.
Trumbull, Jonathan, Jr., of Connecticut, 293; member of first Congress, 24; second Speaker of

House, 25; appreciation of, 30–31.
Trumbull, "Brother Jonathan," 24.
Trumbull, Lyman, of Illinois, 164.
Tucker, John R., of Virginia, 223.
Tudors, the, Speakers of House of Commons under, 3–7, 15.
Tyler, John, 83.

"UNCLE Tom's Cabin," 125.
Union Pacific Railroad, legislation in reference to, 166, 173; part of, in Blaine investigation, 177–178.
United States, 17, 35, 43, 44, 47, 64, 91, 93, 101, 136, 155, 199, 209, 213, 224, 227, 228, 237, 269, 270, 281; Dickens's visit to, 120; slave issue in, 147; corruption in, 183; birth of, as a naval power, 211; Speakership in, contrasted with English Speakership, 285–292.
United States v. Ballin, 224.

VALENTINE, Benjamin, 9.
Vallandigham, Clement L., of Ohio, 124.
Van Buren, Martin, 80.
Vance, Zebulon R., of North Carolina, 124.
Varnum, Joseph B., of Massachusetts, 294; elected Speaker in 1807 and 1809, 30–31; tolerates Randolph, 38.
Vermont, 124, 172, 202; agitation in, against salary bill of 1816, 46.
Verplanck, Gulian C., of New York, 62.
Vinton, Samuel F., of Ohio, 91.
Virginia, 17, 33, 38, 40, 43, 51, 54, 55, 60, 62, 64, 65, 70, 74, 76, 78, 85, 97, 104, 118, 122, 125, 130, 133, 140, 223, 293, 294.

WADE, Benjamin F., of Ohio, 123.
Washington, District of Columbia, 28, 32, 45, 46, 47, 59, 97, 100, 113, 118, 122, 136, 142, 157, 167, 181, 193, 225, 226, 242.
Washington, George, 150; Chairman of Constitutional convention, 20; relations of, with Congress, 23–25, 29; Clay compared with, 34–35.
Waterloo, 252.
Watterson, Henry, of Kentucky, 201, 202.
Wayne, James M., of Georgia, 62.
Weaver, James B., of Iowa, 212, 278.
Webster, Daniel, of Massachusetts, 90, 121, 147; opposed to Clay on tariff, 55; member of twenty-ninth Congress, 87.
Weed, Thurlow, 131.
Weller, John B., of California, 118.
Wellington, Duke of (Sir Arthur Wellesley), 172, 252.
Wells, Daniel, Jr., of Wisconsin, 112.
Wentworth, Paul, 6.
West Indies, 145.
Westminster Palace, 292.
Wheeler, William A., 184, 196, 202.
White, Hugh L., of Tennessee, 68.
White, John, of Kentucky, 294; elected Speaker, 83; vote of thanks to, 85.
Whitney, William C., 211.
Wigfall, Louis T., of South Carolina, 123.
Williams, David R., of New York, 33, 40.
Wilmot, David, of Pennsylvania, 96.
Wilmot district, Pennsylvania, 149.
Wilmot proviso, 95, 97.

Wilson, Henry, of Massachusetts, 123, 172.
Windham County, Connecticut, 149.
Windom, William, of Minnesota, 124.
Winthrop, Robert C., of Massachusetts, 89, 117, 294; criticism of, of Clay, 49; elected Speaker, 90-91; conduct of, in Chair, 93-94, 274; opposition to reëlection of, 95-96; defeated by Cobb, 98-99; compared with Cobb, 100.
Wise, Henry A., of Virginia, 64, 71, 87.
Wolsey, Cardinal, demands subsidy from Commons, 4-5.
Wood, Fernando, of New York, 185.
YORKTOWN, siege of, 33; picture of, in capitol, 221.

POLITICS AND PEOPLE

The Ordeal of Self-Government in America

An Arno Press Collection

Allen, Robert S., editor. **Our Fair City.** 1947

Belmont, Perry. **Return to Secret Party Funds:** Value of Reed Committee. 1927

Berge, George W. **The Free Pass Bribery System:** Showing How the Railroads, Through the Free Pass Bribery System, Procure the Government Away from the People. 1905

Billington, Ray Allen. **The Origins of Nativism in the United States, 1800-1844.** 1933

Black, Henry Campbell. **The Relation of the Executive Power to Legislation.** 1919

Boothe, Viva Belle. **The Political Party as a Social Process.** 1923

Breen, Matthew P. **Thirty Years of New York Politics, Up-to-Date.** 1899

Brooks, Robert C. **Corruption in American Politics and Life.** 1910

Brown, George Rothwell. **The Leadership of Congress.** 1922

Bryan, William Jennings. **A Tale of Two Conventions:** Being an Account of the Republican and Democratic National Conventions of June, 1912. 1912

The Caucus System in American Politics. 1974

Childs, Harwood Lawrence. **Labor and Capital in National Politics.** 1930

Clapper, Raymond. **Racketeering in Washington.** 1933

Crawford, Kenneth G. **The Pressure Boys:** The Inside Story of Lobbying in America. 1939

Dallinger, Frederick W. **Nominations for Elective Office in the United States.** 1897

Dunn, Arthur Wallace. **Gridiron Nights:** Humorous and Satirical Views of Politics and Statesmen as Presented by the Famous Dining Club. 1915

Ervin, Spencer. **Henry Ford vs. Truman H. Newberry:** The Famous Senate Election Contest. A Study in American Politics, Legislation and Justice. 1935

Ewing, Cortez A.M. and Royden J. Dangerfield. **Documentary Source Book in American Government and Politics.** 1931

Ford, Henry Jones. **The Cost of Our National Government:** A Study in Political Pathology. 1910

Foulke, William Dudley. **Fighting the Spoilsmen:** Reminiscences of the Civil Service Reform Movement. 1919

Fuller, Hubert Bruce. **The Speakers of the House.** 1909

Griffith, Elmer C. **The Rise and Development of the Gerrymander.** 1907

Hadley, Arthur Twining. **The Relations Between Freedom and Responsibility in the Evolution of Democratic Government.** 1903

Hart, Albert Bushnell. **Practical Essays on American Government.** 1893

Holcombe, Arthur N. **The Political Parties of To-Day:** A Study in Republican and Democratic Politics. 1924

Hughes, Charles Evans. **Conditions of Progress in Democratic Government.** 1910

Kales, Albert M. **Unpopular Government in the United States.** 1914

Kent, Frank R. **The Great Game of Politics.** 1930

Lynch, Denis Tilden. **"Boss" Tweed:** The Story of a Grim Generation. 1927

McCabe, James D., Jr. (Edward Winslow Martin, pseud.) **Behind the Scenes in Washington.** 1873

Macy, Jesse. **Party Organization and Machinery.** 1912

Macy, Jesse. **Political Parties in the United States, 1846-1861.** 1900

Moley, Raymond. **Politics and Criminal Prosecution.** 1929

Munro, William Bennett. **The Invisible Government** and **Personality in Politics:** A Study of Three Types in American Public Life. 1928/1934 Two volumes in one.

Myers, Gustavus. **History of Public Franchises in New York City,** Boroughs of Manhattan and the Bronx. (Reprinted from **Municipal Affairs,** March 1900) 1900

Odegard, Peter H. and E. Allen Helms. **American Politics:** A Study in Political Dynamics. 1938

Orth, Samuel P. **Five American Politicians:** A Study in the Evolution of American Politics. 1906

Ostrogorski, M[oisei I.] **Democracy and the Party System in the United States:** A Study in Extra-Constitutional Government. 1910

Overacker, Louise. **Money in Elections.** 1932

Overacker, Louise. **The Presidential Primary.** 1926

The Party Battle. 1974

Peel, Roy V. and Thomas C. Donnelly. **The 1928 Campaign:** An Analysis. 1931

Pepper, George Wharton. **In the Senate** *and* **Family Quarrels:** The President, The Senate, The House. 1930/1931. Two volumes in one

Platt, Thomas Collier. **The Autobiography of Thomas Collier Platt.** Compiled and edited by Louis J. Lang. 1910

Roosevelt, Theodore. **Social Justice and Popular Rule:** Essays, Addresses, and Public Statements Relating to the Progressive Movement, 1910-1916 (*The Works of Theodore Roosevelt,* Memorial Edition, Volume XIX) 1925

Root, Elihu. **The Citizen's Part in Government** *and* **Experiments in Government and the Essentials of the Constitution.** 1907/1913. Two volumes in one

Rosten, Leo C. **The Washington Correspondents.** 1937

Salter, J[ohn] T[homas]. **Boss Rule:** Portraits in City Politics. 1935

Schattschneider, E[lmer] E[ric]. **Politics, Pressures and the Tariff:** A Study of Free Private Enterprise in Pressure Politics, as Shown in the 1929-1930 Revision of the Tariff. 1935

Smith, T[homas] V. and Robert A. Taft. **Foundations of Democracy:** A Series of Debates. 1939

The Spoils System in New York. 1974

Stead, W[illiam] T. **Satan's Invisible World Displayed,** Or, Despairing Democracy. A Study of Greater New York (The Review of Reviews Annual) 1898

Van Devander, Charles W. **The Big Bosses.** 1944

Wallis, J[ames] H. **The Politician:** His Habits, Outcries and Protective Coloring. 1935

Werner, M[orris] R. **Privileged Characters.** 1935

White, William Allen. **Politics:** The Citizen's Business. 1924

Wooddy, Carroll Hill. **The Case of Frank L. Smith:** A Study in Representative Government. 1931

Wooddy, Carroll Hill. **The Chicago Primary of 1926:** A Study in Election Methods. 1926